SYNTACTIC THEORY

SYNTACTIC THEORY

Emmon Bach

University of Massachusetts
at Amherst
and
Hampshire College

HOLT, RINEHART AND WINSTON, INC.

NEW YORK, CHICAGO, SAN FRANCISCO, ATLANTA, DALLAS,
MONTREAL, TORONTO, LONDON, SYDNEY

410

B11N

Library of Congress Cataloging in Publication Data

Bach, Emmon W.
  Syntactic theory.

  Bibliography: p.
  1. Grammar, Comparative and general — Syntax.
  2. Generative grammar. I. Title.
P291.B28   415   73-19732
ISBN: 0-03-076715-6

4   5   6   7   8   038   9   8   7   6   5   4   3   2   1

Preface

This book began as a revision of *An Introduction to Transformational Grammars* (1964). It soon became apparent that there was no satisfactory way to revise the earlier book. The present book differs from the earlier one in a number of ways. Most important, the emphasis is much less on the technical apparatus of transformational grammar and much more on the ways in which we use theory construction to find out about the world of language. The hardest thing to teach is how to think, and in a sense it is the only thing worth teaching. Also, I have now tried to make the book largely self-contained. The earlier book was largely written to bridge a gap. In 1963, most students of linguistics had come up through a tradition of structuralism. Now, such training is a rarity. Finally, I have devoted more space to relatively advanced topics, so that the book combines the aims of a textbook with the aim of putting the reader into the world of ongoing research. This double aim is reflected in the structure of the book. The first seven chapters present the reader with a slightly modified version of the theory of Noam Chomsky's *Aspects of the Theory of Syntax* (1965) and give some practice in working within that framework. I have tried to think through the basic questions that arise in justifying that framework and to write about them without glossing over the difficulties. Chapter 8 is a kind of interlude about mathematical linguistics, which is necessary for some of the later sections. The last three chapters deal mostly with modifications in the theory that have arisen in the last few years or are going on at present.

I have not attempted to give exhaustive references, especially in the earlier chapters, where a great deal of the material comes from a kind of oral tradition. Obviously, the book owes most to the work of Chomsky, who started it all.

It is impossible to give explicit thanks to everyone who has helped me directly or indirectly to write this book, but I must mention at least the following colleagues and friends who either gave me helpful criticism of the manuscript at various stages or helped me by talking at length about various problems touched on in the book: Charles Cairns, Helen Cairns, Philip Gough, Maurice Gross, Asa Kasher, Terry Langendoen, W. P. Lehmann, Sam Levin, Marta Luján, Stanley Peters, Carlota Smith, Charles Tang, and Reed Young. Cynthia Allen helped me with the Index. Naturally, all errors and shortcomings are my own. Most of all I would like to thank my students, who have taught me more than they know.

E.B.

Amherst, Massachusetts
November 1973

Contents

SYNTACTIC THEORY

chapter 1
Setting

1.1 Focus and Aim

When people talk they use sounds to convey meanings. Syntactic theory is the result of trying to understand the general principles of sentence construction that people must know in order to accomplish this task.

In the form in which we shall study it, syntactic theory is very young, and the residue of little-understood phenomena vastly exceeds that part about which we feel relatively sure. For this reason, the emphasis here will be more on the way in which we carry out this enterprise than on any exposition of what we know. In the next six chapters we will build up a theory of syntax that has been fairly well worked out and note some of the evidence for particulars of the theory. The reasons for doing this are two: First, in looking at a coherent theory we will learn something about how a theory of syntax can be constructed and how evidence can be found to support theories about particular languages within the framework of such a theory. Second, enough seems secure within the theory that we can consider various aspects of it to be necessary parts of any serious theory of syntax. In the last four chapters we will look at some recent discussions and considerations that point toward insufficiencies of the theory, and at some possible amendments.

The study of syntax forms only a part of linguistic theory, and linguistic theory forms only a part of linguistics. In this chapter we will take up some preliminary questions about the nature of linguistics, its relationship to other studies, and the methods appropriate to its pursuit.

1.2 The Study of Language

Linguistics is the study of language in general. It is comparable to other sciences and disciplines devoted to understanding various phenomena: physics, the study of the structure and interactions of matter and energy; anthropology, the study of man in culture; and so on. As in these other theoretical disciplines, the primary aim of linguistics is understanding. Since most of us are trained to think about language first of all in the schools, where the main concern is (or is said to be) learning languages or learning to use a language well, it usually takes a moderate wrenching of our minds to think about language as a problem to be understood rather than as a tool to be used. Moreover, our use of our language is governed by principles so deep and unconscious that we need to make a considerable effort to see what the problems are. Speaking and understanding a language seem as natural as breathing; it is easy to take them for granted.

To understand language, it is necessary to study languages, but general linguistics is concerned with individual languages only to the extent that they throw light on the nature of language in general.

In popular parlance, "language" often means a written language. The vast majority of languages, past and present, have never been represented in writing. Linguists think of languages as being primarily systems of articulated sounds. (Interesting research is being conducted at present on the "signing" language of the deaf. Such research should throw light on the question of what aspects of language are bound up with its particular manifestation in spoken signals.)

1.21 Synchrony versus Diachrony

All languages have a history and all languages change, both for the individual speaker and as the language is transmitted from speaker to speaker. The study of a language as it changes through time for a group of speakers is called **diachronic** linguistics. If we pretend, for purposes of delimiting our field, that a language can be caught at an instant, as in a photograph, we say that we are doing **synchronic** linguistics. The idealizations that we use in linguistic theory are just like any other idealizations in science. In order to understand any phenomenon it is necessary to make a number of partly arbitrary decisions to separate out aspects that can be studied in relative isolation. A great deal of progress has been made in understanding language by making the assumption that a language can be studied as if it were a fixed, unchanging system.

Diachronic linguistics is interesting and important in itself, but in order to understand how a language changes it is necessary to understand something about what a language can be like at a given point of time. For example, historical linguists are often interested in reconstructing some unattested language by looking at the internal structure of a given language or by comparing several related languages and "triangulating," so to speak, to arrive at a model of the language from which they descended. But if the hypothetical earlier language violates some known principles about the possible variation of language, then the reconstruction simply cannot be correct.

On the other hand, diachronic linguistics offers an important testing ground for notions about synchronic linguistic theory. Ultimately, we have to account for all facts about language. Part of the facts that we know are facts about language change. Diachronic and synchronic theory must jointly account for the possible changes that languages undergo. Hence, to take the converse case, if we have some known principles of language change and put these together with some putative principles of synchronic linguistics to derive some predictions that turn out to be false, we can conclude that something is wrong with our notions about synchrony.

In this book, we shall concern ourselves exclusively with synchronic theory.

1.22 Linguistics and Related Disciplines

The academic divisions that are made in our attempts to understand the world are partly the result of history, accident, politics, individual mistakes, and genius. As human beings we strive to make some sense out of the whole mess by attacking bits and pieces and trying to fit them together. Language has been the object of human speculation from the beginning of our records of human intellectual activity. The people who have worried about language have worn many academic hats: biology, psychology, philosophy, mathematics, anthropology, sociology, and literature, among others. Modern linguistics has its roots in all these fields. But it is not a proper part of any one of them, at least not in the way these fields are usually delimited. We assume that it makes sense to focus on language as such and to look to other fields for corroboration or refutation when we try to put the jigsaw puzzle together in a meaningful way. So far, enough progress has been made under this assumption that it seems promising to continue. I will make in this book two assumptions:

First, I assume that the study of linguistic theory as such is a prerequisite to the study of language in other fields such as psychology or sociology, in other words, that there is a central body of questions and knowledge that is coherent and autonomous enough for us to study it in relative isolation.

Second, because one of the tests of a theory is its goodness of fit with respect to other areas of human knowledge, I assume that in the end we must deal with tangential questions from related fields. We have already considered the relationship between synchronic and diachronic linguistics. Let us name a few of the related fields in which important questions about language have been raised and considered.

Psychology is the study of the human mind. Since one of the most characteristic qualities of the human animal is its ability to use language, linguistics sets a number of central tasks for psychology. The linguistics of the last decade and a half has had a revolutionary impact on psychology, ever since N. Chomsky (1959a)[1] challenged behavioral psychologists (who would presumably object to the first sentence of this paragraph) to account for human linguistic abilities in a simple theory of stimulus and response. Psycholinguistics is a relatively new field in which researchers attempt to understand the acquisition of language by the child, the way in which users of a language process and produce sentences, and so on.

Languages are used by human beings, and all human beings function, more or less, in society. Moreover, a language is one of the important binding forces in a society, both in the large societies we call nations, and in the smaller units of class, ethnic groupings, social clubs, and the like. Sociolinguistics is the study of language in society. Sociolinguists study a variety of questions all revolving around the variations of languages within society and across geographical space (study of dialects).

Philosophers have always been interested in language, especially in the meanings of words and sentences. Recently, there has been a considerable and fruitful interaction between linguists and philosophers. Logicians and mathematicians study various kinds of abstract systems. We will see that there is a very intimate connection between such study and syntactic theory (see Chapter 8).

Since linguistic activity is manifested primarily as speech, that is, as sounds produced by articulations of the human vocal apparatus and heard by the human auditory system, those disciplines that study the physics of sound (acoustics) and the physiology and neurophysiology of phonation and hearing make up an important area of contact between linguistics and the relevant natural sciences. Moreover, as it makes sense to ask about the evolution of the peculiarly human capacity of language, important research on language must be carried out within the context of general biology (Lenneberg, 1967).

Finally, let us note that although we are concentrating here on linguistic theory, and a special part of it at that, there are a vast number of practical concerns in which linguistics can play a role, ranging from speech therapy through social problems of bilingualism and into language teaching. Many pressing problems of the day have their linguistic side.

---

1. References throughout by author and date are to the Bibliography on pp. 281–290.

What should be the medium of education in the early grades? How can developing nations with great diversity of languages solve the problem of finding a common language for administration and education? How can small societies preserve their cultural integrity, including their languages, in the face of urbanization and technological change? Such questions demand answers that cannot wait upon final results to strictly theoretical questions about the nature of language. Moreover, they present important theoretical questions of their own, such as the nature of first and second language learning, and the roles of language in society and society in language. Many linguists are concerning themselves more and more with such questions, and their findings can be expected to play an important part in developing linguistic theory itself. But in all such studies a necessary part will be the process of formulating and testing theories, of thinking rationally about language as such, and it is with this process that we will be primarily concerned.

We have noted just a few of the many areas that impinge on linguistic theory. Let us focus our attention more narrowly now on the kinds of question that we shall consider central to linguistic theory as such.

1.3 The Data of Linguistics

A central part of linguistics is the attempt to answer the question: What is language? We can attack this question by asking two kinds of further questions. What do speakers of natural languages "know" about language? What do speakers of natural languages "know" about their languages? Two terms in these questions are in need of preliminary clarification.

First, by *natural language* is meant one of the thousands of verbal, spoken systems that are used, and have been used, by human beings to communicate with each other and that have not arisen by a conscious act of creation. On the one hand, we delimit such systems from other systems of communication that are used by other species than humans (Sebeok, 1968). On the other hand, we exclude artificial "languages" such as the abstract languages invented and studied by logicians. Thus, we include English, Swahili, Japanese, and so on, as well as more limited dialects and idiolects (the language of an individual).

Second, the verb *know* is used here in a rather special sense. We will take a look in a moment at the kinds of knowledge that native speakers manifest about their languages. But it must be made clear that we do not mean by *know* any necessarily conscious, readily available kind of knowing. It may take a great deal of very indirect evidence to justify the conclusion that speakers of English "know" some particular rule that we are positing. And it may take a considerable amount of reflection and probing even to discover the more direct judgments about sentences and their relationships that speakers may make. In the first question — What do humans know about language in general — I am using *know* in an even more extended sense. The question might be rephrased: What aspects of linguistic ability ought we to attribute to the species-specific ability to learn and use languages?

The idea that a considerable portion of the capacity to use language must be attributed to a general human characteristic is supported by a number of observations. First, even though the thousands of languages that exist show a great deal of variation, we can see that this variation is kept within very strict limits if we consider the logically and physically possible differences that might exist among languages. All languages seem to be cut to the same general plan. That this uniformity is not due to historical accident seems likely when we consider the length of time humans have had language (say half a million years, to be conservative) and the relatively rapid rate of language change. Within a few thousand years two languages can develop from a common source and become so different that it takes considerable ingenuity to discern their common origin. Yet no matter how different in detail, they remain basically the same kind of system. Moreover, we can see similarities in detail developing in totally unrelated languages where there can be no hint of any influence from one to the other.

Second, children learn the language of their environment in a fashion that would be very difficult to understand if we did not assume a heavy contribution from the side of the learner, a kind of built-in capacity that determines the form and, to a surprisingly great extent, the content of the system that is developed. Moreover, this learning takes place in a "natural" way and in a fixed sequence of steps, much more like the species-specific learning of nest-building among birds, say, than like the learning of purely cultural skills, such as typewriting or riding a bicycle (Lenneberg, 1967). Of course, there must be a linguistic environment, but the child is endowed with the ability to learn the language of that environment, whatever it is, in a remarkably efficient and mysterious way. The extent of this accomplishment can be appreciated when we realize that even after a great many years of work linguists are nowhere near providing an explicit account of the grammar of any language. Yet the child acquires the implicit counterpart to the linguist's grammar in the span of four to six years.

Hence, modern linguists follow a time-honored tradition in the history of language study by distinguishing between **universal grammar** and **particular grammars**. The first, the general theory of language, is a theory about what language is and delimits the class of possible natural languages, past, present, and future. A grammar for a particular language is part of a theory about that language in which we try to model or represent what the native speaker knows about his language.

Let us now take a preliminary look at some of the facts about their language that native speakers know. At each point we will notice that some aspects of their knowledge are language-independent, while some pertain to the particular language at hand.

As we noted above, language is primarily manifested as speech, that is, as a series of disturbances in a conducting medium, a series of muscular and neural changes in the speaker and hearer. An important part of linguistics is the study of speech sounds, both in general and for particular languages. One of the first tasks of a linguist studying a new language is to figure out what the sounds are. But what do we mean by "sounds"?

We may study the sounds of a language as physical or physiological events. Such study is called **phonetics,** and it can be carried out from a variety of points of view and in response to a number of different questions. Typically, when a linguist begins to study a language he has not heard before, he will make phonetic transcriptions of short utterances, using a conventional alphabet that purports to record the articulatory characteristics of the utterances he hears. But even such an apparently simple act as making a phonetic transcription of an utterance is shot through and through with hypotheses about language. It is impossible to make a neat separation between "facts" that are "described" and "theories" about them. This point can be made clear by an example: suppose a linguist is told to make a phonetic transcription of a frog-call. He will either throw up his hands in despair or, at best, describe it as resembling roughly what he might transcribe using symbols for human speech sounds. The point is that the phonetic symbols he uses in transcribing even languages completely unknown to him have specific interpretations inextricably bound up with a theory about what is and what is not significant in the sounds of speech, hypothetical entities involved in theories about how sounds are produced, crucial physical parameters in the acoustics of speech (acoustics itself involving a whole intricate theory about sound in general), and so on.

Moreover, it is only within very broad limits that the symbols so used will have the same meaning from language to language. To discover what makes the sound system of Amharic (a language of Ethiopia) different from that of English is to become involved in a second sort of theoretical activity. On the one hand, we have the question: What in general are the possible significant phonetic features of languages? On the other hand, what are the significant features of the English sound system (as opposed to Amharic)? The peculiar structure of linguistic research again becomes apparent: we must have a general theory about language and specific theories about languages.

Let us note next that it is impossible to carry out any kind of linguistic research without becoming involved with the judgments that speakers of languages make about what they say and hear. Linguistics is an empirical science, but its data are not just physical events. What we must account for includes what is known as the native speaker's "intuitions" about his language. Language as a cultural and psychological phenomenon cannot be adequately studied without reference to judgments of native speakers. These judgments range from relatively simple and straightforward ones about the acceptability of certain sentences or sounds to extremely subtle ones that have to be skillfully tapped.

The native speaker judges some utterances to be repetitions of the "same" sentence, phrase, or word. No two utterances are ever exactly alike. But in any speech community some utterances will "count as" repetitions, while others will not, and these judgments of identity of type will vary in general from language to language. To take a standard example, if I say in English the two words *putt* and *but,* they will be judged different, but if I said two words exhibiting the same phonetic difference (voicing and aspiration) in some other language, they might be judged repetitions (nonsignificant variants).

We can conclude from the foregoing considerations that linguistic theory must include an account of the physical and physiological aspects of human speech sounds that allows us to say what possible sounds and distinctions in sounds are available to speakers of languages. It must provide a way of showing how the gamut of possible sounds is organized and used in any particular language and how the sound system of one language can differ from that of another. The theory of some one language, such as English, must show us what selection of all possible sounds is made in that language and what the sound system of that language is in detail. The study of the systematic organization of sounds in linguistic systems is called **phonology.** We call a theory about a particular language the **grammar** of that language; and the part of this theory having to do with its system of sounds is called, again, the **phonology** or **phonological component** of the grammar. Just as the general theory of phonology defines a class of possible sequences of sounds that might be used as utterances in arbitrary languages, the phonology of a particular language defines a class of phonologically possible sequences of sounds for that language. It is a fact of general validity that some language might have an utterance (indicated roughly by a sequence of letters) such as *bradiup iksney,* but hardly *pfttkgkgzk.* It is a fact about English that there might be an English word *skramps* but not *ndafu* (but just the opposite for Swahili). Finally, to take an example from phonetics proper, general linguistic theory must tell us that no language uses a distinctive sound in its phonological system that is made by snapping the fingers against the cheek, while many languages use sounds made by placing the tip of the tongue just behind the teeth of the upper part of the mouth; allowing free passage of air through the nasal cavity; and manipulating the musculature and cartilages of the voice-box (larynx) in such a fashion that the expulsion of air from the lungs, by lowering the rib cage and releasing the muscles of the diaphragm, causes a periodic excitation of the air by rapid successive opening and closing of the passage between the vocal folds (cords): that is, the sound represented in English spelling by *n*.

Next, just as the native speaker is aware that certain sequences of sounds are "pronounceable" in his language, he is also able to judge that certain utterances are genuine utterances of his language, while others are not. Thus, in English we can say

1. The person smoked the cigarette.

but not

2. *The person the cigarette smoked.[2]

But in Japanese the words corresponding to those above can occur in the order of (2) but not of (1):

3. hito wa tabako o nonda   *person* topic-marker *cigarette* object-marker *smoked*

4. *hito wa nonda tabako o

A speaker of Japanese will understand what is intended by (4), probably, but his reaction will be "No, you can't say that that way in Japanese," or "That's the way a foreigner might talk."

Let us pause here again to note a peculiarity of linguistic predictions. It is obviously not the case that an English speaker literally *cannot* say (2) or a Japanese speaker (4). Indeed, I have just pronounced (2) (and if I had a Japanese friend in my study I could probably persuade him to say (4)). What is meant by such a statement is rather something like this: If you want to speak English in the ordinary way you can say (1) but not (2) (or for Japanese (3) but not (4)).

---

2. Sequences of words that are claimed to be impossible sentences in a language are marked here, as is usual, with an asterisk; occasionally, question marks and the like will be used in an obvious manner to indicate questionable utterances.

We cannot say that linguists are describing what in fact speakers of a language do say, for people often make "mistakes," false starts, changes in midstream in a sentence, and so on. It is not inconceivable, for instance, that one might hear, in one day, utterances like these:[3]

  *This form is found in Homer, don't we?
  *Did you both come together?
  *Let us now consider the oh John what the hell are you doing here?

Now it is part of the total job of the study of language to explain how people actually do talk. But a theory of English would simply be incorrect that did not have something to say about the difference between utterances like those just cited and these:

  This form is found in Homer, isn't it?
  We find this form in Homer, don't we?
  Did you two come together?
  Let us now consider the problem of imperialism.

A philosopher (Koller, 1967) has argued on the basis of observations like those just made that linguistics is not and cannot be an empirical science. The results of linguistic study are stated as "rules." Rules can be broken or followed, but are not true or false, hence a "description" of English makes no truth claims. We shall consider more closely in the next chapter the nature of linguistic rules and grammars (which are sets of rules). For the moment let us note that although rules taken in isolation are not statements that can be true or false, the total set of rules forms the basis for predictions that can be verified or falsified. Testing the predictions requires use – direct or indirect – of native speakers' reactions. The fact that such reactions are difficult to come by means that life for the linguist is tough, but not that linguistics is impossible. (On the nature of linguistic rules, see Searle, 1969.)

We call the sentences that are "in" a language the fully **grammatical** sentences of the language. As with many other terms, the term "grammatical" has a presystematic, everyday use and another, technical use. Ultimately, we will restrict the term to mean something like: marked as nondeviant or normal with respect to a theory of a language (a grammar), and not abnormal for reasons of meaning, appropriateness to situation, and so on. It is not clear in general that there is a sharp line separating

3. Something should be said about individual and dialect variation. Many of the judgments about grammaticality will not shared by all readers. My judgments refer to my dialect, although I have checked most examples with several other speakers.

grammatical from ungrammatical sequences, and in particular cases we may be quite uncertain whether to attribute the unacceptability of a sentence to one or another part of our linguistic description. But some clear cases of one or the other match up pretty well with the nontechnical sense of grammaticality that lies behind our technical usage. Thus, most of us would probably agree on the status of these examples:

John Smith is the president of the Chase Manhattan Bank.
Why don't you ever stay home in the evenings?
I believe him to be a fool.
*John Smith are president of the Chase Manhattan Bank.
*Why stay you never home in the evenings?
*Me believe he to be fools.

On the other hand, the following examples have a more shadowy status (and indeed some have played a prominent role in linguistic discussions):

?I remind myself of a gorilla.
?Jones caused a disturbance by his falling asleep at the meeting.
?The man ate the octopuses who was sitting by the fire.

Or consider sentences containing two apparently contradictory time references:

?He saw her yesterday last week.

This may seem like a straightforward example that is to be ruled out by a grammar of English at some level of explanation. But if we grant the possibility of time-travel, we can easily imagine using sentences like this:

Doctor Wonmug is going to see Alley Oop yesterday tomorrow.

We shall make the assumption that it is possible to distinguish between what speakers know about their language and how they actually use this knowledge. The first we call the **competence** of the speaker; the second, the **performance**. That this distinction is reasonable seems to be supported by the observation made above that speakers do make mistakes, that is, often sentences that are clearly ungrammatical are actually used — sometimes deliberately. On the other side, many clearly grammatical sentences are not used because they are too long, too complicated, or too trivial. We shall see some of the advantages of the distinction in further parts of this book. I do not believe that it is possible to do without the distinction at all, although the particular way of applying it, or particular decisions about treating some phenomenon as accountable to a theory of performance or a theory of competence, may be very debatable. In any case, we cannot know in advance what competence and performance are without constructing theories about both and about their interaction. (For some views about the distinction and its problems, see Bever, 1970.) The distinction can be made clearer, perhaps, by the analogy of a game, such as chess. The set of rules defining chess tells you what the initial configurations of pieces and pawns are, what legal moves may be made, and so on. There are exactly twenty possible initial moves. But if you observe actual games you will probably never see more than a half-dozen different first moves. This fact is accounted for not in the theory of what is and what is not a chess game (competence) but rather in a theory of how to win games (strategy). If you make an unusual first move you may be playing a bad game of chess, but if you make an illegal move you are simply not playing chess. (This issue will be discussed further in Sections 2.1 and 2.2.)

From the foregoing discussion we may conclude that a grammar must tell us about the grammaticality of sentences. But speakers of languages know a great deal about their sentences beyond the fact that they are grammatical. Since we want to have as wide a range of facts as possible with which to test our theories, we want to provide some means for representing other aspects of sentences as well, so that we can tie them to further facets of linguistic competence.

Speakers know a good deal about the structure of sentences and their interrelationships. By this I do not mean that speakers have direct knowledge of the sort that we shall try to make explicit in our linguistic theories and grammars, but rather that they can judge some sentences as having the same structure, whatever it is, and they can recognize that whole sets of sentences are related in parallel ways. The first kind of knowledge can be exemplified by these examples:

Boaz watched the harmonium.
The chameleon sitting on the branch captured the fly that had settled on its nose.
Whoever believes that only betrays his ignorance.

All of these sentences exhibit the same gross structure (subject-verb-object), even though their finer structure is quite different. The second kind of knowledge is exhibited when we match up these sentences with their corresponding questions, passives, and so on:

Did Boaz watch the harmonium?
The harmonium was watched by Boaz.
It was the harmonium that Boaz watched.
What Boaz watched was the harmonium.
Boaz watched the harmonium, didn't he?

Knowledge of such regularities can be shown by setting the task of forming corresponding sets of sentences for further specific examples.

Next we may note the rather obvious fact that speakers know a great deal about the meanings of the sentences that they use. Thus they can judge when two sentences mean about the same thing:

1. To live in Manhattan is expensive and dangerous.
2. It is expensive and dangerous to live in Manhattan.

They can recognize when a certain sequence of words has several different meanings:

3. Harry put it in the pen.
4. She was reading the letter to her husband.
5. They saw the man with the telescope.

The last example shows that some ambiguities are quite unobvious. Besides the two obvious meanings, the sentence might mean something like this: *They habitually use a telescope to saw the man.* All of the sentences except (3) show further that meaning relationships and properties are a function not only of the words and other linguistic elements used but also of the structure of the sentences.

Besides the rather direct semantic properties exhibited so far, speakers know about other meaning relationships. A speaker cannot say and believe (6) without becoming committed to the truth of (7):

6. John knows that the earth is flat.
7. The earth is flat.

A speaker who understands the meaning of (8) and (9) knows that if (8) is true, then so is (9):

8. Harriet went downtown and purchased a slide rule.
9. Harriet purchased a slide rule.

A speaker who understands (10) and (11) knows that they cannot both be true:

10. John is a bachelor.
11. John is married.

Further, the speaker knows that (12) cannot be either true or false if (10) is true (assuming in all these examples that *John* refers to the same person):

12. John's wife had apoplexy when he washed the dishes unasked.

Finally, speakers know a great about the appropriateness of various utterances both with respect to other utterances and to the situations in which they are uttered. For example, as speakers of English we know that the (A) answers are inappropriate responses to the questions below, while the (B) answers are appropriate:

1. What did Sally see in the park?
   A. It was in the park that Sally saw a flying saucer.
   B. It was a flying saucer that Sally saw in the park.
      [or simply]
      A flying saucer.
2. Where did Sally see a flying saucer?
   A. It was a flying saucer that Sally saw in the park.
   B. It was in the park that Sally saw a flying saucer.

Or (as an example of the role of nonlinguistic context) at a formal gathering where we are trying to be moderately polite we might make request (1) but not (2):

1. Would you please pass the chutney?
2. Pass the chutney.

Thus, speakers of a language know about the sounds of their language, the structure of its sentences, the meanings of sentences, and their appropriate uses. The complexity and depth of this knowledge can be easily appreciated by trying to give an explicit account of this knowledge. In fact, this is just what we are trying to do when we do linguistics.

In order to give such an account, we require that a grammar provide for each sentence of the language a set of **structural descriptions** related to the various facets of linguistic competence that we have surveyed. These structural descriptions, taken together with our general theory of language, provide us with the means for showing how speakers of a language are able to link sounds and meanings. It is precisely the linkage between the two that it is our job to describe and explain in syntactic theory. The study of meanings as such is called **semantics**. As we shall see, the precise nature of the relationship between syntax and semantics is very unclear (Chapter 9). To make it clear is to construct adequate theories of syntax and semantics.

1.4 Something about Method

In the preceding sections I have repeatedly used words like "theory" and "explain." In this section we shall consider briefly some problems connected with such ideas. The most striking change in the recent history of linguistics, at least in America, has been in the notions that linguists hold about the proper goals and methods of their work.

A scientific theory is a more or less coherent set of hypotheses that is intended to explain a range of phenomena. The tests of a theory are two: the extent to which the theory does explain the facts that it is supposed to explain; the extent to which it fits with other theories that deal with related facts. The methods used in a science must be judged according to whether they lead to results that meet these tests.

The last statement might seem to be a truism. But for a considerable period American linguistics was dominated by the converse idea that the methods should determine the types of theories and explanations that are allowable. The reasons for this situation are understandable. Modern linguistics has grown out of the humanities and social sciences. Once the idea that linguistics is a "science" and not the art of speaking or writing well was accepted, it was natural for linguists (like many of their colleagues in other disciplines that deal with areas formerly considered outside the pale of science) to ask for a definition of "scientific method" that would guide them in their work, and to expect that following such a method would ensure the truth and reliability of their results. Because people have speculated from time immemorial about language, often with no basis in fact, it was natural that linguists would be suspicious of premature generalizations, empty claims, and dubious explanations. Nevertheless, I think it must be admitted that the whole program was misconceived.

The view of linguistic method that was held by many workers was similar to a view of scientific method, which is unfortunately propagated by much teaching of science in the schools and in popular accounts of science. According to this view, the scientist must begin by collecting observations about happenings in the real world. After he has made a large number of such observations or experiments, he proceeds to a "generalization" about these happenings that can be verified by referring to the original observations. After he has repeatedly carried out this process to arrive at a number of such generalizations, he may go on to make a secondary generalization that is "based on" the original generalizations (which are "based on" the original sets of observations). There is supposed to be a method (called "induction") by which one arrives at such generalizations. The classical statement of this view was made by Francis Bacon, an English philosopher and statesman (1561–1626), and we may accordingly call this view of science "Baconian."

This is not the place to give an extended documentation of the thesis that much of modern linguistics has been dominated by an extreme Baconianism (for some remarks see Bach, 1965a). A few examples are, however, in order.

Probably the most influential book on linguistics published in America during the first half of this century was Leonard Bloomfield's *Language* (1933). In his theoretical asides and in the sketch of the history of linguistics (Chapter 1), Bloomfield displays a strongly Baconian view of science. The widespread, if never very explicitly formulated, assumption that linguistic theory should consist of a set of rigorous procedures by means of which utterances could be "segmented" and units "classified" to provide a grammar of a language is clearly based on a notion of Baconian induction ("mechanical discovery procedure"). Finally, one may cite the often reiterated idea that the study of sentence structure can never succeed until we have programmed electronic computers to "handle" the vast bodies of data needed to provide the "basis" for our study. Perhaps these views are an inheritance from the tradition of historical linguistics out of which modern linguistics has grown. Part of historical linguistics deals with the study and interpretation of ancient texts, and one of its chief aims has been to provide compendia of different forms found in the "corpus" (the fixed body of texts that have been preserved). In such a compendium or "grammar" it is indeed important to avoid inventing forms that are not attested. But such a description has no theoretical status; it is equivalent to an organized index to the texts. Even here, however, a theory-free account of allegedly neutral facts is, strictly speaking, impossible.

A more nearly accurate account of scientific method might go as follows. Somehow or other a scientist becomes interested in understanding a certain range of phenomena or in solving a particular problem. How he comes upon the problem is of no theoretical consequence whatsoever. He may be trying to accomplish a certain practical task such as building a rocket that will not burn up when it reenters the atmosphere, or he may notice some unexpected result when performing an experiment — for instance, the unexplained static that led to the development of radio astronomy. Scientific discoveries of the utmost consequence have been made by workers who were systematically working through all sorts of substances in the attempt to find drugs for specific medical treatments, but they have also been made by pure accident. Of course, the accident has to be noticed by the right person, and usually a solid acquaintance with previous work in an area is a prerequisite for good scientific research.

The worker must then formulate some tentative answer to the question or problem, that is, an explanation or "hypothesis." A good hypothesis must meet several requirements. First, it must be precise and explicit enough to allow the deduction of various consequences, typically with the help of other hypotheses and observations. Second, among the possible consequences of the hypotheses there must be some that have some empirical content, in particular, the observations that the hypothesis purports to explain. It is misleading to oppose the deductive method of logic and mathematics to a putative inductive method of empirical science. Deduction plays a central role in linguistics and physics as well as in mathematics. We cannot, of course, deduce theories or hypotheses from observations and statements about them. But we must be able to deduce statements about matters of fact from our hypotheses, or else the hypotheses will be empirically empty. Once again, how we arrive at our hypotheses is insignificant. What is essential is that they say something that can be matched up against facts.

Suppose now that we have made a guess about the explanation of a certain range of facts, made a prediction on the basis of the explanation, and that the prediction turns out to be false. Then we can conclude that one of the hypotheses entering into the deduction is false. That is, we can make an inference of the following sort: If A, B, C, then X (where A, B, C are hypotheses, and X describes some expected result): X is false, therefore: not all of A, B, C can be true. On the other hand, suppose the result (X) does indeed turn out to be true. Can we conclude that the hypotheses (A, B, C) are correct? Not at all. Such an inference would be an instance of a well-known fallacy called "asserting the consequent." (From the statements *If it is raining, then the streets are wet* and *The streets are wet* I cannot conclude that it is raining. Someone might have watered them down with a hose, it might be snowing, a water main might have burst, and so on.) The most we can say is that the hypotheses were corroborated or not disconfirmed.

Two assumptions are made in the paradigm of inference that I have just sketched. First, it is assumed that the chain of deduction involved has been carried out correctly. In simple cases there is no problem in this assumption, but such cases are the exception rather than the rule. Sometimes it is necessary to do a good deal of complicated thinking, and even to use special branches of mathematics (see Chapter 8), before we reach some conclusion that can be related to testable results. Second — and this is really just a special instance of the first assumption — it is necessary that all of the premises of our argument (the *A, B, C* above) be made explicit. More often than not, an argument will make use of hidden assumptions that are extremely difficult to dig out.

A theory is a coherent set of hypotheses that embodies statements of general "laws" or universal statements ("for all *x, P* is true of *x*") meeting certain criteria, which we cannot go into here. Every theory makes use of theoretical terms or "hypothetical constructs," that is, postulated entities and relationships that cannot be directly observed or defined in any simple fashion on the basis of observable characteristics. In physics, such theoretical terms include *mass, negatively charged particle,* and *gravity.* A good part of the following chapters will be concerned with the hypothetical constructs of linguistic theory: *grammar, rule* (of a certain sort), *sentence in L* (where *L* is a "language"; the latter is itself a striking example of a theoretical construct). It has sometimes been argued that science must dispense with such theoretical constructs and replace them by terms that have some observational or operational definition. The inadequacy of such a view has been known for some time (even if not widely appreciated). The main objection to such views is that they fail to characterize correctly the way in which scientists actually construct explanations, and would rule out most of modern science. Once again, the methods of a discipline must be determined by the goals set for it, rather than the other way around. (Hempel, 1966, provides an excellent introduction to the general problems considered in this section.)

Finally, as we shall have occasion to note many times in the sequel, it is rarely the case that some single crucial fact will force us to abandon a hypothesis. Every science comprises an area of fairly well understood facts and a residue of mystery. Ultimately, a whole theory is involved when we come to the conclusion that we are wrong (or hope that we are right). And we hang on to whatever we have until we are offered something better.

BIBLIOGRAPHICAL NOTE

Readers who want a more general introduction to linguistics might begin with three classic works: Sapir (1921), Bloomfield (1933), and Jespersen (1964; originally 1905). Of these Sapir is the least technical and far-ranging. Bloomfield (1933) is a standard work of American structuralism and includes a great deal on historical linguistics. The present work is based most of all on the work of N. Chomsky, to which references will be given throughout. Some more recent general introductions are Lyons (1968) and Langacker (1968); for syntax, Langendoen (1969). A convenient summary of much of the transformational literature on English syntax is Stockwell, Schachter, and Partee (1973) (this work presupposes familiarity with syntactic theory), and as an introduction to a number of problems in English syntax and to the transformational approach in general, see Langendoen (1970). Readers should supplement the point of view followed here by study of such works as Gleason (1961) and Hockett (1958). We will consider mostly examples from English. An important part of beginning work in linguistics is an acquaintance with a variety of problems in various languages; sets of problems for such purposes can be found in Koutsoudas (1966) and Langacker (1972).

Problems and Questions

1. Comment on the statement: "*ain't* isn't English."
2. Give a list of what you feel to be the characteristic properties of human language.
3. A certain linguist studies an Indian language of the Pacific coast. He notes (a) that he has a great deal of difficulty in gaining a practical control of the language; (b) that only the oldest generation speaks the language with fluency, the middle generation (about age 30–45) is more hesitant in its use, while the children do not speak it at all, although most understand a considerable amount; (c) that everyone except for a few old people speaks and understands English. He concludes that the language is so difficult that it takes about thirty years to learn it. Argue against his conclusion, and try to think of evidence that could be found to refute his theory.
4. Argue against the notion that children learn language by imitation.
5. In what disciplines besides linguistics might one want to make a distinction between "competence" and "performance"?
6. Comment on the statement: "Every language is like Latin."
7. Find examples of impossible sequences of sounds for English speakers.
8. Find examples of impossible sequences of words in English.
9. Describe a system of communication that might be used by beings who

   a) had only a sense of smell.
   b) could only touch and feel, but not see or hear or make noises.

10. All languages apparently have pronouns like *I, you,* "third person" (*he, she, it*), with or without further distinctions of number, gender, and so on ("we including you," "we excluding you"). Invent a system of pronouns that is based on some other set of distinctions than that underlying the examples above.

11. Catalog some of the ways in which language functions as a tool in social interaction, to mark social status, sex, and so on.

12. Comment on the following definition of a standard meter: "A meter is exactly equivalent to the length of a platinum-iridium bar of a certain diameter at a certain temperature, suspended across two supports exactly 0.572 meters apart."

13. Why is, if it is, the study of linguistics important?

chapter

2

Grammars and Languages

2.1 Why Study Grammars?

In much linguistic work of the last decade and a half, the question "What is language?" has been turned into the question "What are grammars for natural languages like?" In this chapter we will take up some fundamental notions about grammars and languages, but before doing so we might ask whether this way of attacking our subject is a reasonable one. Chomsky's framing of the question in this way (1957) represented a major break in the history of linguistics, and it is by no means the case that there is a consensus among linguists that this road is the best one to take (see, for example, Hockett, 1968).

The decision to study the structure of language by examining the structure of grammars might seem to be a matter of choice. If this were the case, we could argue for it only on grounds of practical considerations. An alternative approach might go like this: since we know nothing whatsoever about many of the world's languages and since many are facing extinction as the juggernaut of Western Kultur rolls over the deserts and jungles, the best thing for linguists to do might be to equip hundreds of sound trucks to go to every linguistic community and simply record as much as possible (or one might try to stop the juggernaut). But no matter how useful such a project might be, we can argue that it would be insufficient. Presumably one reason for such a project would be to gather information about many languages while there is still time to do so. But collections of tape recordings of texts or conversations can form only a very limited part of the data required to understand the structure of a language. It is necessary in addition or instead to go to the field with certain questions in mind, and these questions always presuppose some theory of what languages are like. Once we admit that we want to understand languages and their structures, we must commit ourselves to constructing some kind of theory or theories about them.

But the decision to study languages in a theoretical way does not yet tell us how to go about doing it. At different times in the history of linguistic research quite different approaches have been made.

One such approach is that of what is often called traditional grammar. Grammarians such as G. O. Curme (writing on German and English) or Otto Jespersen (English) produced voluminous works containing observations and generalizations about syntax that have hardly been approached in their attention to detail. But the bases for these works are largely unexplored; that is, the work took for granted most of what we are trying to understand. The presentation is informal, and very little attention is paid to general, cross-linguistic concepts. It is assumed that the reader knows roughly what is meant when a term like "verb," "pronoun," or "relative clause" is used. Once again, we can conclude that, no matter how useful and important such work is, it must be supplemented by an attempt to lay bare the foundations upon which it rests. (This necessity was obviously recognized by Jespersen, who wrote many works dealing with problems of general linguistics.)

Another approach might be to ask if we could program a computer to take as input transcriptions of utterances from a language, supplemented perhaps by information about certain aspects of the meaning of these utterances, and produce descriptions, or grammars, of languages as output. One period in American linguistics seems to have been dominated by the attempt to provide such "discovery procedures" (see, for example, Harris, 1951). But if we examine the basis for such "structural grammars" we can see that they presuppose a theory of language that can be shown to be false.

Every general theory about language requires some universal concepts. We can discard immediately the notion that there are no language-independent categories or theoretical terms. Even though it has been seriously claimed that "languages can differ without limit and in unpredictable ways" (Joos, 1957, p. 96; attributed to what Joos calls the Boas tradition), every linguistic theory makes some universal claims; for example, there is the claim that every language is organized on at least two levels, as a system of sounds and as a system of grammatical elements that combine in certain partially fixed ways. The question then is not: Are there linguistic universals? but rather: What linguistic universals are there?

Suppose that we confined our general cross-linguistic concepts to those that refer only to types of categories rather than categories themselves, and suppose we limited ourselves to concepts that can be operationally defined on the basis of the techniques we use to arrive at these categories (for example, the instructions that we would give our grammar-producing computer). Thus, we might define *phonemes* as classes of sounds that figure as units in a language, and that meet certain operational tests; *morphemes, morpheme classes,* and the like as classes of sequences of phonemes; and so on.

There are two fatal difficulties with the theory underlying such approaches. First, no known operational tests lead mechanically to the categories, classes, and other discriminations that are required for the grammars of arbitrary natural languages. The hope that they can be provided seems totally unjustified. Concepts such as *phoneme* and *morpheme* are hypothetical constructs that cannot be operationally determined. They must be defined not only within a general theory of language but with respect to theories of particular languages. But this requirement implies that we must have some general hypotheses about grammars to start with. Second and worse, even if we could provide some discovery procedures for the basic categories and define the units and classes of languages on the basis of these procedures, we could discount the theory on which they are based as making much too weak claims about natural languages. (One theory is said to be weaker than another if the class of natural languages defined by the first is properly included in the class defined by the second.) Empirical studies of language after language have corroborated the idea that languages bear similarities to each other going far beyond the existence of classes of sounds and so on. Another way of seeing this is to note that substantive concepts like *consonant, vowel, verb, noun,* and *sentence* have considerable validity across languages. If our theoretical terms were limited to formal ones such as *phoneme* and *word-class,* we would not have any way of explaining such similarities (and finding new facts of this order). (I am not claiming that such substantive categories are the same in detail from one language to another, but rather that they are far from totally different.)

To put the last point in a slightly different way, the alternatives are not between studying grammars and doing something else, but between two different substantive theories about what grammars are like. One theory projects a much wider set of possible grammars than the other one. We choose, on the basis of known facts, that theory which makes more specific claims about natural languages. Even if we had no factual basis, we would choose the more specific theory simply because it tells us more and hence can be refuted (or corroborated) more easily by examining new facts (the basis for such an argument is discussed in Sections 7.76 and 9.2).

We might admit or decide that the most fruitful approach to studying the structure of language is to study the possible systems that underlie languages, but it would still be possible to take an alternative approach to the study of grammars, namely, to try to study utterances directly in some unified way. Such an approach would dispense with the competence-performance distinction entirely. (Some linguists, for example, Sydney Lamb, have represented their theories in this way.) The only way to decide between the two approaches, as far as I can see, is to suggest alternatives and see which ones provide the more revealing account of language, open more avenues to new questions, and so on. But, in fact, it seems that the choice is not really between making or not making the competence-performance distinction, but rather between making it in one way or another. Once we admit that a single factor is a problem of language *use,* rather than *knowledge* of language, we have drawn the distinction. Then the question becomes not whether to draw it, but how to draw it in particular areas. Presumably no one would propose to include directly in the description of a language the distortions and errors in speech that occur under the influence of alcohol. Once we decide to exclude those facts, as I think everyone would, we have committed ourselves to studying competence apart from performance. (Notice that the decision, even in this case, does not entail that we ignore the study of the effects of inebriation on speech or possible inferences we might draw *about competence* from such study.)

Let us consider a more interesting example and at the same time use our conclusions to learn something about a specific requirement that can be placed on a theory of grammars.

2.2 Finite and Infinite

One of the central facts about the way people talk is their creativity, by which is meant the ability to invent and understand novel utterances and to use them appropriately. We might ask whether this aspect of natural languages implies that the number of different sentences of a language is infinite or merely very large.

If we think about this question for a moment, two apparently contradictory results emerge. On the one hand, there seems to be no longest English sentence. If we admit that, given any English sentence, we can concoct some way to add at least one more word to the sentence and come up with a longer English sentence, then we are driven to the conclusion that the set of English sentences is (countably) infinite. For example, given a sentence like *It's raining,* we can add *Harry thinks that* . . . , to which we can in turn add *Sally says that* . . . , and so on. On the other hand, we could name some arbitrarily high number, say one billion, and feel confident that no person would ever utter a sentence containing more than one billion words. But if there is an upper limit to the length of English sentences, no matter how large we care to make it, then the set of English sentences is finite.

There is evidently no direct empirical evidence that will settle the question whether the set of English sentences is finite or infinite (contrary to the assertion in Hockett, 1968, p. 60). This follows from the fact that the set of English sentences is not something that exists apart from theories about language and about English. We cannot identify the set of English sentences as the set of utterances that have been used, for reasons mentioned in Chapter 1 and in the last part of Section 2.1. If it were so identified, then the set of English sentences would be finite.

The only way in which we can decide the question is to ask about the kinds of theories that would lead to one or the other answer. If a theory asserting that the set of English sentences is infinite can be justified on some grounds, then we will choose that theory.

Recall that we need to resolve an impasse. On the one hand, it seems that there is no longest English sentence; on the other hand, this seems to lead us to say that there could be an English sentence a billion words long. The way out of the impasse is to follow the lines we have already indicated by separating out a theory of grammar from a theory of performance. The set of grammatical English sentences is infinite; there is no longest English sentence. But the set of actually usable English sentences is finite, not because of the grammar of English, but because of other factors, mostly completely nonlinguistic: limitations on attention span, facts about the length of human life, and so on. We can calculate approximately how fast it is possible to speak and how many seconds a human being can be expected to live, and make a very confident prediction that no English utterance can be used that would require a length beyond the life span of an individual. But this is not a fact of grammar; it is a fact about human longevity, which would also play a role in determining the maximal length of symphonies, ping-pong games, and sexual unions.

We can support the decision to consider the set of English sentences infinite by looking at alternative theories of grammar. One of the central facts about language structure is that it is possible to construct complicated sentences by putting simpler sentences together in various ways. Constructing grammars that specify exactly how to do this seems to provide a revealing explanation for this facet of language structure. If we decide to treat the obvious limitations on length and complexity as a matter to be dealt with in theories of performance, we can account for the way in which sentences are used as fundamental building blocks for other sentences, and in addition we will be able to account for other facts. If limitations of length and complexity are a function of language use rather

than knowledge about language, then changing the conditions of performance ought to result in changes in those limitations, and this indeed seems
to be the case. If we allow people increasing lengths of time to prepare
an utterance, or if we furnish them with external aids to memory, they
can produce and understand longer and more complicated sentences.

All of this points up the fact that the set of English sentences is a
theoretical construct rather than something directly observable or given.
The set of acceptable utterances of English is another theoretical construct that involves, presumably, both a theory of English grammar and
theories about other factors affecting performance. The set of actually
used English utterances is a finite set (for any stretch of time) that forms
part, but only part, of our empirical basis for testing the adequacy of both
theories of competence and theories of performance. Suppose I ask
whether a particular English sentence, *The macaque overturned the bowl
of chicken soup,* is grammatical and acceptable. To find a transcription
of this sentence in some record of actual utterances would not tell me that
the sentence in question is grammatical, and failing to find it (as I undoubtedly would) would certainly not permit me to conclude that it is ungrammatical or unacceptable. (The disagreements about whether to consider limitations on length and complexity part of a grammar, as evidenced
in such writings as Hockett, 1968; Reich, 1969; and Olmsted, 1967,
compared to the more or less standard transformational view expressed
here, seem to stem largely from differences in the meaning of such
terms as "English language" and "English sentence." It is "empirically
absurd" to think that there could be an English sentence a million words
long, as Hockett writes, only if you mean by "English sentence" either
actual utterance or acceptable sentence.)

2.3 Languages

In the remainder of this book, we will take a **language** to be a set of
sentences and a **grammar** to be some explicit account of (among other
things) the sentences of the language. We consider each sentence to be a
string or sequence of zero or more elements put together by an operation
of **concatenation** (literally "chaining together"). The elements might be
anything whatsoever; in our discussions of natural languages we may
think of them as representing distinctive sounds (phonemes) or other
linguistic elements (words, morphemes), depending on the focus of our
discussion. We call the set of basic elements the **(terminal) alphabet** or
vocabulary of the language (and its grammar). Very often we will deal with
simple artificial examples, in which the alphabet consists of arbitrary
letters *a, b,* and so forth.

Consider any alphabet—say, the alphabet consisting of just the letters *a*, *b*. Then there is an infinite language made up of all strings of these elements of any length: *a, b, aa, bb, ab, ba, aaa, . . .* Moreover, any subset of this set will be a language. For each such set we may try to give a grammar, which is just an explicit account of the particular subset we want. In general, and certainly in the case of natural languages, not all sequences of the basic elements will be permitted. There are no English sentences *The the the* or *Come why the house*. Often, and again this will hold for a natural language, the number of permitted strings will be infinite. Therefore a grammar for a natural language cannot be just a list of the basic elements nor a list of the sentences. A grammar is an explicit statement that provides such a list.

But what exactly do we mean by "explicit"? The only good answer to this question is to actually set down a general theory of what a grammar is, how the grammar is used to specify exactly a set of sentences, how we are to interpret the grammar and the sentences it describes, and so on. We will be doing this in detail in the next few chapters. But we can perhaps get used to the idea by contrasting an informal statement about English with the ideal that we have in mind. A description of English might contain the following statement:

> Interrogative questions in English begin with the interrogative phrase, for example, *Who said that? What did Kant propose? Why do you always talk too loud?* etc.

This description is perfectly clear to anyone who knows English, but since in a grammar we are trying to give an account of what an English speaker knows, we cannot presuppose this knowledge in our grammar. A grammar by itself must show what a question is and what an interrogative phrase is, and must (in order to correctly capture the English speaker's ability to construct an indefinite number of questions of this sort) replace the "etc." by some predictive statements or rules.

The requirement of explicitness is exactly whatever we need to replace informal statements like the one just given by a complete account of what is presupposed in such a statement. One of the primary characteristics distinguishing the theories that we will study from traditional or pedagogical grammars is this requirement of explicitness. For this reason, such grammars are sometimes called **generative grammars**. The term "generative" is borrowed from mathematics and means only what I have just said. A grammar defines precisely and explicitly—"generates"— the sentences of the language. No connotations about actual production are intended. A speaker of a language knows various things about stretches of sounds and noises, in particular, whether they are sentences of her language or not. A grammar taken together with a general theory about grammars models this knowledge in such a way that we can tell from the grammar what the language that it defines is. In principle, it should be possible to give a few mechanical directions and use a grammar to grind out sentences of the language it purports to describe. Only if everything is made explicit can we test the correctness of a grammar as an account of the native speaker's knowledge.

2.4 Generative Grammars

To recapitulate, a grammar of a language is a theory or set of statements that tells us in an explicit way which strings of the basic elements of the language are permitted. This is a necessary but not a sufficient criterion for an adequate theory of a natural language. In subsequent chapters we will add further requirements that go toward meeting some of the desiderata outlined in Chapter 1, that is, means for providing various further structural descriptions for the sentences. Here we will concentrate on the single structural description that assigns some value of **grammaticality** to strings of elements.

There are innumerable ways in which we might state a theory about a language explicitly. For instance, let us imagine a language L made up of strings of the letters a and b up to any desired length, and subject only to the requirement that the number of a's and b's in any sentence be exactly the same. The preceding sentence is a grammar of L in a perfectly real sense. Yet it still conceals certain assumptions about the contribution of a "user" of the grammar; for example, that he knows how to count. Let us consider two other grammars for the same language in which we try to make a little more explicit the way in which the grammar itself defines or generates the language.

Our first grammar consists of three statements:

1. ab is a sentence.
2. For any string x, if x is a sentence then axb is a sentence.
3. For any string x, if x is a sentence, then y is a sentence, where y is the result of rearranging the elements (the a's and b's) of x.

By ordinary use of logic and with the understanding—which amounts to a fourth statement—that nothing is a sentence in our language except by virtue of a deduction from 1–3, we can use this grammar both to construct sentences in L and to test whether strings presented to us are in L. Notice that we can do these tasks by means of any number of procedures, which may or may not draw directly on the statements of the grammar (in the terminology of Chapter 1, these are questions of performance).

Our second grammar takes a form that is more in line with the current conventions of linguistic theory. In place of the statements of the first grammar, we have a series of **rules.** Instead of using variable symbols like *x* and *y* (as above), we make use of special symbols in an alphabet distinct from the symbols of the sentences in our language. These **auxiliary** or **nonterminal** symbols will play a very important role in our later refinements of the system. One of these symbols, in particular, and the only one that we will need here, is *S* — the **initial symbol** — which may be thought of as standing for *Sentence.*

Rule 1. *S* → *aSb*
Rule 2. *S* → *ab*
Rule 3. *ab* → *ba*

We interpret this grammar as follows: A **derivation** from a grammar is a sequence of strings of symbols, each of which is formed from the preceding one by applying some rule of the grammar (the ordering of rules plays no role). We apply a rule "*x* → *y*" by looking through the string for the symbol or symbols to the left of the arrow (*x*), then writing down a new string that is just like the old one except that we have replaced the string to the left of the arrow (*x*) by the string to the right (*y*). The sentences of the language defined by our grammar are all and only the strings of terminal symbols for which there are derivations beginning with the string *S*. Notice these two conditions: (1) the string must consist of non-auxiliary or terminal symbols and (2) it must be derivable from *S* by rules of the grammar.

Here are several derivations of sentences of *L* from the grammar just given:

S	*S*	*S*
aSb	*aSb*	*aSb*
aaSbb	*aabb*	*aabb*
aaabbb	*abab*	*abab*
		baab

Once again, we can check the assertion that these are derivations of sentences from the given grammar in a number of ways. We can also stipulate a number of different ways for "producing" sentences from the grammar, each of which might be the analog of a theory of performance. One such explicit procedure might be the following:

1. Write down an arbitrary string of *a*'s and *b*'s.
2. Find a part of the string corresponding to the right side of a rule in the grammar.

3. Write down a new string just like the first one except that the part found under instruction 2 is replaced by the left side of the rule found under 2.

4. Continue steps 2 and 3 until the original string has been reduced to a single occurrence of the symbol *S.*

5. If step 4 is successfully concluded, then the original string is a sentence in the language of the grammar.

Of course this is not a very efficient procedure. Notice, however, that it does use the rules of the grammar in a direct way. It is possible to imagine performance theories for this language that would bypass the rules of the grammar completely. For example, an obvious procedure for checking whether a given string is a sentence of the language would be simply to count the occurrences of *a*'s and *b*'s. One of the interesting questions of a theory of performance is just the question whether speakers of a language "use" the rules of the grammar postulated by the linguist in any direct way.

Before turning to an example of a grammar for a bit of natural language of the sort just introduced, let us notice that we might sometimes wish not only to replace a string of symbols by another string of symbols in a rule but to delete one or more symbols. Recall that I introduced the term *string* above to mean a sequence of zero or more symbols. The string consisting of no symbols at all is called the **null string.** Let us refer to it by the symbol "ø." Now we can think of a rule that deletes some symbol as a rule in which the symbol is replaced by ø. A rule saying "delete an occurrence of *a*" will be written as follows:

$$a \rightarrow \emptyset$$

Applying this rule to a string *bab* would yield the string *bb*. In the underlying system of concatenation that must be included in a formal development of the ideas outlined here, the null string plays the same role as does zero in arithmetic (an identity element): for any string *x,* $\emptyset + x = x + \emptyset = x$. (In most of our examples it will not be necessary to use any special symbol for concatenation. Traditionally, a plus sign or an arch is used: $a + b$ or $\overset{\frown}{a\ b}$ is the string formed by letting *b* follow *a*.)

2.5 Example

Let us now consider an example of a grammar of this sort for some English sentences. Suppose we wish to describe a small segment of the English language (as a written system) consisting of sentences of the following sorts:

Example   31

John loves Mary.
John hates Mary.
John says that Mary loves Harry.
Harry knows that Mary loves John.

One grammar for this language might take this form:

1. $S \rightarrow N\ V_1\ N$ 5. $N \rightarrow$ Harry
2. $S \rightarrow N\ V_2$ that S 6. $V_1 \rightarrow$ hates
3. $N \rightarrow$ John   7. $V_1 \rightarrow$ loves
4. $N \rightarrow$ Mary   8. $V_2 \rightarrow$ knows

9. $V_2 \rightarrow$ says

We can derive each of the sentences above from this grammar, but also some sentences that were not in our original list, as in this derivation:

$$S$$
$N\ V_2$ that S (choosing Rule 2)
$N\ V_2$ that $N\ V_2$ that S (Rule 2)
$N\ V_2$ that $N\ V_2$ that $N\ V_1\ N$ (Rule 1)
Mary V_2 that $N\ V_2$ that $N\ V_1\ N$ (Rule 4)
Mary says that $N\ V_2$ that $N\ V_1\ N$ (Rule 9)
Mary says that $N\ V_2$ that Harry $V_1\ N$ (Rule 5)
Mary says that Mary V_2 that Harry $V_1\ N$ (Rule 4)
Mary says that Mary knows that Harry $V_1\ N$ (Rule 8)
Mary says that Mary knows that Harry hates N (Rule 6)
Mary says that Mary knows that Harry hates John (Rule 3)

In this grammar, the terminal symbols are the English words *John, Harry, Mary, hates, loves, knows, says, that*. The auxiliary symbols are S, N, V_1, V_2. Notice the similarity between a derivation from a grammar and a proof in a mathematical system. S – the initial string – plays the same role in the derivation as might an axiom in a mathematical system. Further steps in the derivation follow in each case by applying a rule in accordance with a general principle, much like a rule of inference in a mathematical proof. In fact, a grammar is a particular kind of formal system, and some developments in linguistic theory have drawn heavily on certain branches of mathematics and formal logic. (The foregoing comparison is included at this point solely in order to clarify the nature of a grammar for readers who come from a background of logic or mathematics. There is, in fact, a branch of mathematics devoted to the abstract study of "grammars," which we will take up in Chapter 8.)

What exactly do the rules of our grammar mean? We can agree to the following interpretations:

I. To say that S is the initial string of our grammar is to say that the string S is *generated*.

II. To have a rule of the form "$x \rightarrow y$" is to say that if a string "$\ldots x \ldots$" is generated then the string "$\ldots y \ldots$" is also generated.

III. If a string is generated and also consists wholly of terminal symbols, then that string is in the language defined by our grammar; no other strings are in the language defined by the grammar.

It is easy to construct simple grammars for invented "languages," or segments of real languages, like the ones considered so far. Obviously the grammar just given defines only a very small part of English. The problem of the linguist is to discover the grammar that defines *all*, and *only*, the grammatical sentences of given languages such as English.

2.6 Unrestricted Rewriting Grammars

We have just sketched a primitive linguistic theory. The description of grammars of the general sort just considered, the definition of the ways in which these grammars can be interpreted, and so on can be taken as a theory about the possible grammars that speakers of natural languages might "have." To what extent is such a theory confirmed? We can answer this question by asking how well the grammars defined by the theory meet the requirements outlined in Chapter 1 and in the first part of this chapter.

To begin with, the grammars we have looked at are certainly explicit. We noted earlier that most informal grammars presume that the reader already knows a great deal about language. In the grammars just presented, all that is presumed is explicitly built into the lists of assumed elements and the definitions of "grammar," "derivation," "sentence of the language defined by the grammar," and so on. We saw also that the principal virtue of explicitness is the vulnerability of the grammar to testing. In the grammar for a fragment of English just given, it is extremely easy to see its failures as a description of English. The grammar certainly describes *only* sentences of written English, but hardly approaches a description of *all* the sentences of written English. Notice, however, that these failures are failures of the particular grammar, not necessarily of the theory behind it. It is a much more difficult task to show that a theory about grammars is defective. To show the failure of a theory, it is necessary to show that every one of the whole class of grammars defined by the theory is defective in some way.

In Chapter 1 we saw that grammars for natural languages must tell us what is and what is not a sentence of the language described, or, in the terminology of Section 2.3, they must provide for statements about the grammaticality of strings of elements. It is easy to see that the grammars considered for the simple languages above meet this requirement. But what about the much harder question of the adequacy of the class of grammars for describing natural languages in general? That is, can we show that a grammar of the sort described above will be able to pick out the sentences from the nonsentences for any natural language that we might care to describe? The answer to this question seems to be yes, as we will see in a moment. Grammars of the class described fail in important respects, but not in their ability to cope with the requirement that grammars provide predictions about grammaticalness.

The grammars described above consist simply of an auxiliary vocabulary, a terminal vocabulary, and a set of *rewriting rules* that apply to strings of elements, with no special stipulations about the form of the rules. Such grammars are called **unrestricted rewriting systems** (or **grammars**).[1] It can be shown that the following statement is true:

If a language (that is, a set of strings) can be defined by any explicit formal system at all, then it can be defined by an unrestricted rewriting system. (We will return to this statement in a more formal discussion in Chapter 8.)

Now, if we were to deny that grammars of the sort discussed above can specify or describe all and only the sentences of some natural language, we would have to deny that natural languages can be described by explicit grammars. But why should we believe that languages can be described by grammars at all? One could argue that this is simply the fundamental assumption of linguistics and without it we would have no reason to continue our activities. But however enticing such an argument may be, it has no force, since exactly the same argument could be used to justify the theory that the motions of the stars influence the development of human character: without this assumption there could be no "science" of astrology. Rather, we must consider the assumption a working hypothesis for which there is a certain amount of evidence. First of all, children do learn to speak and understand natural languages in a relatively short time (compared to their life spans). Second, by and large, speakers of a language can tell the difference between sentences of their language and gibberish. It is difficult to reconcile these two sets of

---

1. The specimen grammars above do not make use of the full power of unrestricted rewriting grammars and actually belong to a restricted subclass of such grammars.

data with the notion that a language cannot be described by some sort of a system of rules. Third, the mistakes that children make during acquisition of their native language show clearly that they are learning systematic rules: *he goed* for *he went,* and the like. Finally, linguists have managed to describe large parts of natural languages with considerable success using grammars of one sort of another. If we make the underlying assumptions and the form of such grammars explicit, we find that they fall well within the bounds of the hypothesis that languages can be described by unrestricted rewriting systems.

It was argued above that a grammar must have the capacity to define an infinite number of sentences. The unrestricted rewriting systems we have considered meet this aim. For example, the fragment of English described by the grammar above consists of an infinite number of sentences. To see this, notice that the symbol *S* is reintroduced in Rule 2, so that it is possible to continue applying this rule as often as desired to derive longer and longer sentences. In order for a grammar to generate an infinite number of sentences, it is necessary that it contain some element from which we can derive further instances of the same element, so that the rules can apply recursively. We call an element of this sort a **recursive element.** As long as nothing in the grammar sets a limit to the number of times the element can recur, the grammar generates an infinite number of sentences.

We have seen that the unrestricted rewriting systems given above meet the requirements that a grammar be explicit and that it provide information about grammaticality. Let us now consider some inadequacies in the system of grammars that we have looked at.

The argument mentioned above to show that unrestricted rewriting systems are capable of describing any language that can be described by any formal system at all can be considered as an argument against the adequacy of such grammars. For without further specifications of the form of a grammar, our theory fails to distinguish natural languages from other kinds of systems. To say that a grammar is an unrestricted rewriting system is to say nothing more than that a language is a definite system of some sort. We might imagine a language in which the number of sounds in each word increases exponentially from the beginning of each sentence, or in which the number of words in each sentence must equal some prime number, or in which every sentence must have an even number of words. All of these are perfectly well-defined systems that could be described by a formal system, and hence by an unrestricted grammar of the type described. But we know from our experience with natural languages that no natural languages exhibit such regularities. With an unrestricted grammar it is possible to describe all manner of systems: chess games, systems of equations, logical systems of various sorts, the set of all possible football scores, and so on. But our linguistic theory should narrow this list down to capture just the set of possible natural languages. The net we have looked at has too wide a mesh.

On the other hand, our theory has had nothing to say about other aspects of the native speaker's competence. We need theories that will give us grammars yielding all the other sorts of information sketched in Chapter 1: sets of structural descriptions, relations between sentences, meanings, and the like. Thus, unrestricted rewriting systems fail in both directions. They provide too broad a class of possible languages (as sets of sentences) and are hence too powerful. And they fail to provide enough information to account for many of the most important parts of a native speaker's knowledge, and are hence too weak. In subsequent chapters we will examine a selection of more richly structured theories, which seem to come closer to the ideal requirements of a syntactic theory.

Problems and Questions

1. For each of the following grammars, describe the language generated (in these and following examples, capital letters stand for auxiliary symbols and small letters, for terminal symbols).

Example:
$$S \rightarrow AB$$
$$A \rightarrow aA$$
$$A \rightarrow a$$
$$B \rightarrow bB$$
$$B \rightarrow b$$

This grammar generates the language consisting of all and only the strings consisting of one or more a's followed by one or more b's. (A handy notation for a string of n a's is a^n, so that we may describe this language as consisting of strings of the form $a^n b^m$, where n and m may be any numbers greater than zero, or in shorthand $n, m > 0$.)

a) $S \rightarrow aSb$
$\quad S \rightarrow ab$

b) $S \rightarrow aSa$
$\quad S \rightarrow bSb$
$\quad S \rightarrow aa$
$\quad S \rightarrow bb$

c) $S \rightarrow abSc$
$\quad S \rightarrow abc$

d) $\quad S \rightarrow aSBC$
$\quad S \rightarrow aBC$
$\quad CB \rightarrow BC$
$\quad aB \rightarrow ab$
$\quad bB \rightarrow bb$
$\quad bC \rightarrow bc$
$\quad cC \rightarrow cc$

2. On pp. 28–30 above we discussed a language consisting of all and only the strings of a's and b's containing equal numbers of these symbols. Write a set of rewriting rules that will take this language as input and reduce every sentence in the language (and no other strings) to the null string.

3. Write grammars that generate the following languages (see Problem 1 for the notation):

    a) ab
    b) $ab, aabb, aaabbb$
    c) $a^n b^m a^m b^n$ $(m, n > 0)$
    d) $a^n b^m a^n b^m$ $(m, n > 0)$
    e) John ate the fish.
       The fish ate John.
       The fish who said that John ate the fish ate John.
       John said that John ate the fish.
       John said that the fish ate John.
    f) An infinite number of sentences like the sentences of Problem 3e.

4. Show that a grammar with no recursive symbols will generate only a finite number of sentences.

5. Show that a language is finite if and only if there is a longest sentence in the language.

6. What evidence and arguments can you give against the idea that speakers of natural languages simply memorize long lists of sentences?

chapter

3

Phrase-Structure Grammars

3.1 Phrase-Markers

When we examine an English sentence such as *Harriet tried to swallow the goldfish,* we find our judgments about the structure of the sentence include two sorts. On the one hand, we consider certain words to be grouped together more closely than others. For example, *the* and *goldfish* seem to go together in a way that *to* and *goldfish* or *swallow* and *the* do not. Moreover, certain of these groupings are again grouped into larger constituents, and so on. As long as we restrict our groupings to adjacent elements, such judgments can be represented by bracketings, or in the form of a so-called tree-diagram:

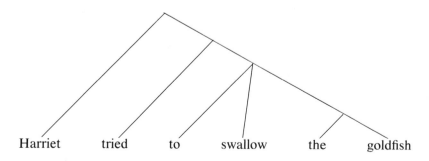

[[Harriet] [[tried] [[to] [swallow] [[the] [goldfish]]]]]

On the other hand, we judge the words and the groupings of words to be examples of different types or categories of phrases. The whole sequence above is a sentence, *Harriet* and *goldfish* are nouns (of different types), while *Harriet* again and the phrase *the goldfish* are obviously units of a single type that we call (following usual terminology) a noun phrase, and so on. We can combine both kinds of information into a single representation by attaching labels such as *Sentence* (*S*) or *Noun-Phrase* (*NP*) to the nodes of our tree-diagram or to the brackets of our bracketing:

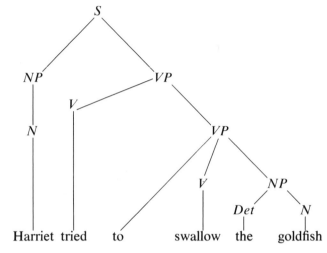

[[[Harriet]] [[tried] [[to] [swallow] [[the]
S NP N   VP V   VP   V   NP Det

[goldfish]]]]]]
N

S: sentence
VP: verb phrase
NP: noun phrase
N: noun
Det: determiner

A structure of the sort representable by a labeled bracketing or a labeled tree-diagram is called a **phrase-marker** (*P-marker* for short). A P-marker is a linguistic reconstruction of the notions embodied in the traditional exercise of parsing sentences. In this chapter we study a class of grammars that provide P-markers to represent such information about the sentences generated by the grammar. First we shall examine more closely the nature of P-markers, and then ask what kinds of grammars might provide P-markers for the sentences generated by the grammar. Then we shall consider some evidence for the reality of the hypothetical constructs embodied in P-markers. Finally, we will ask again about the adequacy of the whole class of grammars considered.

Phrase-markers provide two basic kinds of information. As we have seen, they provide an analysis of the sentence into parts that are classified as to type. The basic relationship here is that of being a constituent of a certain type. This relationship is called **dominance.** In the phrase-marker above, one occurrence of the label *NP* dominates the element *Harriet,* another the phrase *the goldfish.* We interpret this linguistically to mean that in this sentence, with the particular analysis represented by the P-marker, *Harriet* and *the goldfish* are constituents of the type *NP.* In addition, the P-marker gives a formal representation to the linear ("left-to-right") relationships of the elements, called **precedence** relations. Thus, if we transposed the branch ending with *Harriet* to the end of the sentence, we would have a different P-marker (in this case it would directly represent no English sentence). The difference would not be in the relations of dominance, since they would remain the same, but in the order from left to right.[1]

Moreover, it is possible to define certain other relations on P-markers in a straightforward way. Thus, we might define the relation "subject-of" as the relation holding between the *Noun-Phrase* immediately dominated by an *S* and the sentence dominated by that *S.*

3.2 Phrase-Structure Grammars

In the last chapter we looked at a class of generative grammars called "unrestricted rewriting systems." These grammars include both terminal symbols and auxiliary symbols. We identified the terminal symbols with the actual bits of linguistic material that occur in sentences of a language. Suppose we identify the auxiliary symbols with the labels on the nodes of P-markers. Now it is possible to describe a class of grammars that will not only meet the requirement of defining a set of sentences, but also assign a P-marker to each generated sentence. Grammars of this sort will go at least part way toward meeting the goal of providing a representation for the speaker's knowledge of the structure of sentences.

We noted above that P-markers provide information about groupings of constituents and types of constituents. We can ensure that a grammar

---

1. Obviously, the terminology "left-to-right" is arbitrary (and ethnocentric). What is meant is an abstract ordering that corresponds ultimately and indirectly to an ordering in time for utterances.

will provide this information by restricting the rules of our grammar to those in which only a single symbol is replaced at each step and no terminal symbol is replaced by anything. If these restrictions are followed, it is easy to define a way of assigning P-markers to sentences. Reading off the terminal symbols from left to right gives the sentence, and the P-marker itself gives a direct representation of the structure of the sentence.

Grammars of this general class are called **phrase-structure grammars.** They are a special subset of the set of unrestricted rewriting systems (the grammar given on p. 31 above happens to be a phrase-structure grammar). That is, we can take our description of unrestricted rewriting systems and add more restrictions to yield the class of phrase-structure grammars. Hence every phrase-structure grammar is an unrestricted rewriting system, but there are unrestricted rewriting systems that are not phrase-structure grammars.

We can use phrase-structure grammars to define P-markers as follows. Suppose there is a rule

$$A \rightarrow B_1 B_2 \ldots B_n$$

We know that A is a single symbol in the auxiliary alphabet of the grammar. We can construct a piece of a P-marker directly from this rule:

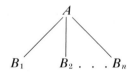

or using the equivalent notation,

$$[\ B_1 B_2 \ldots B_n]$$
$$A$$

Suppose there were a rule like this in our grammar:

$$A \rightarrow \emptyset$$

Then our associated P-marker would take the form

A

Since we are interested in constructing a theory with some linguistic interpretation, we need to ask how we would interpret P-markers with branches of this sort, that is, branches terminating in the null string. One interpretation of such a branch might be that there is actually a constituent in the given sentence with no phonetic representation. For example, a traditional account of imperatives is to say that there is an "understood" subject. So the P-marker for a sentence like *Shut the door* might be of this form:

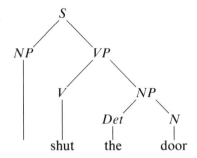

At this point in our discussion there is little direct linguistic motivation to prevent us from allowing rules of deletion in our grammars. But later chapters will argue that the correct reconstruction of notions like "understood subject" or "zero constituent" is done better in terms of transformational rules (see Chapter 5). We shall see that there need to be heavy restrictions on the allowed deletion rules. On the other hand, one can argue that what should be deleted in the imperative example (and others like it) is not a category but an actual terminal element *you*. If we were to allow a rule

you $\rightarrow \emptyset$

we would be claiming that there is a branch

in our tree; that the null string is a constituent of the type *you*. But *you* is not a constituent type at all. Thus, if we restrict our rules to rules for replacing auxiliary elements, then we cannot include the desired sort of deletion anyway.

There is another argument against the use of deletion rules in phrase-structure grammars. In the last chapter we saw that the class of unrestricted rewriting systems allowed a much too wide class of possible natural languages. To claim that grammars for natural languages are just unrestricted rewriting systems is to claim only that languages are systems of some sort. But it is possible to prove that the class of languages generable by phrase-structure grammars with free deletion rules is exactly the same as the class of languages generable by unrestricted rewriting systems. We are looking for restrictions on grammars that will narrow down the class of possible languages. But by including deletion rules in our phrase-structure grammars, we would open the back door after carefully closing the front door. This argument must be taken on faith at this point. In Chapter 8 we shall return to this essentially mathematical argument.

Phrase-structure grammars (PSG) themselves can be divided into several different types, of which we shall here consider two: **context-free** (CF) and **context-sensitive** (CS) phrase-structure grammars. Since both are PSG, they both meet the restriction that only single auxiliary elements are replaced in rules, but, as the names suggest, in the latter type we allow specification in the rule of the context in which it is to apply. A rule in a context-sensitive grammar can have the form

$$A \rightarrow X \text{ in the environment } Z - W$$

or more briefly

$$A \rightarrow X/Z - W$$

In a context-free grammar, on the other hand, every rule has the form

$$A \rightarrow X$$

In both, again, A must be a single nonterminal symbol (in linguistic grammars, S, NP, V or the like) and X a nonnull string of elements, terminal or nonterminal. We can see that the class of CS grammars properly includes the class of CF grammars, since the environment in which a rule applies *need* not be specified in a CS grammar (and *must* not be specified in a CF grammar), and it can be shown (see Chapter 8) that this is an essential difference.

Context-sensitive rules can find an immediate interpretation and use in many linguistic situations. For example, suppose we wish to account for the facts illustrated in these sentences and nonsentences of English:

I saw a boy.
I saw the palm tree.
I like Mary.
*I like boy.
*I saw the Mary.
*I saw a Harry.

Evidently there are two types of nouns in these examples: common nouns like *boy* and *palm tree* that occur after determiners and proper nouns like *Mary and Harry* that do not. Starting from a type of phrase called *NP*, a context-free grammar might include these rules:

$NP \rightarrow Determiner \quad Common\text{-}Noun$
$NP \rightarrow Proper\text{-}Noun$
$Common\text{-}Noun \rightarrow$ boy, tree, . . .
$Proper\text{-}Noun \rightarrow$ Mary, Harry, . . .

Now we have ensured the proper distribution of the two types of nouns, but our grammar fails to show any connection between them. This failure depends on two characteristics of context-free grammars: the category symbols like *NP* or *Proper-Noun* are simple, unanalyzable elements, and it is impossible to show how a single category can be represented by different subcategories in different contexts. We will take up the question of further analyzing the elements in a grammar in the next chapter. But even with simple elements it is possible to remedy the second defect with context-sensitive rules. A context-sensitive set of rules for English noun phrases of the type illustrated might take this form:

$NP \quad \rightarrow Det \; Noun$
$NP \quad \rightarrow Noun$
$Noun \rightarrow Common\text{-}Noun/Det -$
$Noun \rightarrow Proper\text{-}Noun/X_1 -$
$Noun \rightarrow Proper\text{-}Noun/X_2 -$
$$\vdots$$
$Noun \rightarrow Proper\text{-}Noun/X_n -$

where $X_1, X_2, \ldots X_n$ are all the other categories in the grammar after which *Noun* might stand, such as *Verb* or *Adjective*. Now not only have we achieved the correct distribution of items, but our rules will directly reflect the judgment that both types of nouns are indeed nouns, as for instance in these partial P-markers:

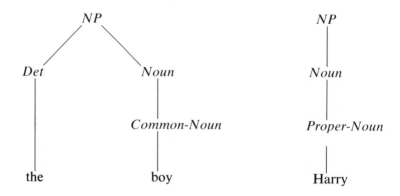

3.3 Ordering of Rules

As we have defined them, PSG include sets of rules that are *unordered*. That is to say, whether we use the rules to give derivations, as in the last chapter, or to construct P-markers, all we need to do at each step is to look through the rules to find some element (perhaps in some context) matching the final line of the derivation or the sequence of lowest elements in our P-marker. If we find such a rule, we know how to take the next step. The very nature of the rules imposes an ordering of possible steps. For example, if we have not yet applied a rule giving the element *NP*, we obviously cannot apply any rule with this element on the left of the arrow. As opposed to this kind of **intrinsic** ordering, however, it is possible to define grammars in which the rules must be applied in conformity with an explicitly specified **extrinsic** ordering. Most linguistic grammars using context-sensitive rules have in fact used an extrinsic ordering of the following sort:

> Assume that all the rules of the grammar are ordered from 1 to *n*. If a rule in a certain place in this ordering is applied, then no rule ordered earlier may be applied until all the rules have been applied (if applicable) and we start over again with Rule 1. Further, if several adjacent rules apply to the same symbol in the same context, then one of these rules must be applied before going on to the next rule.

Suppose we have a grammar with these rules (with *a, b, c* terminal):

1. $S \rightarrow B\ C$
2. $S \rightarrow B$

3. $B \rightarrow a/-C$
4. $B \rightarrow b$
5. $C \rightarrow c$

If the rules are ordered in the sense just defined, there will be these possible derivations:

```
    S         S
 B    C      B
 a    C      b
 a    c
```

But if the rules are unordered, there will be in addition a derivation leading to the string bc. Thus, imposing an extrinsic ordering on the rules can make a difference in the language generated.

Now we need to ask whether grammars for natural languages should impose an extrinsic ordering on their rules. We can return to this question in detail only in Chapter 6, when we have built up a picture of a complex grammar consisting of a number of different components. For now, let us consider very briefly the kind of argument that might be used to support extrinsic ordering of rules in context-sensitive grammars.

Recall the partial grammar for English *NP*'s in the last section. In order to ensure that those unordered rules produced the proper result we had to include not only a rule that forced us to choose common nouns in the context of a determiner, but a number of rules allowing us to choose proper nouns in all the other possible contexts of the grammar:

Noun $\rightarrow$ *Common-Noun/Det* $-$
Noun $\rightarrow$ *Proper-Noun/Verb* $-$
Noun $\rightarrow$ *Proper-Noun/Adjective* $-$

and so on. These rules fail to characterize the difference between essential and accidental connections among linguistic items. It seems reasonable to say that there is a restriction on common nouns such that they must stand after a determiner (in phrases like these), but hardly reasonable to say that after verbs, adjectives, and other categories we must have proper nouns. If we impose an ordering of the sort just considered on the rules, however, we can express the relations as follows:

1. $N \rightarrow$ *Common-noun/Det* $-$
2. $N \rightarrow$ *Proper-noun*

These rules say, in effect, that after a determiner you must choose a common noun, but everywhere else you may have a proper noun. Notice that the rules do not make any claims about the actual production of sentences (the speaker's performance). It would surely be nonsense to say that speakers of English, in producing sentences, first choose to use a determiner and then are forced to use a common noun. What the rules do express about the speaker's knowledge is something like this: "There are two kinds of English nouns (in this artificially limited type of noun-phrase), one of which must stand after a determiner, the other of which may not stand after a determiner." Notice further that the ordered rules make different predictions than the unordered rules. Suppose we find some new category in our grammar that we had overlooked in giving the rules of the unordered grammar. There is no basis in the rules for deciding whether it should go with common nouns or proper nouns. In the ordered rules, however, we can predict that it will be covered by the second, "elsewhere" rule.

3.4 Abbreviatory Conventions

In writing grammars, linguists make use of a number of abbreviatory conventions for collapsing partially similar rules. Let us define two such devices and then consider the theoretical status and justification for these abbreviations.

Suppose two rules differ only in the presence or absence of some item, for example:

$$S \rightarrow aSb$$
$$S \rightarrow ab$$
or
$$NP \rightarrow Det\ Noun$$
$$NP \rightarrow Noun$$

Then we can enclose the optionally present item in parentheses and write the two (or more) rules as one:

$$S \rightarrow a(S)b \qquad\qquad NP \rightarrow (Det)\ Noun$$

Second, suppose two rules differ only in that one has some item standing in the same place as another item in the other rule, for example:

$$A \rightarrow XYZ$$
$$A \rightarrow XWZ$$
or
$$NP \rightarrow Pronoun$$
$$NP \rightarrow Det\ Noun$$

Then we can enclose the different parts in (curly) braces and write

$$A \rightarrow X \begin{Bmatrix} Y \\ W \end{Bmatrix} Z \qquad\qquad NP \rightarrow \begin{Bmatrix} Pronoun \\ Det\ Noun \end{Bmatrix}$$

Combining the two devices, we might write a rule like this:

$$NP \rightarrow \begin{Bmatrix} Pronoun \\ (Det)\ Noun \end{Bmatrix}$$

We have already used another abbreviatory convention in our discussion of context-sensitive rules. Notice that the first of these two rules abbreviates the second:

$$A \rightarrow B/C - D$$
$$CAD \rightarrow CBD$$

Are these abbreviatory devices of any significance except as conveniences for making rules easier to read, or for saving space? If they are merely such ink-saving devices, then we need spend no more time on them. But there is some reason to think that they are more than that. That is, it is possible to justify the devices as theoretical constructs of some importance in characterizing the competence of native speakers of natural languages. One kind of justification can be taken up only in connection with a discussion of the so-called evaluation metric, which we will consider in Chapter 10. But at this point we can already offer a certain amount of justification.

If abbreviatory devices like those above were merely conveniences that said nothing about the nature of human languages, then any abbreviation would be just as valid as any other. For example, we could define an abbreviation for the two following rules that would make use of the fact that the same elements occur on the right in a certain order and its reverse:

$$A \rightarrow BCDE$$
$$A \rightarrow EDCB$$

These we might abbreviate, say, as

$$A \rightarrow [*BCDE]$$

Or, to take an example from Kiparsky (1968), we might abbreviate the following two rules as the third:

$$X \to Y$$
$$Z \to X$$
$$Z \to \left[X\right]^{\to Y}$$

Why have linguists adopted parentheses, braces, and a few other devices that we will take up later, but not the devices that I have just mentioned? The reason seems to be that the devices adopted express something valid about the way human languages work and the way in which learners of such languages make generalizations on the basis of limited data. Specifically, we may make the following claims about the structure and working of natural languages:

   I. Linguistic constructions, units, and so on typically have variants that are determined by other elements in the linguistic environment.
  II. Constructions typically contain optional elements that do not change the basic character of the larger construction.
 III. Constructions, items, and so on can often be grouped into classes that can stand in the same sorts of environment, but may differ among themselves in their internal structure.

It is fair to say that proponents of every serious linguistic theory have recognized claims I, II, and III as characteristic of natural languages. And the abbreviatory devices introduced here find a certain amount of justification in the fact that they make it possible to express "linguistically significant generalizations" such as I–III.

3.5 A Phrase-Structure Grammar for English

Let us now consider an extended example of a phrase-structure grammar for a small part of English. In our rules we will make free use of the abbreviatory devices just introduced, and the rules will be ordered.

1. $S \to NP\ VP$
2. $VP \to V\ (NP)\ (PrepP)$
3. $PrepP \to Prep\ NP$
4. $Prep \to \begin{Bmatrix} \text{to} \\ \text{for} \\ \text{by} \\ \text{at} \\ \text{about} \end{Bmatrix}$

5. $V \rightarrow$ $\begin{cases} V_1/-NP \quad \text{to} \\ V_2/-NP \quad \text{for} \\ V_3/-NP \quad \text{by} \\ V_4/-NP \quad \text{at} \\ V_5/-NP \quad \text{about} \\ V_6/-\text{to} \\ V_7/-\text{for} \\ V_8/-\text{by} \\ V_9/-\text{at} \\ V_{10}/-\text{about} \\ V_{11}/-NP \\ V_{12} \end{cases}$

6. $NP \rightarrow \begin{cases} Pronoun \\ (Det)\,N \\ \text{that } S \end{cases}$

7. $N \rightarrow \begin{cases} N_1/Det- \\ N_2 \end{cases}$

8. $Det \rightarrow \begin{cases} Def \\ Indef \end{cases}$

Instead of giving long rules in braces we can simply give lists for the actual lexical items:

N_1: boy, girl, palm tree, fly, stick, . . .
N_2: Henry, Vanessa, Harry, Sally, . . .
Pronoun: he, she, it, I, you, they, . . .
Def: the, this, that
Indef: a, some
V_1: gave, showed, sent, explained, . . .
V_2: thanked, bought, substituted, . . .
V_3: laid, put, . . .
V_4: threw, caught, saw, . . .
V_5: told, reminded, . . .
V_6: spoke, ran, . . .
V_7: asked, sang, . . .
V_8: sat, swore, . . .
V_9: whistled, shouted, . . .
V_{10}: spoke, swore, . . .
V_{11}: saw, hit, killed, surprised, amused, . . .
V_{12}: elapsed, slept, shouted, sang, ran, existed, . . .

With this grammar we can derive sentences like the following:

Henry sang.
Mary spoke to the fly.
That the fly elapsed surprised a palm tree.

and an infinite number of others, some sensible, some not. Moreover, our grammar will assign P-markers to those generated sentences that have a certain measure of plausibility:

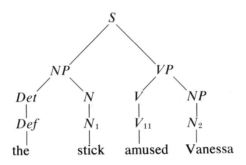

Let us now consider the problem of validating a grammar like the one just given. A large part of the justification for the rules derives from the justification that we can give for the P-markers assigned by the grammar to the sentences it generates. We will consider in a separate section below the problem of justifying P-markers. For now, what direct evidence can we give about the rules?

First of all, it is easy to show that the grammar does not generate only sentences of English. For instance, the grammar will provide the following strings of words.

1. *Vanessa reminded he about she
2. *I gave that the boy slept to that the stick existed

(1) is clearly ungrammatical because the forms *he* and *she* must appear in this position in a different form. If we substitute *him* and *her* the sentence is perfectly grammatical. (2) is impossible because we cannot sensibly talk about *giving* a fact to a fact. Are these mistakes simply inadequacies of detail, or are they indications of deeper inadequacies in the theory of phrase-structure grammars? On the face of it, it looks as if we could simply make a more detailed set of rules to accommodate these facts. For mistakes like those of (1) we can add context-sensitive rules that will ensure the correct distribution of the forms *I* and *me, he* and *him,* and the like. For problems like those of (2) we can simply provide a more detailed subclassification of verbs according to whether they can occur

with *that*-clauses as subjects and objects. I shall show in subsequent chapters, however, that both kinds of facts are better handled by proposing a different theory than the theory of context-sensitive phrase-structure grammars. Notice that, with regard to the adequacy of a general theory, it is a virtue rather than a defect to be able to show so easily that the grammar generates nonsentences.

Second, the grammar obviously does not describe *all* sentences of English. For instance, none of these sentences is generated by the rules:

1. Vanessa thanks you for the stick.
2. Did Henry swear at Sally?
3. The palm trees exist.
4. Charlotte danced.

There is a clear difference in importance between (1)–(3) and (4). The last sentence can be included in the list of generated sentences by the trivial modification of adding the items to the lists of lexical items at the appropriate places. We would not feel that the structure of English would be much affected if there were no word *Charlotte* in the language. On the other hand, we would judge inadequate an account of English grammar that failed to show that sentences can occur in other than the past tense or that in certain tenses the form of the verb is affected by the number of the subject (1); that included no description of questions (2); or that had nothing to say about the fact that most English nouns have a plural as well as a singular form (3). Once again, we will ultimately conclude that the addition of details like these entails deep modifications in the theory of grammar. But for the moment, it seems as if we could simply provide a more detailed set of rules of the same sort to include these different kinds of phrases and sentences.

Beyond these considerations, little can be said directly for or against particular rules of the sort we have considered. We consider next the validity of the structural descriptions assigned by the rules.

3.6 The Reality of P-Markers

What kind of evidence can we find relating to the validity of P-markers? It is obvious that no one can see or hear P-markers. That is, they have the status of theoretical constructs that can be justified only indirectly. There is, however, a considerable amount of evidence that these abstract characterizations of the structure of sentences do have psychological reality.

Justifications for the assumption that P-markers "exist" fall into three categories: direct judgments by native speakers about the structure of sentences, the role of phrase structure in the perception and production of sentences, and the role of P-markers in the system of linguistic theory. We consider each of these categories in turn.

As we saw in the first chapter, native speakers do have judgments about the structure of sentences. The intuitions of speakers must be used with care as evidence, but it would be foolish to deny their existence. Consider the example of an ambiguous sentence:

I saw the pigeons in the park.

This sentence can have (at least) two interpretations, equivalent to these two sentences:

In the park, I saw the pigeons.
I saw the pigeons that were in the park.

Corresponding to these interpretations are two distinct P-markers, roughly as follows (I omit irrelevant details in giving P-markers for many examples; the use of a triangle indicates that the internal structure of the constituent plays no role in the discussion at hand):

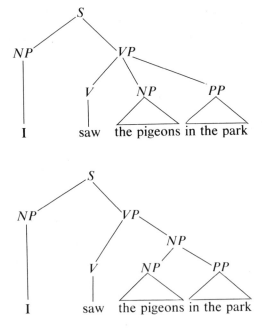

Moreover, most speakers of English would agree that only the second, unit-*NP* interpretation is manifested also in a sentence like this:

The pigeons in the park are multiplying rapidly.

Judgments of this sort provide very indirect evidence for the reality of P-markers. The judgments themselves tell us that there are differences and similarities in the structures of sentences that are not part of the actual physical signal. P-markers provide a representation for such differences that is sufficient to account for the judgments in cases like these. But innumerable other constructs would achieve these results. And beyond establishing very gross similarities and differences, judgments of speakers fail to give us any help in establishing the detailed characteristics of P-markers. In order to find evidence for the specific kind of construct embodied in a P-marker, we must look beyond direct intuitions about structure.

If P-markers do indeed represent essential information about sentences, then it is possible that they play a role in the perception and production of sentences. Psycholinguistic experiments have been carried out that can be interpreted as supporting the correctness of some aspects of P-markers.

In a number of experiments, subjects listened to English sentences with a simultaneous brief noise or click located at various points in the stream of sound. It was discovered that the syntactic structure of the sentence plays a large role in determining the point at which the click is heard. Fodor and Bever (1965), for example, were able to show that the same physical signal would be heard differently depending on context. Roughly, the click is heard as located at a point where there is a major syntactic break. To the extent that P-markers provide a precise basis for defining major syntactic breaks, experiments of this sort tend to support the correctness of the concept in general. Similarly, if subjects are asked to provide the next word in a sequence of words from a sentence, there is a fluctuation in the transition probabilities that fits the syntactic structure as represented in a P-marker (Johnson, 1965). Finally, the amount of nesting or self-embedding in a sentence plays an obvious role in difficulties of comprehension as well as production; self-embedding and nesting are concepts that can be directly defined on the basis of P-markers.[2]

---

2. A construction is said to be **nested** if it is interrupted by a smaller constituent. If, in addition, the smaller constituent is one of the same type, the construction is **self-embedded.** For example, the phrase *look the number up* is nested; the sentence *the fact that he is here disturbs me* exhibits self-embedding (see Miller and Chomsky, 1963).

Probably the most important arguments for the correctness of P-markers as elements in the structural description of sentences are those that depend on the role P-markers play within the structure of a grammar and within general linguistic theory. Since the following chapters will contain many examples of the dependence of various aspects of linguistic theory on P-markers, we can limit ourselves here to a few examples.

Part of the task of a grammar is to supply a set of possible "pronunciations" for each generated sentence; that is, an essential part of a grammar is a phonology. Studies of the phonology of various languages have shown that the syntactic structure of sentences plays a large role in determining various aspects of the phonological structure of sentences. One particularly clear example is provided by the rules for breaking up a sentence into possible intonational units or phonological phrases. Thus, consider the ambiguous sentence given above. If the whole sentence is pronounced under one intonation curve, it remains ambiguous. If we break up the sentence, however, we find a differentiation according to the syntactic structure:

1. I saw the pigeons in the park.
2. I saw the pigeons|in the park.
3. I saw|the pigeons in the park.
4. I saw|the pigeons|in the park.

(2) must go with the interpretation in which *in the park* is not a constituent of the second *NP,* (3) with the unit-*NP* interpretation, and (4) again with the interpretation of (2). (See Bierwisch, 1966, for a discussion of such optional phrasing rules for German.) Further, certain intonation breaks are obligatory. For example, in each of the following sentences there must be such breaks at the indicated points:

5. John,|shut the door!
6. Mary,|who lives in Connecticut,|is leaving at three.
7. I went downtown,|and John went home.

It has been shown that these obligatory phrase boundaries can be predicted on the basis of the presence of "root" sentences, meaning roughly *S*-nodes that are not within the predicate of a sentence (Downing, 1970). The first set of examples, (1)–(4), provides support for the bracketing made explicit in a P-marker, while the second, (5)–(7), provides support for the particular labeling that is assigned by the grammar of English to certain sentences. Another sort of example is provided by rules for stress in English. What the exact rules are for predicting stress in English is still unclear, but it is certain that the correct rules will have to differentiate between compounds and phrases: *bláckboard* versus *black bóard*. But there are independent syntactic reasons for assigning a label *NP* to the second and a label *N* to the first of these and similar examples, and this is again a representation in terms of P-markers.

The burden of the preceding paragraphs was to show that P-markers receive partial justification in the phonological rules of a language. Let us consider one example of the way in which other parts of a linguistic description might depend on the information embodied in a P-marker. Consider the two examples:

I talked to John about myself.
*I talked to John about the policeman that arrested myself.

By and large, reflexive pronouns like *myself* in English must stand within the same simple sentence (in some sense) as their antecedents. Again, this restriction can be described in various ways, and there are considerable difficulties in providing an exact account of reflexives in English. But it is difficult to see how any account could dispense with the notion "in the same simple sentence," a notion that depends essentially on the sort of structural description given by a P-marker. (See Sections 5.4 and 6.3 for a discussion of reflexives.)

Digression

It is worthwhile to pause for a moment and reflect on the nature of the question we have just been asking and the nature of the answers we have tried to give. The question was a typical one in science: We have proposed a certain theoretical construct (P-marker). We ask what evidence there is for the reality or the correctness of the construct. By the very nature of a construct, there is no direct way of observing the entity in question. Thus, we are restricted to justifying it in an indirect way. The construct fits into a complicated structure of theory, and we can ask questions about the construct in question only by making assumptions about the correctness of other aspects of the theory. Ultimately, we are left with the need to justify the whole theory rather than any one part of it. We must build all parts of the theory simultaneously. We are rarely presented with a situation where we can find crucial evidence about one small part of the theory. The individual parts of the theory receive indirect justification to the extent that the whole theory provides a satisfying and fruitful account of the whole range of questions presented to it, and to the extent that it leads to new questions.

3.7 The Adequacy of Phrase-Structure Grammars

If the evidence considered in the last section (and other evidence of the same sort) is valid, then we must conclude that some mechanism for providing P-markers for sentences is necessary in an adequate grammar. Correspondingly, general linguistic theory must define grammars in such a way as to make it possible to use the grammars for this purpose. The theory of phrase-structure grammars does meet this necessary condition for a linguistic theory. We shall see in the next few chapters that the theory is deficient in many ways, that is, the theory is not sufficient to meet all requirements for a grammar. Eventually we will define a class of transformational grammars. Such grammars include a component that is almost a phrase-structure grammar.

Problems and Questions

1.   Examine the following sentences and provide P-markers for them that seem to be reasonable in the light of your intuitions about English structure:

a) Harry loves Sally.
b) The girl and the tiger stared at each other.
c) I gave the man a dollar.
d) The big house is on the corner.
e) A good job is hard to find.
f) Try to persuade Sally to go home.
g) John ran away.
h) Away ran John.

2.   The following sentences are ambiguous. Provide P-markers for them that might be correlated with the different meanings of the sentences:

a) Harry kissed the girl in the park.
b) The fox saw the goose swimming in the pond.
c) Time flies like an arrow.
d) The president's fiscal policy is wrecking the economy.

3.   Determine the classification of English nouns that is evident in the following examples, and then modify the ordered rules given in the text, p. 49, to include these types:

I saw blood.
I saw the blood.
*I saw a blood.
I hear the air-conditioning.
*I hear an air-conditioning.
*I hear air-conditioning.
I see people.
I see the people.
*I see a people.
I like trees.
*I see Marys.

4. Expand these abbreviated rules into all the simple rules from which they have been formed:

a) $A \rightarrow \left(\left\{ \begin{matrix} B \ (C) \\ D \end{matrix} \right\} \right) G$

b) $A \rightarrow \left\{ \begin{matrix} B(C)\mathrm{D}/X - Y \\ F \end{matrix} \right\}$

5. Show how the resultant strings ("sentences") of a grammar containing the rule of Problem 4b would differ according to whether the rules abbreviated are ordered or not.

6. Revise the grammar of Section 3.5 to include the rule or rules that will ensure the correct distribution of pronoun forms: *I see him*, but *he sees me*, and the like.

7. The grammar of Section 3.5 includes no provision for plural nouns nor for present tense. If we include present tense, there needs to be some provision to ensure that verbs in it agree with the subject: *they sleep* vs. *he sleeps*. Discuss the difficulties that might arise if we attempt to extend the grammar of Section 3.5 to include these possibilities.

8. Show that labeled bracketings and tree-diagrams are equivalent, that is, that every P-marker that can be represented by one type of device can be represented by the other.

9. Discuss the following statement: "Theory A is superior to Theory B because it is harder to show that Theory A is incorrect, hence Theory A stands a better chance of surviving."

10. Describe a procedure for constructing P-markers on the basis of the rules of a context-sensitive PSG.

4

The Nature of Linguistic Elements

4.1 Formatives

In this chapter we will examine a little more closely the nature of the linguistic elements that enter into our rules. We will see that there are serious inadequacies in the account given so far, and we will undertake some revisions of that account. First we consider the nature of the terminal elements of our grammar—the elements corresponding to English words, suffixes, and so on, like *big, -ed, of*—and then the categorial elements like *NP, S, V.*

Let us first settle a matter of terminology. We call the terminal elements that correspond more or less directly to bits of sentences in some language **formatives.** Thus, in the fragmentary phrase-structure grammar given in Chapter 3, the English words listed at the end of the grammar are formatives. (Formatives correspond roughly to what are called *morphemes* in structural grammars.)

It is important to remember that formatives are hypothetical constructs like other elements in our grammars and are not given to us by any direct observation. For example, it is a question of theory whether we identify as instances of the same formative the underlined items in these English sentences:

I saw a <u>man</u>.   <u>Man</u> the lifeboats!
You really im<u>press</u> me.   She sup<u>press</u>ed a smile.
John went <u>to</u> the store.   I want <u>to</u> go swimming.

It is a question of theory whether the English words *railroad, cranberry, slimy,* and *formative* are to be considered simple formatives or sequences of formatives. It is even a question of theory whether we consider the English phrase *an apple* to be derived ultimately from a formative *a/an* plus a formative *apple* or a formative *a* plus a formative *napple* (to say nothing of the other logical possibilities: *anapple, anapp + le, an . . . le + app,* and so on).

Suppose we have agreed that there exists an English formative corresponding more or less directly to the word that we spell *sing.* What kinds of information are required to ensure that a grammar of English will generate sentences in which this formative is used correctly?

Most obviously, the grammar must tell us something about both the sound and the meaning of the formative. To meet the first aim, somewhere in the grammar we associate with each formative a phonological representation, which will provide the input to a set of phonological rules that ultimately yield a phonetic representation for the sentence. Let us assume that this representation takes the form of a phonological matrix in which each column relates to a **phonological segment** or **phoneme** and each row specifies, for the given segment, whether it does or does not partake of some phonological (ultimately phonetic) property. For example, it is possible to justify something like the following matrix for the formative *sing:*

	s	i	n	g
vocalic	−	+	−	−
consonantal	+	−	+	+
high		+		
back		−		
low				
anterior				−
coronal				−
voiced	−			+
continuant	+			−
nasal			+	−
strident	+			
tense		−		

The plus and minus signs in the cells of this matrix indicate values for the phonological property or **feature** in question. Notice that some cells are empty. These empty cells indicate points at which regularities of English or of language in general allow us to predict the value for the segment from other properties of the segment or of its context. For example, it is possible to predict that the nasal *n* will be specified for the features *anterior* and *coronal* in agreement with the following *g*, as we can see by comparing the point of articulation for the nasals in words like *sink*, *pump, hand, paint*. (Consonants are classified as [+ anterior] if they are formed in the front half of the mouth, as [+ coronal] if they are formed in the area reaching from the teeth to the hard palate. For explanations of these and other phonological terms the reader may consult Chomsky and Halle, 1968.) English does not have any simple formatives in which the nasal differs in point of articulation from a following stop, that is, there are no simple words or formatives like *simk, punp, haŋd* (where ŋ refers to the velar nasal of *sing, sink*). There must be some reflection of regularities like this in phonological theory and in a grammar. If we simply listed the terminal phonetic form of a word like *sing* with all features specified, we would have no explanation of the fact that new words in a language tend to sound like old words.

The kinds of rules that are needed to account for facts of phonology are different from the kinds of rules that we have considered so far. I do not wish to enter into the many questions that arise in justifying the form and content of phonological rules or other parts of a phonological theory (see Chomsky and Halle, 1968; Harms, 1968). We will be concerned with phonology only to the extent that it interacts with the rest of a grammar. For now, let us merely note that it is well established that a grammar must contain some rules and devices such that they relate to phonological segments and can insert segments, change their feature composition, delete them, and interchange their positions in the string of elements. When we refer to an element like *sing*, then, we are assuming some minimal phonological representation such as the one given above and further rules that will translate this matrix of features into a phonetic representation giving us the information for predicting the way the item will sound in a given context. The phonological representation of a formative has some phonetic consequences, that is, there is a relation of some restricted sort between the features of a phonological representation and phonetic features. But the representation is abstract in the sense that it must be translated by a set of well-justified rules into a phonetic representation. For example, the phonetic representation of the ultimate result of the element *sing* consists of only three phonetic segments. Well-motivated rules of English serve to produce the following steps:

s i n g
s i ŋ g
s i ŋ

A grammar can be characterized as a device for relating sounds and meanings. We have seen that part of what an English speaker knows about the formative *sing* is that it consists of a sequence of segments such that application of the rules of the language will produce a phonetic representation. However, there are properties of the formative that are not given in the phonological matrix but must still be associated with the formative in order to get a correct "pronunciation." If we compare sentences like the following ones, we see that it is necessary to know that certain rules apply to certain formatives and not to others, not just by virtue of their phonological form but by virtue of their membership in some nonphonological class of English formatives:

I sang the song yesterday.
I played the song yesterday.

The past tense of *play* is *played*. The past tense of *sing* is not *singed* but *sang*. How do we know that this is not the result of the phonological shape of *sing*? We are led to believe that the property is not purely phonological by the following consideration. There are formatives that appear to have exactly the same phonological form, but show up in different shapes in various inflections. Take for instance the three homonyms *wring, ring* (a bell), *ring* 'to encircle'. Their base forms appear to be the same, namely /ring/. Yet they appear in different paradigms:

Present	Past	Participle
wring	wrung	wrung
ring	rang	rung
ring	ringed	ringed

It would be possible, of course, to set the items up with different phonological forms but, as far as I know, only in an ad hoc way. Rather than do this we assume that formatives may have associated with them **morpheme features** that play a role in the operation of certain phonological rules. For example, we might assume that the first *ring* above is characterized, say, [+R 57], where R 57 refers to a certain rule of English of limited extent, the rule being a **minor rule** (see G. Lakoff, 1970a) with application only to verbs that act like *ring* in formation of their past tenses and participles: *sing, ring, sink, stink,* and so on. (Notice that one can provide some justification for the representation of *sing* and *ring* as ending on a nasal plus stop by reference to this rule.) Again, we are not interested in the exact details, but only in the conclusion that the formative *sing* has certain properties besides its strictly phonological ones that have to do with peculiarities of its inflections and so on.

Next, the element *sing* has a certain meaning by virtue of which speakers of English are able to understand sentences incorporating this word rather than others. *I sang a song* means something different from *I heard a song* or *I played a song*. Thus the formative must have associated with it somewhere in the grammar (using this word, as usual, in a very broad sense to mean roughly "total description of a language") some elements by means of which we can represent its potential contribution to the meaning of sentences using it.

Just as in the case of the phonological makeup of a formative, we assume that the element *sing* is not an indivisible semantic whole but rather a complex of simpler semantic elements. The *Oxford English Dictionary* includes the following under its entry for the intransitive verb *sing:*

> To articulate or utter words or sounds in succession with musical inflections or modulations of the voice, so as to produce an effect entirely different from that of ordinary speech. . . .

Such a definition provides many clues to the basic semantic representation of *sing,* but it obviously cannot be taken to be identical to such a representation, since it is simply a paraphrase into other English words. Just as the phonological features must have language-independent meanings, the ultimate semantic units must reflect universal elements of meaning. For the time being let us assume these "atomic" elements to be features, possibly complex, that provide the input to a set of semantic rules, which derive a **reading** for each sentence generated by the grammar in some sort of compositional process.

Finally, as we saw in the previous chapter, the formative has various syntactic properties. Let us list a few:

1. Sing is a verb. It is by virtue of this property that it can occur in contexts like these:

He is _____ing.
_____ me a song!
To _____ is more fun than to be silent.

but not like these:

The best _____ is *Home on the range.*
John is _____er than Mary.
The extremely _____ man told me a long story.
2. Sing is a verb of the class that can occur in the progressive aspect (*He is singing a song*), as opposed to verbs like *know* (**He is knowing the answer*).
3. Sing can occur in an imperative (as above (1)), unlike verbs like *know:* **Know that it's hot!*

4. Sing can occur in the passive: *This song was first sung by Rudy Vallee.* (**This man is resembled by his mother.*)
5. Sing can stand with two *NP*'s in its predicate: *She sang me a song* (compare **She saw me a sailboat*).
6. Sing takes as object nouns like *song,* not nouns like *alarm clock* or *boy.*
7. The subject of *sing* must ordinarily be an animate being, except in metaphorical use.
8. Sing does not demand an object (unlike, say, *compel: *John compelled* vs. *John sang*).
9. Sing can stand in the *-ing* form as modifier of a noun: *the singing boy* (vs. **the hitting boy*).

Let us summarize what we have seen to be some of the characteristics of the formative *sing:*

1. Phonological characterization sufficient and necessary to ensure correct phonetic representation by means of phonological rules.
2. Representation of the membership in nonphonological classes for predicting inflectional characteristics.
3. Meaning characteristics sufficient and necessary to characterize the contribution of the formative to the meaning of sentences in which it appears.
4. Syntactic characteristics, that is, information about the kinds of structures in which it can occur.

At the date of this writing, there is a great deal of discussion going on about the exact nature of the relationships between (1) and (2), and (3) and (4), respectively. We shall consider the latter pair in subsequent chapters (Sections 6.5, 9.62).

4.2 Formatives as Complex Objects

In the grammars we have considered up until now, the elements of the rules were simple unanalyzed units. We will now see that our picture of a grammar must be revised in such a way that the elements that enter into the rules are complexes of more fundamental elements.

It is easy to see that formatives must be complex objects at least to the extent that we distinguish between the phonological aspect of the element and other properties. This follows directly from the fact that phonological properties are independent of and not directly related to other properties, such as properties of meaning. Suppose we have a phonological rule of a general sort, for example, the rule in German that devoices the final obstruent (stop or fricative): roughly, when a word ends on an obstruent, then that obstruent must be voiceless. Thus the German words on the right are pronounced with a final voiceless consonant, whereas when some vocalic ending follows, as on the left, the stops and fricatives in some words are voiced, in some voiceless:

Räder 'wheels'	Rad [t] 'wheel'
Räte 'councillors'	Rat 'councillor'
sagen 'say'	sag [k] 'say'
Säcke 'sacks'	Sack 'sack'

The rule in question applies to every word in the German language that ends on an obstruent, and this property cuts across all other classifications; nouns, verbs, prepositions, articles, intransitive verbs, proper names, and so on may or may not end on obstruents. But even if we could manage to construct a very complicated phrase-structure grammar in which we accounted for the fact that voiced obstruents do not appear in final position, we would be missing the point. An adequate grammar for German must be able to account for the distribution of formatives in sentences independently of their phonological shape, and for the alternation of voiced and voiceless sounds independently of syntactic and semantic facts. This can be accomplished only if we admit that a linguistic formative is complex to the extent that it has a phonological side plus another side (at least) related to its meaning and syntactic privileges. Thus every formative is a pair, one part a phonological matrix (as sketched above) that is itself complex, and another part.

Now we will see that the "other part" is also complex. In a phrase-structure grammar we account for syntactic properties like those listed above by breaking down a certain category, say *Verb,* into subcategories, say *Verb-Transitive* and *Verb-Intransitive,* by means of a rule that effects this change, perhaps in a certain environment, for example:

$$Verb \rightarrow \begin{Bmatrix} Verb\text{-}Transitive/ - NP \\ Verb\text{-}Intransitive \end{Bmatrix}$$

Notice that the symbols *Verb-Transitive* and *Verb-Intransitive* are simply handy labels that have no systematic significance. As far as the grammar is concerned, they could just as well be P and Q. As a consequence, if we wish to refer to both kinds of verbs again in our rules, we need to name them both. Suppose, for example, both kinds of verbs need to be divided according to whether they can take as subject a *that-*

clause. In English, we do need such subclassifications, as shown by these examples:

It surprises me that she is in New York.
*It dislikes me that she is in New York.
It happens that she likes raw oysters.
*It sings that she likes raw oysters.

(*It* in each sentence "stands for" the *that*-clause. See Chapter 5 for an explanation.) We can make such a subclassification into verbs (of type "1" and type "2," say) in a phrase-structure grammar either before or after we have divided verbs into transitive and intransitive verbs. But by either choice we must name several classes in exactly parallel rules:

$$Verb\text{-}Transitive \quad \rightarrow \begin{cases} Verb\text{-}Trans\text{-}1/\text{that } S- \\ Verb\text{-}Trans\text{-}2 \end{cases}$$

$$Verb\text{-}Intransitive \rightarrow \begin{cases} Verb\text{-}Intr\text{-}1/\text{that } S- \\ Verb\text{-}Intr\text{-}2 \end{cases}$$

Or alternatively:

$$Verb\text{-}1 \rightarrow \begin{cases} Verb\text{-}Trans\text{-}1/-NP \\ Verb\text{-}Intr\text{-}1 \end{cases}$$

$$Verb\text{-}2 \rightarrow \begin{cases} Verb\text{-}Trans\text{-}2/-NP \\ Verb\text{-}Intr\text{-}2 \end{cases}$$

In this situation we can draw only one conclusion. There is something wrong with the basic framework within which we are working. The choice of one classification over the other as primary is arbitrary. In either case we are missing generalizations. The generalizations needed are these:

I. Verbs (in general) are classified according to what kinds of subjects they make take.
II. Verbs (in general) are classified according to whether or not they may take objects.

The generalizations cannot be stated without making reference to certain syntactic properties independently of others. Our theory should allow us to refer to these properties independently. We conclude that the elements of our rules should be considered complexes of properties rather than simple unanalyzed units. Notice that this argument is exactly parallel to the argument used above to establish that formatives should be considered complexes of phonological and nonphonological properties.[1]

The existence of such cross-cutting classifications of linguistic elements is a pervasive characteristic of natural languages and not at all an isolated phenomenon. Consider a somewhat more complicated example. In German it is necessary to classify verbs according to all of the sorts of criteria we have listed above (pp. 62–63) and in addition according to these (among others):

1. Whether or not there can be a prepositional object (as in our fragmentary grammar for English in Section 3.5).
2. If there can be a prepositional object, just which preposition can occur with the verb.
3. In addition, for some prepositions, whether the preposition takes one or another case.
4. If there is an ordinary nonprepositional object, which of three cases is assigned to the object.

Since each of these classifications involves from three to a dozen or so characteristics, and various combinations, it is obvious that a phrase-structure grammar for German verb classifications would be extremely complicated. But it is important to remember that we cannot argue that a theory is wrong from the fact that the grammars that we construct within that theory are complicated. We do not have any advance knowledge about how complicated a grammar should be. After all, a natural language is a very complicated system. But we can argue that the theory is wrong if it leads us to *arbitrary* complexities and classifications and fails to capture generalizations that appear to lie behind the complications of the system. Notice that an argument like this is considerably different from most of the arguments we have seen before. The argument rests on the requirement that a certain correspondence should obtain between the form of our grammar and certain facts about language that we feel to be true or significant generalizations.

4.3 Syntactic Features

The arguments just considered support the hypothesis that formatives (at least) are complex elements made up of "smaller" characteristics. Just what form the representation of these smaller properties should take

---

1. The cross-classification problem was first used to establish the complex nature of syntactic elements by G. H. Matthews; see Chomsky, 1965, pp. 79, 213 (fn. 13).

is very much an open question. Phonological theory had developed a fairly good picture of the nature of phonological segments as complexes of binarily specified features ($\pm$ features), as sketched above, at the time when the first arguments for complex syntactic elements were presented. There are direct arguments for considering phonological properties to be features taking one of several values. On the model of phonological features, syntactic properties are usually considered to be of the same sort. For example, if we consider that verbs may be classified as to whether or not they take objects, we may assume that they are marked [+transitive] if they do, [−transitive] if they do not. But it must be admitted that there is very little evidence one way or the other for this conception of most syntactic features.

Many syntactic features are represented by the following notation: suppose an element can stand in a certain environment, say $X - Y$, then we may mark it as positively specified for the feature "$X - Y$," that is, we mark it $[+X - Y]$, using a kind of picture of the environment as a name for the feature. For example, suppose we wish to assign a feature to nouns according to whether they can stand with a determiner (see Sections 3.2 and 3.3 and Problem 3 in Chapter 3). Then we might mark various nouns as follows:

boy $[+Det-]$
Mary $[-Det-]$
blood $[-Indef-]$

Notice that we might also have decided to consider definiteness in the determiner as a feature. Then the last feature might be represented in this way:

$[-[+Indef]-]$

That is, we have gone inside another complex element in our picture of the environment in which the noun in question may or may not stand. Whether these notations are merely handy mnemonic devices or have some systematic significance is again a theoretical question about which we have no very good evidence.

4.4 Grammars with Complex Symbols

Let us now modify our picture of a grammar as follows. On the basis of the evidence and considerations presented in Chapter 3, we assume that a grammar for a natural language will include some rules of the sort that can be used to determine P-markers. On the basis of the considerations given so far in this chapter, we assume that the formatives are not simple unanalyzed elements but complexes of phonological, syntactic, and semantic features. Each such **complex symbol** for a formative is a set of features. At least some features are themselves bipartite, that is, they consist of a specification (perhaps + or −) for a particular property. Thus we revise our picture of a P-marker to include such complex symbols as terminal elements. The P-marker for the first sentence diagrammed in Chapter 3 is roughly as follows:

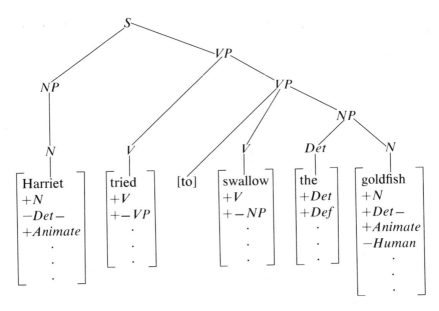

Several different theories of grammar conform to this rough general description. We will return to several alternatives after we have modified our picture of a grammar even more drastically in the next chapter. For now, we assume that the grammar that assigns P-markers like the one above to sentences is divided into two main parts: a set of context-free phrase-structure rules and a lexicon. The lexicon consists of a set of entries, one for each formative, and each containing a number of feature specifications for the phonological, syntactic, and semantic properties of the formative. Among the syntactic features are some that determine, in a way as yet to be explained, the placement of the formative in a P-marker. Thus, for sentences like the one diagrammed we can assume these rules:

1. $S \rightarrow NP\ VP$

2. $VP \rightarrow V\ (NP)$
3. $NP \rightarrow (Det)\ N$

These rules will determine P-markers for sentences with transitive and intransitive verbs:

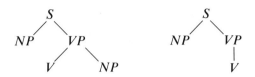

Each NP can be represented as either a simple noun or a noun with a determiner:

In our lexicon there will be, among others, entries of the following form, where I indicate phonological matrices by underlined representations in conventional orthography:

Harriet, $+Noun$, $-Det-$, $+Proper\text{-}Name$, $+Female$, $+Human$, $+Animate$, ...
the, $+Det$, $+Definite$, ...
goldfish, $+Noun$, $+Det-$, $-Proper\text{-}Name$, $+Animate$, $-Human$, ...
try, $+Verb$, $+-$to VP, $+[+N$, $+Animate]\ -$, ...
swallow, $+Verb$, $+-NP$, ...

Besides this apparatus, we assume the existence of a set of phonological rules that operate on the phonological part (at least) of the P-marker to provide a final phonetic specification for the sentence. A derivation from such a grammar includes a derivation of a prelexical P-marker and then the addition of appropriate entries from the lexicon to provide a full P-marker like the one above. We can call the final P-marker that results from adding these lexical entries the **syntactic structure** of the sentence.

The reader will notice that I have included in the entries above certain feature specifications that seem to be closely related to, if not identical with, certain aspects of the meaning of the item. The exact nature of the relationship between syntactic and semantic features is a largely unsolved problem. We shall return to it in Chapter 9. For now, we can simply note that some syntactic features cannot be identified with semantic features, for example, gender specifications for languages like

German and French. Whatever the correct semantic description of an entry like *table* may be, it is surely incorrect to imagine that it would differ between English, German, and French in such a way that tables were interpreted *semantically* to be sexless, male, and female in these three languages respectively, or forks, knives, and spoons to be feminine, neuter, and masculine respectively in German!

4.5 Categorial Elements

Besides the formatives, which we have just discussed, phrase-structure grammars contain auxiliary symbols like *Sentence, NP,* and *VP.* In the last chapter we saw that these elements have a natural interpretation as designations for classes of linguistic elements in languages. In the present chapter we have seen that there are many good reasons for believing that the terminal elements or formatives of a grammar are complex rather than simple. The question arises whether the auxiliary symbols are themselves also to be redefined as complexes of features. We shall continue to assume that they are simple elements, although some more recent discussions have thrown this question open (see McCawley, 1968a; Chomsky, 1970). However, a number of other questions about the status of such symbols need to be touched upon.

The initial symbol *S* has a special status in the theory as that symbol which figures essentially in the definitions of "derivation," "language defined by a given grammar," and the like. But the other auxiliary symbols have no such status. Should they be considered completely arbitrary symbols that have meaning only ad hoc from language to language, or should they have some language-independent interpretation?

On a priori grounds we prefer a theory in which these symbols have some language-independent interpretation. The reason is that we can make stronger claims about the nature of human language if we give some substantive meaning to the symbols of our grammar. Consider two theories and two possible worlds: in one theory the categories (except *S*) of our rules have no interpretation apart from the rules for that language; in the second they do have some independent interpretation. In one possible world there are no similarities among languages as to the classifications of formatives and the structures in which they occur; in the other there are strong similarities, even when the languages are not related. It is obvious that the first theory does not distinguish these two possible worlds, since it could happen by chance that the languages described by the set of possible grammars in that theory were in fact very similar. But in the other theory it is possible to rule out the first possible world by postulating some substantive constraints on the rules.

Now in fact, it appears that the real world of human languages is more like the second than the first of these possible worlds. By and large, we find we can make many predictions about classifications of formatives and structures across unrelated languages. At the same time, it is obvious that various languages cannot be described by exactly the same sets of phrase-structure rules, or else we would be able to map sentences from one language to another formative by formative and preserving order, which is manifestly false.

We can draw several conclusions from the above considerations. We need to search for some substantive and language-independent interpretations for our categorial symbols. In other words, it should be possible to give some meaning to the notions *Noun, Verb, Adjective, . . .* that will enable us to account for the fact that in many languages the constructions in which these categories figure are similar, and for the fact that often words like *man, hit,* and *hot* will enter into similar relationships with one another across languages. But within the theory we have considered so far, namely, the theory of complex phrase-structure grammars, there is no basis for accounting for these similarities. Thus, the theory must be inadequate.

Problems and Questions

1.   Write lexical entries for the formatives of the grammar given in Section 3.5.
2.   Write phrase-structure rules for the fragment of English given by the grammar of Section 3.5, according to the modifications of this chapter. Assume that there are separate lexical entries for prepositions and give them (that is, your grammar will include something like Rule 3 but not Rule 4).
3.   Using symbols like *NP, S, VP,* describe the kinds of constructions in which the following verbs in English can occur:

elapse	happen	like	get
surprise	remind	interest	manage
entail	forget	be	seek
seem	remember	have	know

4.   Consider two theories of phonology: (1) The features or elements by which we describe formatives have no particular phonetic interpretation except by virtue of the phonological rules into which they enter. (2)

Every feature or element used to describe a formative must occur in at least one form of the formative as a phonetic characteristic. Which theory makes stronger claims about the nature of phonological representations? Show.

5. State what additional assumptions must be made to show that the following principles lead to the conclusion that the categories of a phrase-structure grammar should have some language-independent status:

    i) Rules for giving the interpretations of sentences must make use of the relations *Subject, Main-Verb, Object* (of a sentence).

    ii) Rules for giving the interpretations of sentences must be language-independent.

6. Which of the following general statements are readily translatable into phrase-structure rules? For those that are not, give a general explanation in terms of the facts involved and the properties of phrase-structure grammars. For those that are, write a rule.

    a) Questions in English begin with an interrogative word such as *who, what, when,* or in the case of yes-no questions with some verb or verbal auxiliary such as *be, can, do.*

    b) A sentence (in a certain language) may consist of an optional sentence adverb followed by a *Subject* noun phrase, a verb, and (optionally) an *Object* noun phrase.

    c) There is a certain class of verbs that can occur with complement sentences or with a "prosentence" like *so: know, believe, think.*

    d) (In a certain language) adjectives that modify nouns must agree with the noun in number, gender, and case.

    e) (In a certain language) nouns are divided into animal, vegetable, and mineral; verbs are divided into transitive and intransitive, and are also classified according to whether their subjects (and objects) are animal, vegetable, or mineral.

    f) (In a certain language) transitive verbs all have a suffix $-t$; intransitive, a suffix $-u$.

    g) The intransitive suffix $-u$ (of Problem 6f) disappears if the following formative begins with a vowel.

    h) In English, the indefinite article is *an* before a vowel, *a* before a consonant.

chapter

5
Grammatical Transformations

5.1 Some Further Inadequacies of Phrase-Structure Grammars

In the last chapter we sketched a theory that counters some of the difficulties inherent in the notion of grammars as phrase-structure grammars with simple unanalyzed elements. In the present chapter we shall look at a radically different kind of rule that goes a long way toward meeting other difficulties in the phrase-structure theory of linguistic structure. We can see some of the properties of the new kind of rule by looking at some further difficulties and inadequacies in PSG and considering ways to overcome them.

The most serious defect of PSG is the fact that they assign only a single structural description to each sentence, in the form of a phrase-marker. In Chapter 1, we noted that some sentences seem to have basic similarities even though they have widely disparate forms, while others that appear to be very similar or identical have deep-seated differences in the organization of the constituents and their meaning relationships. Some further examples of the first sort are these:

That he is sick disturbs me.
It disturbs me that he is sick.

John kissed Sally.
Sally was kissed by John.

Harry captured the castle.
What Harry captured was the castle.
It was the castle that Harry captured.

John saw the fish.
. . . the fish that John saw . . .

Melissa caught something.
What did Melissa catch?

The parakeet is choking.
Is the parakeet choking?

Examples of the second kind are these:

This question is hard to answer.
This man is anxious to escape.
The lobster is too hot to eat.

I persuaded Mary to leave.
I promised Mary to leave.
I expected Mary to leave.

What he said was idiocy.
What he said was "Idiocy."

Crashing into the house, Harry saw an elephant. (*two meanings*)
She hates visiting relatives. (*two meanings*)

    The facts illustrated by these sentences suggest that a grammar should assign two structural descriptions to each sentence. If we had a pair of phrase-markers for every sentence, we could exhibit the similarities among sentences like those in the first set here as similarities between one member of each pair, and the differences as differences in the other member. Likewise, for sentences like those in the second set, we could show the differences by means of one kind of phrase-marker and the similarities by the other.

    In Chapter 3 we considered some evidence for the reality of P-markers as representations of the syntactic structure of sentences. Suppose we agree to call a P-marker corresponding more or less directly to the phonetic form of the sentence a **surface structure.** Then we can say that the sentences in the first set above differ in their surface structure, while those in the second are similar in their surface structure. We call the other P-markers associated with each sentence the **deep structures.** Thus, the groups of sentences in the first set have the same or very similar deep structures; those in the second set, different deep structures.

We have begged an important question in the above paragraph by assuming that the deep structure of each sentence is a P-marker of the same general nature as the surface structure. The grammars we will study in the next few chapters are based on this assumption. I will not attempt to give a complete defense of this view here (we will consider the assumption in Section 9.62). Here we may simply note that it is a very natural assumption and one that makes strong claims about deep representations. Several different considerations converge on the same general conclusion, as we shall see.

There is no obvious way in which PSG as such could be used to assign pairs of P-markers to sentences. What is needed is some way of relating P-markers and P-markers.

Let us look again at some sentences in the first set considered above (pp. 73–74). We have described them as being sentences with similar deep structures and different surface structures. The surface structures for them have roughly this form:

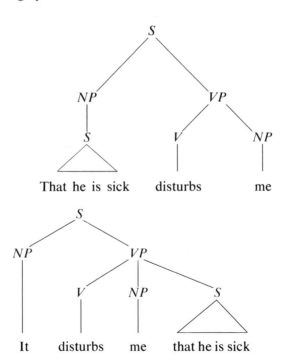

Within a phrase-structure theory of grammar, these sentences must be described in completely independent ways. However, it seems as if sentences like these two are not accidentally related. It is a fact about English that for many sentences of the form *X that S Y* there are also English sentences of the form *X it Y that S:*

That it is raining is false.
It is false that it is raining.

That Murgatroyd was the murderer was proved by Nigel.
It was proved by Nigel that Murgatroyd was the murderer.

I revealed that you were a Boy Scout to the F.B.I.
I revealed it to the F.B.I. that you were a Boy Scout.

It is clear that a grammar describing the members of these pairs of sentences independently is missing an important generalization about English. Suppose we were to add to our grammar rules or statements of the form: "If such-and-such a kind of sentence is grammatical, then such-and-such another kind of sentence is grammatical." Then it might be that we would also be able to solve the first difficulty, the necessity of assigning pairs of P-markers to sentences.

Finally, consider some difficulties in English grammar that were glossed over in the fragmentary rules of Section 3.5. In general, verbs and auxiliaries in the present tense in English agree with the subject; that is, if the subject is third-person or first- or second-person plural, the verb is unmarked (for most verbs), while if the subject is third-person singular, the verb must have a suffix *-s* (*-es*). Agreements of this sort are a very common feature of languages. How would we account for this fact in a PSG for English? Since the facts of number agreement are completely independent of any other classifications of verbs in English, we have a typical case of the cross-classification problem considered in Chapter 4. For some classification *X,* we may classify verbs as *X* or non *-X.* Then we must describe the facts of agreement twice, once for *X*-verbs, once for non-*X*-verbs. Or we may describe the agreement facts first by dividing present tense verbs into singular and plural, according to their subjects. But then we must describe the classification *X*/non-*X* twice. It would seem that a solution might be forthcoming by recourse to complex symbols, as sketched in Chapter 4. That is, we might assume that there is a feature rule of this form:

$$\begin{bmatrix} +Verb \\ +Present \end{bmatrix} \rightarrow \begin{cases} [+Plural] \ / \ \begin{bmatrix} +Noun \\ +Plural \end{bmatrix} - \\ [-Plural] \end{cases}$$

This approach would resolve the cross-classification difficulty, but it merely leads to a new problem. What kind of rule will now actually introduce the suffix -*s* (in some appropriate phonological form)? The rule might be something like this:

$$\begin{bmatrix} +Verb \\ -Plural \end{bmatrix} \rightarrow \begin{bmatrix} +Verb \\ -Plural \end{bmatrix} + s$$

But this is obviously not a phrase-structure rule. We might argue that the rule is a phonological rule, that is, we might set up our theory in such a way that the phonological rules could include rules like this. But there is still a difficulty.

Notice that the agreement rule given introduces a feature specification in a present-tense verb according to the form of the preceding noun. But as a moment's reflection will show, it is not true that the subject — that noun or noun phrase which determines the form of the present tense verb — always immediately precedes the verb in English sentences. Notice the following, where the verb and its controlling subject are underlined:

John unfortunately is an idiot.
John, even though you may think he is smart, is an idiot.
The man that the police are looking for has left.
The man that is looking for the police has left.
Never has an idiot made so much money.
Who does Harry like?
There were fourteen dead men on the floor.
There is in the back room if I am not mistaken about the contents of that foul-smelling den of iniquity a copy of *Pride and Prejudice*.
The man who said that . . . is here.

These examples show that to describe the facts of English number agreement is literally impossible using a simple agreement rule of the type given in a PSG, since we cannot guarantee that the noun phrase that determines the agreement will precede (or even be immediately adjacent to) the present-tense verb. We could use such a rule, if we also had rules that would rearrange elements in the structures that underlie sentences. But such rules are not countenanced in PSG. Phrase-structure rules as defined do not include rules of the form $AB \rightarrow BA$.

If we do include rules for rearranging elements, they will have to be of a completely new kind. Suppose, for example, that we want to have a rule for inverting the subject and the verbal auxiliary to describe questions in English:

He is an idiot.   Is he an idiot?

Mary can speak Swahili.   Can Mary speak Swahili?

Let *Aux* stand for the relevant part of the verbal complex; then we might have a rule like this:

$$NP + Aux \rightarrow Aux + NP$$

How are we to interpret this rule? If we interpret it as we do a phrase-structure rule, that is, as a rule in a rewriting grammar, the rule will define sub-sequences of derivations like this:

$$\ldots NP + Aux \ldots$$
$$\ldots Aux + NP \ldots$$

If we continue with such a derivation, we are back to the difficulty encountered above. To describe facts of agreement we must give two rules, one for sentences to which this rule has not applied, and one for sentences to which it has, since in some derivations the subject *NP* will precede, and in others follow, the *Aux*. What we need for the inversion is some sort of rule applying to constituents that have already been developed. In other words, we want to have a rule that applies not to strings of elements, but to strings of elements with a particular analysis, that is, to P-markers.

Let us sum up what we have considered so far in this chapter. First we noted that phrase-structure grammars assign only a single structural description (in the form of a P-marker) to sentences, and seem to be defective in that single P-markers cannot show both the differences between sentences and their similarities. Next, we saw that unnecessary duplications and failures to represent important generalizations arise in PSG dealing with sets of sentences that differ in systematic ways. Finally, we have seen that certain kinds of operations on the structures underlying sentences are not possible with PSG and that there seem to be situations in natural languages that are simply not describable (or not describable simply) within the limitations of PSG. These considerations all point in the same direction: we should revise our conception of a grammar to include a new kind of rule, one that can operate on P-markers rather than on strings of elements as such. Such rules, called transformations, have given the name to the kind of grammar we will will consider in this and the next chapters. The grammars we will study still contain complex PSG and phonological rules, but add a new kind of rule in a special component of the grammar.

5.2 Grammatical Transformations

The basic purpose of including transformational rules in a grammar is to make it possible to describe one type of structure directly and to describe other structures as modifications of structures of the first type. The most well-known transformations are rules that relate different types of sentences. We will examine several examples of transformational rules in order to show something about the properties of this new type of rule.

Consider again pairs of sentences of the following type:

That you would say that amazes me.
It amazes me that you would say that.

Let us assume that we want a rule that will relate these two types of sentences, and let us further assume that the rule operates to derive sentences of the second type from sentences of the first type. Such a rule has been called Extraposition.

The first thing to note is that the rule must be one that operates on P-markers rather than on strings of elements. In the last section we saw that we cannot intersperse rules of this general form throughout the phrase-structure rules of a grammar, but must allow them to operate on P-markers in order not to lose generalizations and fall into unnecessarily complicated formulations. We can see this again in the case of Extraposition. We can characterize verbs such as *disturb* that can take sentential subjects — for example, *that*-clauses — by means of a syntactic feature, for example [+*That-S* −]. Suppose we had a rule that simply changed the order of a string of category symbols (in the PS-rules): *That-S VP* → *it VP that S*. Then we would have to include another different syntactic feature to allow *disturb* to appear in the second type of context as well. But if we allow the *S* to develop, and think of the rule as a rule that operates on a P-marker, then no such otiose duplication of information is necessary.

On the other hand, we cannot think of the rule as operating on a *sentence,* that is, an actual terminal string of formatives. The reason is that there is no way to tell that a given string of elements is an *S, NP,* or whatever apart from the P-marker assigned to the sentence by a grammar. We can demonstrate this by showing how the same sequence of words can have a totally different status in two different structures. For example, we can break up the sequence of English words given above to conform to different analyses:

"That," you would say, "that amazes me."
That you would — say — that amazes me!
That you would say that — amazes me.

Only the last of these has the proper structure to undergo Extraposition. It is for this reason that we must, when speaking carefully, talk about transformations as applying to "the structure underlying" a given sentence, rather than the sentence itself. The reader may object that the three sentences above would have radically different phonetic forms. There are two answers to this objection.

The first is that there are many cases of phonetically identical sentences with different analyses and different transformational properties. For example, the following sentence is ambiguous (as to whether the adverb *yesterday* is in the inner or the outer clause):

I promised to wash the car yesterday.

But only one structure can undergo the operation of the rule that preposes adverbs, as we can see by noting that the next sentence is unambiguous:

Yesterday, I promised to wash the car.

This sentence is incompatible with a reading in which I promised, say, last week to wash the car yesterday.

The second answer to the objection is that it is the syntactic form that dictates the phonetic form, rather than the other way about. If we need a representation of the syntactic form for the proper operation of the phonological rules, then we have this form available for transformational rules like Extraposition.

We can thus see that the input to the transformation must be a P-marker. The last argument shows that the output must also be a P-marker. If the phonological rules require a representation of the syntactic structure, a point that has been well established (see Chomsky and Halle, 1968), and if the transformations operate on P-markers to give alternative sentences, then the result of a transformation must also be a P-marker. But there is an additional argument that the output must be a P-marker. Transformations can be compounded, that is, some structures can be satisfactorily explained only if we assume that they have undergone several transformations in sequence. Let us look at an example.

There is a transformational rule of English called Passive (see Chapter 7 for a detailed justification for the existence of this rule). There are sentences in English that involve both Passive and Extraposition in their derivations (or "transformational history"):

It was proved by Nigel that Fergus had left the party.
That Fergus had left the party was proved by Nigel.
Nigel proved that Fergus had left the party.

The last sentence represents the form of the sentence that results most directly from the grammar, without either rule, while the second sentence involves Passive but not Extraposition. This example does not in itself show that transformations must be compoundable, since it is possible to imagine that the two rules somehow operate simultaneously on an underlying P-marker to provide a surface sentence. But there are in fact several arguments that these rules must apply in sequence (I will not give the rather complicated arguments here). Part of the justification for the conclusion is that if we make the assumption that transformations are compounded, we can explain why there is no sentence of the form to which Extraposition alone has applied:

*Nigel proved it that Fergus had left the party.

We could provide even stronger evidence that transformations must be compoundable if we could show structures that actually are created only by transformations and to which other transformations apply. Several such structures will be discussed in Chapter 7 in detail.

For now, let us just sketch one example without attempting any very elaborate justification. It is usually assumed that sentences like the first of the following ones are derived by a transformation called Raising from structures like the next sequence (Postal, forthcoming).

John believed Harry to be an idiot.
John believed [Harry be an idiot]
    S

Raising has the effect of detaching the subject of an embedded sentence and making it into a single constituent NP in the embedding sentence. When, as in the above case, the resultant structure has this NP in object position, the structure may undergo the passive transformation:

Harry was believed by John to be an idiot.
These grapes are claimed to be delicious.

We can give very strong evidence for analyses of these sentences in which the two transformations, Raising and Passive, apply in turn (see Sections 7.3 and 7.5 for a detailed discussion of these rules).

Thus, a transformation is a rule that takes a P-marker and gives us another P-marker, or, as we usually say, that maps P-markers into P-markers. Given this assumption, we can begin to see what a transformation must be like: it must first of all tell us what P-markers it can apply to, and it must tell us what the resulting P-markers will look like. We call the first part of the rule the **structural analysis** (SA, sometimes called "structural description" or "structural conditions"). The second part, which tells us what the resulting P-marker must be, is called the **structural change** (SC).

In order to show what P-markers a transformation can apply to, we can make use first of all of the nodes of our P-markers. Let us assume that the structural analysis of a transformation will apply to a sentence, that is, the P-marker to which it will apply must be an S. To say that a transformation applies to a P-marker with n terms: $A_1, A_2, \ldots A_n$ is to say that we can divide up the final line of the P-marker into n pieces such that the first piece can be traced back to a node labeled A_1, the second to a node labeled A_2, and so on. For example, suppose the SA of a given transformation is this: NP, VP. To decide whether a given P-marker can undergo the transformation, we must look to see whether it can have the analysis specified. Of the following P-markers, only the first fits this structural description:

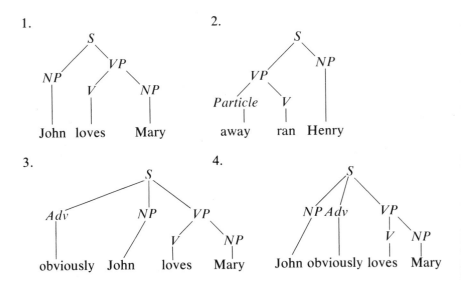

The second fails because the constituents are in the wrong order; the third, because there is an element preceding NP, and the SA specifies only NP at the head (that is, the $NP\ VP$ sequence is not exhaustively dominated by S); and the fourth, because there is an intervening element.

These last examples suggest that it might be useful to modify our picture of a structural analysis to allow the appearance of arbitrary bits and pieces, in other words, that we be allowed to separate out essential from irrelevant material. We can do this by allowing some terms in our SA to be *variables* (X, Y, or the like). For example, if we wanted to allow for the possibility of both preceding and intervening matter in the SA given above, we could expand the terms to (X, NP, Y, VP). Now the transformation in question might apply to all of the above P-markers except the second. As this example suggests, the presence of a variable like X means that in that part of the P-marker anything or nothing at all may appear without affecting the applicability of the transformation.

The use of variables is not just a handy device to save ink or even an abbreviation that can be justified as expressing true generalizations (although it can be defended on both grounds). There appear to be transformations that cannot be correctly stated without the use of variables. One such is the rule of *WH*-movement, which moves an interrogative element to the head of a sentence in a question. It is literally impossible to give all of the environments over which an interrogative may be moved, since it may occur arbitrarily deeply embedded:

Who(m) did you see?
Who(m) did you say Mary saw?
Who(m) did you say Mary thought Bill saw?

Following the usual analysis of such sentences, we must have a rule with something like this SA: X, *WH-NP*, Y. We cannot replace the variable X by any finite sequence of constituents or any disjunction of such sequences (such as: either A or B). (For a different formulation of this rule, see Chomsky, 1973.)

Finally, since the terminal elements of the grammar are complex elements, as we saw in our last chapter, the SA of a transformation may define some subpart of the P-markers to which it applies in terms of features of some sort. For example, if we wish to restrict the formation of imperatives to verbs like *learn* and *look* (which are −Stative) as opposed to verbs like *know* and *resemble* (which are + Stative) (see G. Lakoff, 1970a), we may include the feature specifications [+*Verb*, −*Stative*] in the SA of the transformation for imperative.

With these revisions, then, we can state that the structural analysis of a transformation is a sequence of terms each of which is either a variable, a node symbol, or a set of feature specifications. To decide whether a given transformation applies to a given P-marker, we simply look to see if the P-marker can be exhaustively divided into a sequence of strings such that: for terms in the SA that are node symbols, that substring can be traced back to a node with the given label; for terms that are sets of feature specifications, the relevant part of the P-marker has the appropriate specification; for terms that are variables, any string at all (including $\emptyset$) can satisfy the analysis.

We need next to look at the changes that can be effected by a transformation. A transformation is a very powerful kind of rule, so it will be desirable to restrict the types of changes that are countenanced by the theory as severely as possible. A step in this direction can be made by first requiring that it be impossible to state ad hoc for each transformation any arbitrary kind of SC in P-markers, and then stating once and for all a limited number of possible changes. Then, by looking at a P-marker analyzed in a particular way according to the SA of a transformation, we can determine the form of the P-marker that results from applying some combination of these operations.

We call the possible simple operations on P-markers **elementary transformations.** What the necessary and sufficient elementary transformations are is a difficult empirical question, still very much unsettled. But there is some evidence that they can be limited to four basic types. For each one we need to state what the effect of the transformation will be in specifying the P-marker that results from the application of the given elementary transformation. Each elementary transformation tells us what happens to one piece of the P-marker as analyzed by the SA of the transformation.

Before describing the elementary transformations, let us introduce a technical term. Suppose we have a branch of a P-marker of the form:

$$\underset{B_1 \; B_2 \; \ldots \; B_n}{\overset{A}{\diagdown\!|\!\diagup}}$$

or equivalently in a part of a labeled bracketing:

$$[\ldots B_1, B_2, \ldots B_n \ldots]$$
$$A$$

where the only elements standing between "[" and "B_1" and "B_n"
$$A$$
and "]" are left and right brackets respectively. Then we say that A **dominates** $B_1, B_2, \ldots B_n$ (when $B_1, B_2, \ldots B_n$ is a string of formatives, we say that the string is a constituent of type A).[1] We shall also say that A

---

1. Compare Section 3.1. The reader should be warned that the term *dominates* is sometimes used in a different sense to mean the relation between a node A and any node or terminal element or sequence of these in a structure dominated (in our sense) by A.

dominates itself. Thus in this P-marker S dominates (AB), $(A \ CD)$, (S), but A does not dominate B, nor does S dominate A:

Now we can return to our elementary transformations. The easiest type of elementary transformation to describe is **deletion.** If the elementary transformation of deletion applies to a piece A of a P-marker, we simply remove everything dominated by A and everything that dominates it. For example, suppose a transformation specified the deletion of the first term of a P-marker with the analysis:

SA: you, VP

then the transformation would operate as follows:

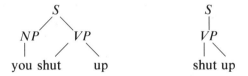

"You" is deleted (because "you" dominates "you") and so is the NP that dominates "you" (but not S).

The next type of elementary transformation is the **substitution.** In a substitution of a term A for a term B, we simply replace B by whatever is dominated by A in such a way that whatever dominated B now dominates A. Thus, if we wanted to substitute the third for the first term in a P-marker fitting the analysis:

SA: A, X, C

we would effect this change:

We may substitute a term *A* by simply attaching another item *B* to it in such a way that *A* and *B* are dominated by the same node. Two constituents immediately attached to the same higher node are called **sisters**. Hence, this special case is sometimes called **sister-adjunction** (on the left or right). Suppose we want to assume that the rule of adverb movement produces changes like this:

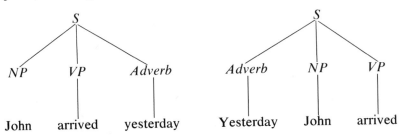

Then we can say that the adverb is sister-adjoined to the left of the initial *NP* (*Adverb* plus *NP* is substituted for *NP*) and the original adverb deleted.

The third type of elementary transformation is called **Chomsky-adjunction** (to the right or left). It is defined for terms of the SA that are node labels. In Chomsky-adjoining on the left an element *E* to a node branch labeled *A*, we first create a new, higher copy of the node *A* and then let *E* plus the branch labeled *A* be sisters underneath this new node *A* (and correspondingly on the right for right Chomsky-adjunction). For example, to Chomsky-adjoin the third term to the left of the first term in P-markers meeting the SA: *A*, *X*, *C* would have this result:

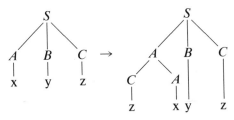

Finally, if we wish to specify a change in the feature composition of some terminal item in a P-marker, we simply let that item conform to the feature specification mentioned in the change. If the item had a different specification for that feature, it now assumes the new one. If it had none, now it has one. Thus, we might mark nouns as [+*Pronominal*] by some rule with the SA: *NP*, *X*, [*Y*, *N*], *Z*. (It is sometimes assumed that
$$NP$$
there is a fifth type of elementary transformation, **daughter-adjunction**,

with the result of adding a new term as a **daughter** to — that is, directly dependent on — one of the nodes of the SA. We shall ignore this possibility here.)

Now we are ready to say what a transformation does. The output of a transformation (the **transform**) will be a P-marker that looks exactly like the input P-marker, except as elementary transformations are specified that bring about one or more of the changes just described. A handy notation for a transformation, and one that I shall use throughout, is as follows. I give on one line the sequence of terms in the structural analysis, numbered beneath from 1 to *n* (for *n* terms), followed by a double arrow ⇒ to indicate the structural change. Under each of these numbers I indicate the elementary transformation as follows: If there is no change, I simply repeat the number. If there is a substitution, I put the substitute under the substituend (using the same numbers to refer to terms of the analysis, or the formative that is introduced by the rule, and plus signs to connect a sequence of such). If there is a Chomsky-adjunction, I use an asterisk. If there is a feature change, I simply put beneath the item to be changed a feature specification. Here is an example:

SA: *A,* *X,* *B,* *Y,* *C,*   *N*
       1   2   3   4   5   6 ⇒
SC: 1*a 2   ∅   4 5+3 [+*F*]

This example is interpreted as follows. The transformation applies to a P-marker that can be analyzed as (1) a piece that is dominated by *A*, followed by (2) anything, followed by (3) a piece that is dominated by *B*, followed by (4) anything, followed by (5) a piece that is dominated by *C*, followed by (6) a terminal element which is an *N*. The structural change is as follows: No change takes place in the second and fourth terms. The item *a* (notice this is a new element) is Chomsky-adjoined to the right of the first term *A*, thus creating the structure:

The third term *B* is deleted, while the fifth term is replaced (substituted) by itself followed (sister-adjoined on the right) by a copy of the third term *B*, and the sixth term is now specified [+*F*]. For example, given the first P-marker below as input, we would derive the second as the output of this rule:

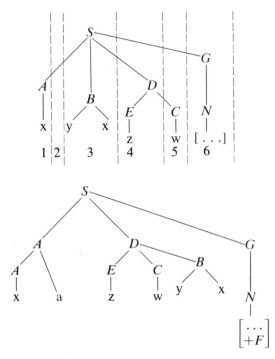

The reader should be warned that many discussions of transformations for various languages are stated in a very informal and rough way, so that the exact effect of a given transformation is often unclear. The reason for this is not always a vagueness of style but, more often, a lack of evidence on what the best formulation of the rule should be. The difficulty of finding good evidence for or against formulating a certain change as a Chomsky-adjunction or a sister-adjunction is not very surprising when we consider the difficulties in finding evidence for the necessary and sufficient elementary operations that should be allowed in a grammar. We have no direct evidence about rules, P-markers, or syntactic classes.

Given the addition of transformations to a theory of grammar, it is possible to describe many situations in a satisfying way. There are some transformations that may or may not apply to a given structure. These we call **optional** transformations. They account for many variations in sentences like the ones given in the discussion of Extraposition above. Others must apply, or else the result will simply not be a sentence. These we call **obligatory.**

It is still the case that various conditions must be met for transformations to operate correctly. Some of these are general conditions, some special. We shall consider in some detail in later chapters the problem of restricting transformations. Even as we have described them, it will be obvious that they are very general and powerful devices.

5.3 Some Examples of Transformations

I give here a few examples of transformations in English, mainly for practice with our new notations and concepts. We shall not attempt to justify the existence or form of the rules. Let us take up first the Extraposition transformation discussed earlier in this chapter. The rule may be formulated as follows:[2]

> *Extraposition*   Optional
> SA: X, [it, S], Y]
>   *NP*   *VP*
>   1   2   3   4 $\Rightarrow$
>   1   2 ϕ 4 + 3

The rule allows one to transpose an S within a noun phrase next to the special formative "it" to the end of the *VP*. For example:

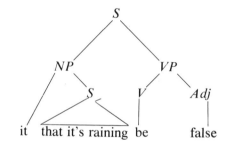

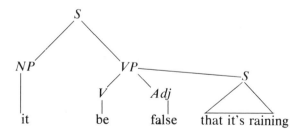

Notice that the rule depends on a particular assumption about the form of

---

2. This SA can be satisfied by P-markers in which the matching left *VP* bracket is covered by X or Y; thus it is an abbreviation for two SA's

$$X_1, [_{VP} X_2, [_{NP} IT, S], Y]_{VP}$$

or

$$X, [_{NP} IT, S], Y_1 [_{VP} Y_2]_{VP}.$$

the underlying P-markers, namely, that the relevant *NP*'s have the form "it" + *S*. We shall not try to defend this analysis here, but simply note that the addition of transformations to a grammar makes it possible to posit quite "abstract" underlying forms, that is, forms that are quite different from the surface form of sentences. This analysis necessitates another rule of *It*-deletion (ordered after Extraposition; see Chapter 6 on various ordering hypotheses) to disallow sentences like **It that it is raining is false* and to get the unextraposed form *That it is raining is false:*

It-deletion Obligatory
SA: *X*, [it, *S*], *Y*
        NP
    1   2   3   4 ⇒
    1   ∅   3   4

It-deletion is an example of a typical kind of "housekeeping" rule that arises in a grammar with underlying structures that do not look quite like surface structures.

One of the most often quoted and still least understood transformations is Passive. It serves to relate sentences like these:

John saw the fish.
The fish was seen by John.
The police picked up the baby.
The baby was picked up by the police.
No one reckoned on the storm.
The storm was reckoned on by no one.

One version of the Passive transformation is this:

SA: *X, NP,   Aux,   V, (Prep), NP, by, Agent, Y*
     1 2   3   4   5   6   7   8   9 ⇒
     1 6   3+be+-en   4   5   ∅   7   2   9

Assume an underlying P-marker for the first sentence above like this:

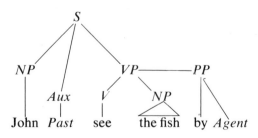

Application of Passive will yield this P-marker:

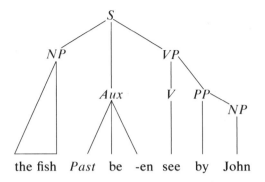

the fish *Past* be -en see by John

In Section 7.5 we will use Passive as an example for a detailed justi-fication for the existence and form of a transformation. Let us here notice only two things about the rule.

First, the presence of the prepositional phrase *by + Agent* is an exam-ple of setting up a hypothetical element that exists solely for the purpose of providing a place for a substitute in a transformation. If we did not have this element — that is, if we tried to state the rule by a structural analysis lacking terms 7 and 8 of the rule above — we would meet a technical difficulty in assigning what we know on other grounds to be the correct constituent structure of passive sentences. There are various reasons for believing that the agent phrase — *by John* — has the same structure as other prepositional phrases like *with John, from Henry, to Mary*. The node *PP* cannot be introduced transformationally, as a review of the elementary transformations given above will show. The only way to create new nodes is by Chomsky-adjunction, and that way is apparently not open to us here. This is an important restriction on transformations. If we do not severely limit the way in which new structures can be created by transformations, we will be hard put to say what transformations cannot do. In general, we want to limit the power of our grammars as much as possible. Thus an instance like the present one can become crucial for a question of theory. If on the other hand we allow ourselves to create new "empty" nodes in the basic structures every time we run into a difficulty about derived structure like the present one, we will have lost whatever limits we thought we had gained by restricting the power of transformations. Sev-eral suggested analyses get around the present difficulty. One made by John Ross (1967a) is as follows. Prepositional phrases share many properties with *NP*'s. Suppose we reanalyze prepositional phrases as *NP*'s with this structure:

Now it would be possible to introduce the higher structure of the agent phrase by means of Chomsky-adjunction, one of the permitted elementaries. Put another way, the restriction of node-building to the special case of Chomsky-adjunction requires us to assign this structure to new constituents consisting of an *NP* plus an introduced element like "by." To the extent that we can find evidence for the correctness of this assignment, we can say that this restriction on the general theory is supported. Another possibility was suggested by Charles Fillmore (1971). Noting that many pairs of sentences seem to be related in which one sentence has an *NP* as subject and the other that *NP* in the verb-phrase preceded by a preposition, Fillmore suggested that all subjects are marked with *by* in underlying structures and that this *by* is deleted exactly when the phrase stands in subject position. Examples of the first sort are these:

> The room is hot.
> It's hot in the room.
>
> Bees swarm in the garden.
> The garden swarms with bees.
>
> The shelf has some books (on it).
> There are some books on the shelf.

The passive examples would fall in line with these.

The second thing to point out about the Passive rule is again an instance of a more "abstract" underlying structure to which the rule applies. The second term *Aux* has no overt realization in many sentences. Let us look briefly at English auxiliary elements. There are very good reasons for separating out the underlined portions of the following English verbal phrases and considering the remainders independent constituents (in underlying structure):

> <u>has been</u> running
> <u>may have</u> tried to open the door
> opened the door
> opens the door

For example, we can describe verbs in terms of the constituents with which they can occur in the verb phrase and quite independently of whether they are in the past or present tense, whether their subjects are singular or plural, or whether they occur in the progressive (*be* + *-ing*), perfect (*have* + *-en*), or with modal verbs like *can, must, will, may*. Given the decision to separate out these elements and consider them possible developments of an abstract underlying element *Aux*, we can provide a very elegant analysis for several phenomena of English (see Chomsky, 1957, for the first presentation of these arguments). Yes-no questions in English are formed by inverting the first *NP* and the first element in this auxiliary. Note these pairs:

John can open the door.
Can John open the door?

Harry is marrying a belly dancer.
Is Harry marrying a belly dancer?

You have seen the opera.
Have you seen the opera?

We might formulate a rule as follows:

Inversion
SA: *NP,* [*X, Y*], *Z*
         Aux
SC: 1   2   3   4 ⇒
      2+1   ∅   3   4

(In order for the rule to operate correctly, we must add a special condition to ensure that the added part, *X*, of the first term is a single constituent. We shall consider later the status of such special conditions; see Chapter 9.)

Now suppose the rule is allowed to operate on structures without any overt auxiliary verbs, for example, the structures underlying sentences like these:

1. John likes fish.
2. Mary went home.
3. Seagulls love oysters.

Assume that tense in English is represented by formatives *Past, SG,* and *PL,* all derived from an element *Tns,* and that *SG* and *PL* represent singular present and plural present. Assume that the inversion rule applies to strings in which these elements are standing at the head of the *Aux* constituent. Then for structures underlying the three sentences above we get:

4. *SG* John like fish.
5. *Past* Mary go home.
6. *PL* Seagulls love oysters.

In the analysis followed here, affixes like the tense elements just mentioned, and the *-ing* and *-en* suffixes for verb forms like *singing, broken* (as well as variants like *-ed*), are positioned ahead of the verb forms to which they will eventually be attached. Thus we need to have a rule attaching the affixes to the next verb or auxiliary to the right. An example of the successive operation of this rule is the following:

John *Past* have -en be -ing run to the store
John have *Past* be -en run -ing to the store
(ultimately: John had been running to the store.)

For purposes of phonology, let us assume that this rule (perhaps in conjunction with some other rules) has the effect not only of Chomsky-adjoining the affix to the following verb but also of introducing a special word-boundary symbol "⊕" after the shifted affix:

Affix-shift
SA: *X*, [+*Affix*], [+*Verb*],   *Y*
       1   2   3   4 ⇒
       1   ∅   3*2 +⊕   4

Notice that this rule cannot apply to the structures (4)–(6), since the affixes are now separated from their neighboring verbal elements (I assume that all auxiliaries are specified as [+*Verb*]). But now we can explain another phenomenon of English by adding to our grammar an obligatory rule to supply the "dummy" auxiliary *do* for all unattached affixes:

Do-support Obligatory
X, ⊕, [+*Affix*, +*Verb*], ⊕, *Y*
1 2   3   4 5 ⇒
1 2   do+3   4 5

Additional support for this analysis comes from the fact that *Do*-support applies to other instances of sentences where affixes become separated from the following verb, for example in other inversions, insertion of negatives, and so on:

Not only did he go home . . .
He did not go home.
Mary went home and so did he.
Mary went home, didn't she?
Mary did go home.

(In the last instance one might assume that a special *Emphasis* formative has been introduced, which also separates the tense affix from the following verb.)

The analysis just given dovetails with another decision about English grammar. Notice that plural subjects select verb forms with no overt affixes:

The boy likes . . .   The boys like . . .
John sleeps . . .   John and Mary sleep . . .

Two possibilities suggest themselves. We could think of the plural verb form as being simply an absence of a certain suffix. Or we could think of it as being, in its underlying form, composed of a verb plus an affix that happens to have no phonetic substance (that is, must be deleted before we have a surface phonetic form); thus, for example, *sleep* above could have these possible interpretations:

sleep *vs.* sleep + *PL*

But if we adopt the former analysis we must introduce unnecessary complications in our grammar. If we have an overt plural present affix, the rules of *Subject-Aux* inversion and *Do*-support will apply uniformly to all of the appropriate sentences. If we have no such affix, then we shall have to deal with sentences with plural subjects in a special way.

In this section we have looked at several transformations that have been posited for English. We have done this mainly in order to illustrate some of the typical situations in which transformations have been used: to explain optional variants of sentences (Extraposition, Passive), obligatory changes like *Subject-Aux* inversion, and various "housekeeping" rules like *It*-deletion, *Do*-support, and Affix-shift. It should have become clear through the discussion that analysis of a language must be carried out on all fronts at once. Decisions about transformations depend on and influence decisions about the underlying structures we posit (as in Chomsky's analysis of the auxiliary). Decisions about one transformation affect and are affected by decisions about other transformations. What we are attempting is to construct a coherent theory that provides the maximum amount of insight into the structure of the languages we are analyzing. In later chapters we will consider a number of further transformations for English.

5.4 Restricting Transformations

As we have described them, transformations are extremely general and powerful devices. Nevertheless, some restrictions have been built into the definition. Let us consider these limitations, and then go on to look at a few more restrictions. As we will see in later chapters, the principal problem in the theory of transformational grammars at present is the formulation of restrictions that will limit their power sufficiently to explain why languages are the way they are. Recall once again that our general aim is to describe a class of grammars that is just powerful enough to accommodate known facts about languages.

A transformation is a rule relating pairs of P-markers. Part of each rule is a structural analysis defining the class of P-markers to which the given rule can apply. The other part is the structural change, a set of elementary transformations telling what happens to each term of the analyzed P-marker as we construct a new P-marker, which is its image under the mapping. Certain limitations are built into each of these two parts.

First of all, notice that the structural analysis consists of a *finite* number of terms. This does not mean that the rule applies to only a finite number of P-markers, nor that there is some finite bound on the length of the P-marker analyzable by the SA. For example, a variable like X or a category symbol like NP could cover an infinite number of different pieces (and hence unboundedly long P-markers or pieces of them). But in any transformation, as defined, there is a fixed, finite number of terms, whether four (as in Affix-shift) or nine (as in Passive). This means that it is impossible to state transformations corresponding to informal rules like these:

Delete all but the first of an indefinite number of verbs in conjoined verb-phrases just so long as the verbs are all identical

An indefinite number of conjoined sentences of the form X-Y-Z and X-Y'-Z and X-Y''-Z . . . where the X's are identical, the Z's are identical, and all elements Y, Y', Y'', and the like are constituents of the same type, can be reduced to a sentence of the form X Y and Y' and Y'' . . . Z.

As these examples show, it is not at all unreasonable to imagine that there might be a need for rules of this more powerful and general type. But the point is that transformations as strictly defined (by Chomsky and others) do not admit structural analyses with indefinite numbers of terms like these. We shall discuss in Chapter 9 some possible ways in which this and other restrictions might have to be relaxed.

The second limitation is that a structural analysis contains a simple set of conditions that must be met by P-markers in its domain of application, each of these conditions being a statement of whether the piece in question is a constituent of a certain type, is *not* a constituent of a certain type, is a constituent of a certain type *and* a constituent of a certain other type, or is a constituent of a certain type *or* a constituent of a certain other type. That is to say, we can build up a structural analysis for a transformation by making conditions based on the notion of being a constituent of a certain type or by combining these conditions by means of the logical elements *not, or,* and *and.* A logic or system making use of connectives with the formal properties of *not, or,* and *and* is called a Boolean system. Hence, this property of transformations is usually stated by saying that the structural analysis of a transformation is a set of Boolean conditions on *analyzability* (this term refers to the relation involved in assigning a piece of the terminal string of a P-marker to a category). Practically speaking, this means that we can have SA's like the following:

$$\underset{1 \quad 2 \quad 3 \quad \quad 4 \quad \quad 5}{\underset{A}{[}\ B,C\ ],X, \left\{ \begin{matrix} D \\ E, F \end{matrix} \right\} Z}$$

where 3 is not dominated by NP

The analysis not only says that the first elements (1, 2) in the P-marker to which the rule applies must be a sequence analyzable as a *B* followed by a *C,* it also says the whole sequence must be an *A;* this is an *and* statement. The fourth term is a familiar representation (using the notation of Chapter 3) for an *or* statement: the fourth term must be either a *D* or a sequence of an *E* followed by an *F.* Finally, the condition on the third term is a typical *not* statement.

What kind of structural condition would fall outside of the limitation to such Boolean combinations of conditions? Ruled out is any kind of statement involving what logicians call *quantifiers,* that is, statements involving the logical quantifiers of existence (*there is an* x such that . . .) or universality (*for all* x . . .). Thus, it is impossible to state transformations involving conditions like these:

The third term must be immediately dominated by S.
The NP dominated by the highest S . . .

In the first instance, for example, we would have to be able to state a condition roughly like this: There is a node S such that this node S dominates the third term and there is no node Y such that S dominates Y and Y dominates the third term and is not identical with the third term (recall that every node dominates itself). Once again, it is not immediately apparent that we should limit transformations in this way. We shall take up later some cases that seem to demand violations of this restriction to Boolean statements.

Let us now consider some limitations on the SC part of the transformation. We have already seen that the restriction to four types of elementary operations provides some restrictions. Many logically possible types of operations are impossible within these limitations. For instance, we cannot arbitrarily create new nodes. The most we can do is create copies of nodes in a limited way by Chomsky-adjunction. Nor can we create new types of nodes. As formulated, the categorial possibilities are strictly limited by the categories made available in the rules defining underlying structures. Moreover, if we take the limitations on elementary transformations together with the limitations on possible structural analyses, many other possible types of operations are ruled out as transformations.

Notice that every element that is adjoined or substituted in a transformation either is present already within the P-marker undergoing the transformation or is a constant new terminal element. Thus, it makes no sense to state a transformation like this:

$$NP, \quad VP$$
$$1 \qquad 2 \Rightarrow$$
$$NP+1 \quad 2$$

This attempt to introduce a new NP at the head of a sentence is an illegitimate rule, since there is no specified source for the new NP. The only interpretation we should give to it would be to assume that "NP" is a special formative of some sort (not to be identified with the node NP) and that the rule would have this sort of effect:

We shall see later (Chapters 8, 9, 11) that transformations as defined are still much too powerful. At that point we will consider a number of possible restrictions that can be placed on them. For now, let us look at one important restriction that has been hypothesized, without going into a detailed justification.

The elementary transformations of deletion and substitution both allow us to perform transformations such that we can define some relations between sentences that seem empirically unjustified. Notice that we can arbitrarily delete any elements we like. Consider the following putative imperative transformation, for example:

SA: *NP, Tns, VP*
     1   2   3 $\Rightarrow$
     $\emptyset$ $\emptyset$ 3

This rule will produce strings that have the proper external form to be imperatives:

Go home!
Be a slob!
Shut up!
Open the door!

But the rule makes no claims whatever about the possible *NP*'s that could stand in the subject position. Thus, we might relate the above sentences by the rule with, for example, the following:

Mary went home.
Richard III was a slob.
All the little green elves shut up.
The lock opens the door.

If we require that the rule delete not just any *NP* but only, say, the specific element *you,* and not just any tense but (perhaps) the present tense, then we will have much more intuitively satisfying sentences to relate to the imperatives:

You go home.
You be a slob.
You shut up.
You open the door.

Much other evidence can be adduced to show that this decision is correct.

Similarly, suppose we allow a rule that supplies a reflexive pronoun (*himself, herself,* and so on) by substitution for an arbitrary *NP* object. Then we will not only be setting up relations between deep and surface structures that seem unreasonable, do not satisfy semantic requirements, and so on, but we will actually be producing ungrammatical sentences like these:

> *Mary shaved himself.
> *The conclusion that pigs can fly revealed himself to be false.
> *The girl told her mother about himself.

Situations like these provide part of the justification for the so-called recoverability condition. The intent of the condition is to limit the possible relations between deep structures and surface structures. Since ambiguous surface structures exist, it is impossible to state a condition ensuring that we can always recover a single deep structure for a given surface structure. But a partial solution is to require that we be able to tell, for a given transformation and a given P-marker that has just undergone the transformation, what the input P-marker was. We can insure this by restricting certain kinds of substitution and deletion. Let us call a deletion of an element that has not been copied somewhere else in the transform, or a substitution of a constant element for a full piece of a P-marker that has not been copied somewhere else, an **information-losing substitution** (in the case of deletion, we are substituting the null string). The **recoverability condition** states that we can perform an information-losing substitution in only two situations: (1) the element to be replaced or deleted is identical to some other element in the P-marker, or (2) the element to be replaced or deleted is a constant single element. Application of this principle can be illustrated in the cases above. If we require that the reflexivized *NP* be identical to an earlier *NP* in the sentence (under appropriate further restrictions), then we will have derivations like these without the unfortunate results above):

Mary shaved Mary	→	Mary shaved herself.
The conclusion that pigs can fly revealed the conclusion that pigs can fly to be false	→	The conclusion that pigs can fly revealed itself to be false.
The girl told her mother about the girl	→	The girl told her mother about herself.

These fall under case (1). The formulation of the imperative rule suggested above falls under case (2).

The recoverability condition entails that we be able to add one new kind of structural condition to the statement of a transformation: restrictions of identity. Such a restriction is usually given as an addendum to an SA (introduced either by *where* or *Condition*). For an example, we may take the reflexive rule just referred to:

SA: *X, NP, Y, NP,   W*
    1   2   3   4   5 $\Rightarrow$
SC: 1   2   3 4+self 5
    Where 2 = 4

(Actually, this rule merely adds a formative *self*—we might also have marked the *NP* [*+Reflexive*]—and it is only later that the *NP* itself is reduced with loss of information.)

5.5 Another Argument for Transformational Grammars

At the close of Chapter 4 we considered briefly a major defect in phrase-structure grammars even as extended there to include complex elements. They provide no basis for understanding why languages show similarities in their systems of categories and the types of constructions into which the categories enter. A very strong argument for transformational grammars can be made because they do provide such a basis. A full development of this argument must be delayed until Chapter 11. But for now we can make a few observations that will serve to prepare us for our later discussion and at the same time underscore an important property of transformational grammars.

The essential thing that separates transformational grammars from alternative grammars that we have considered is that they provide (at least) two systems of syntactic rules: complex phrase-structure rules that define a basic set of representations, and transformations that extend this set by operations on the underlying (and derived) representations. Languages show many similarities both in the deeper representations provided by the complex phrase-structure rules and in their surface structures. It is only by means of grammars of at least the complexity of transformational grammars that we can hope to account for the similarities as well as the differences among languages. An important property of transformational grammars is the interplay between the phrase-structure rules and the transformations. We find much of the justification for particular hypotheses about deep categories and constituents in the behavior of these hypothetical elements under transformations. Moreover, we find that across unrelated languages, similar if not identical transformations operate to fulfill identical functions, and do so in similar circumstances.

Let us consider one example. The category NP figures typically in many transformations in English, among them a Relative-clause transformation of roughly this sort:

> *Relative-clause*
> SA: X, [NP, [$\quad Y$, $\quad NP, Z$]] W
> $\quad\quad\quad NP \quad\quad S$
> $\quad\quad$ 1 $\quad$ 2 $\quad\quad$ 3 $\quad\quad$ 4 $\quad$ 5 $\quad$ 6 $\Rightarrow$
> SC: 1 $\quad\quad$ 2 $\quad\quad WH+4+3 \quad \emptyset \quad$ 5 $\quad$ 6
> *where 2 = 4*

It is claimed by this rule that the underlying structure for an NP like (1) is something like (2):

> 1. . . . the man that Harry saw . . .
> 2. . . . the man [Harry saw the man] . . .
> $\quad\quad\quad\quad\quad S$

We find rules essentially like this in language after language (see Bach, 1965). We can account for this fact if we consider both the terms of the transformation's structural analysis and the transformation itself to have some language-independent interpretation. Without a theory of grammar at least as complex and rich as that of transformational grammar, it is difficult to see how we could account for the cross-linguistic similarities. Of course, merely postulating a theory of this sort does not suffice to explain such similarities. We will consider in Chapter 11 attempts to provide a theory of transformational grammar that gives us not only the necessary but also the sufficient conditions to explain such phenomena.

Problems and Questions

1.   Construct underlying and derived P-markers illustrating the effect of Extraposition (p. 89), *It*-deletion (p. 90), Passive (p. 90), Inversion (p. 93), Affix-shift (p. 94), *Do*-support (p. 94), Reflexive (p. 101), Relative-clause (p. 102).

2.   For Extraposition, *It*-deletion, Passive, Inversion, and Relative-clause, provide examples showing that the rules in question must be stated as affecting P-markers rather than terminal strings or strings of lexical categories like *Noun* and *Verb*.

3.   What syntactic properties are shared by *NP*'s and prepositional phrases? What are some differences between them?

4.   Which of the following hypothetical rules can be formulated as transformations? For those that can be so formulated, write the transformation. For those that cannot, explain why they cannot.

a) Delete every other constituent of a sentence starting with the first.

b) If an *NP* in a prepositional phrase is deleted, the preposition is adjoined to the right of the verb of the verb phrase in which the prepositional phrase stands.

c) A preposition preceding another preposition is deleted.

d) Questions are formed by moving the verb from its normal place at the end of the sentence to a position immediately preceding the two *NP*'s that immediately precede the verb for transitive, or the single *NP* for intransitive, verbs.

e) If any sentence within the main sentence contains a sentence adverb, that adverb must be placed after the first constituent of the highest (main) sentence.

5.   Give evidence in support of the identity condition given with the Relative-clause rule as stated on p. 102.

6.   Discuss the difficulties that result in an analysis of English in which the plural present form of verbs (*see, go, . . .*) consists of just the verb stem without a "zero"-affix.

7.   Argue for or against an analysis of English in which the singular form of nouns has the representation *Noun + Singular.*

8.   Use the Relative-clause rule to argue for the correctness of the recoverability condition.

chapter

6

A Theory of Transformational Grammar

6.1 Introductory Outline

In this and subsequent chapters we will be examining various proposals about the general theory of language. They all include the assumption that a grammar for a natural language contains several different
components, among them being a set of transformational rules of the sort
described in the last chapter. It is evident that a wide variety of hypotheses falling within this general framework can be entertained. In the
present chapter I will outline one such hypothesis about the form of a
transformational grammar. I call this theory (following Chomsky, 1971)
the **standard theory**. It represents fairly, I believe, one of the hypotheses
set forth in one of the basic works on transformational syntax, Noam
Chomsky's *Aspects of the Theory of Syntax* (1965), together with a few
elaborations introduced by later workers. In presenting the standard
theory we will pay attention to the evidence that can be given for various
points in the hypothesis, and we will also note where the theory makes
certain assumptions that do not seem to have any very strong arguments
in their favor. In the next chapter we will look at some analyses of
English that have been carried out within the standard theory.

The standard theory of transformational grammar makes the following assumptions about the components of a grammar. The grammar for a
natural language contains these parts:

    I. The base
        A. Base rules
        B. Lexicon
    II. The transformational component
        A. Precyclic rules

B. Cyclic rules
   1. Ordinary cyclic rules
   2. Last-cyclic rules
III. Phonological component
IV. Semantic component

Parts I and II together make up the **syntax**. The grammar specifies in its syntax pairs of P-markers called **deep structures** and **surface structures**. The **semantic component** determines for each deep structure a **semantic reading**, while the **phonological component** takes each surface structure and associates with it a **phonetic representation**. Both the semantic and the phonological rules are **interpretive** in the sense that the choice of a particular pair in the syntax determines a meaning and a pronunciation. We consider each part in turn.

6.2 The Base

The base consists of a set of context-free phrase-structure rules and a lexicon. The category symbols of the base rules (sometimes called **branching rules**) are simple unanalyzed elements, chosen in part presumably from a fixed set of universal categories. The elements of the lexicon are complexes of features. Among the terminal elements of the base rules is a **boundary** symbol "#," which plays a special role. First of all, we assume as the initial string that stands at the head of every well-formed derivation one occurrence of the sentence symbol flanked by boundary symbols: $\#S\#$. In addition, certain rules reintroduce the sentence symbol, and each time they do so the S appears between a pair of boundary symbols. Since the rules contain at least one recursive element, S, they will define an infinite set of P-markers. The rules are assumed to apply over and over again until there are no more occurrences of the symbol S that have not been fully developed. The rules are unordered (extrinsically). When no more rules can apply, we perform a lexical insertion for every final node that corresponds to a lexical category. Among the features making up a lexical entry are contextual features that limit the possible contexts in which an item can appear. When we have made all possible lexical insertions, we have what we will call a **base phrase-marker** (sometimes called a "generalized phrase-marker"). The base phrase-marker is subject to the operation of the transformational rules in a way to be explained below.

A possible set of base rules for English might be the following:[1]

---

1. These rules are adapted from the rules of Chomsky (1965), pp. 106–107. They are given mainly for illustration. The rules can be justified only in part, but represent at least tenable speculations. A number of the specific features and problems of the rules will be discussed below.

1. $S \rightarrow (Sentence\text{-}Adverb) \ NP \ Aux \ VP \ (Location) \ (Time)$

2. $VP \rightarrow \begin{cases} V \ (NP) \ (NP) \ (Adverb) \\ Copula \ Predicate \end{cases}$

3. $Predicate \rightarrow \begin{cases} NP \\ Adjective \\ Location \\ Time \end{cases} \left(\begin{cases} NP \\ \#S\# \end{cases} \right)$

4. $NP \rightarrow \begin{cases} NP \ \#S\# \\ (Det) \ N \ (\#S\#) \end{cases}$

5. $Aux \rightarrow Tns \ (Modal) \ (Perfect) \ (Progressive)$

6. $Tns \rightarrow \begin{cases} Pres \\ Past \end{cases}$

Most of the symbols used are self-explanatory or have been discussed already. A few remarks are in order. By *Sentence-Adverb* (*SA*) is meant the adverbial elements (*unfortunately, possibly,* and so on) that seem to modify the sentence as a whole. I include among them a special element *Neg*, which underlies negation in most sentences with negative elements. An example of a sentence in which each of the elements of Rule 1 is chosen is this:

Unfortunately, John   is   sleeping here today.
    SA   *NP Aux   VP   Loc Time*

The *Adverb* of Rule 2 is a so-called manner adverbial like *cleverly, gladly.* A major problem of English syntax is the analysis of adverbs of various sorts. The above rules do little more than indicate that several classes of such elements exist. In the remainder of the top line of the verb-phrase rule, we distinguish three basic types of verbal constructions: those without any nominal complement (intransitive verbs) and those with one and two such complements. The rules follow an analysis in which prepositions are attached to noun phrases by transformational rules. A few examples of each sort are these:

Intransitive:
    John is sleeping.
    The time has elapsed.

Transitive (single object):
    Hans followed Gretel.
    The customers complained about the bloody hamburgers.
    The monster killed Marco Polo.

Transitive (double object):
    Harry gave the sandwich to his son.
    Mary talked about the crisis to the governor.

The analysis of *NP*'s followed in Rule 4 distinguishes two ways in which an *NP* can contain an embedded sentence: the *NP* may have attached to it a relative clause (top line), or it may contain a **complement** sentence together with some nominal head noun like *fact* or *suggestion*. We follow the "traditional" transformational analysis of English, which posits an abstract noun *it* that appears in sentences like those discussed in connection with Extraposition in Chapter 5 (see, for example, Rosenbaum, 1967). By applying Rule 4 one or more times we can derive (via a Relative-clause transformation) sentences like these:

The man who said that is an idiot.
The horse that finished last that was running closest to the rail was Alice B. Toklas.

Complement sentences (again via various transformations to be discussed below) in various *NP* positions are illustrated by these sentences:

It disgusts me that you feel that way.
That he is here proves that he is a fool.
I believe that you have no other recourse.
I don't want to go home.
For me to say this is extremely difficult.
I prefer being independent and broke to selling my business and being rich.

The copula of Rule 2 is *be*. The predicate types given in Rule 3 are illustrated in these sentences:

John is a doctor.
Sally is intelligent.
Sally is angry at Harry.
Leander is afraid that Hero will be asleep.
I am at home.
The concert is at three.

The various types of *Auxiliary* phrases are these:

Tns: John went home.
Tns + Modal: John must go home.
Tns + Perfect: John has gone home.
Tns + Progressive: John is going home.
Tns + Perfect + Progressive: John has been going home.
Tns + Modal + Perfect: John must have gone home.
Tns + Modal + Progressive: John must be going home.
Tns + Modal + Perfect + Progressive: John must have been going home.

Other modals in English are *can, may, shall, will, should, would, might, could.* (In present-day English it is unlikely that the last four should be analyzed as past forms of the others.)

Finally, for every lexical category there is a general rule deriving a special **dummy symbol** △. Specifically, for our grammar:

Let $B = N, V, Adjective, Adverb, Time, Location, SA$
$B \to \triangle$

From these rules we can derive a prelexical P-marker like this:

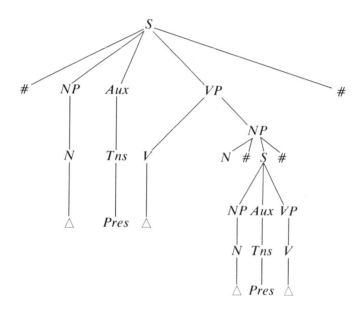

Lexical entries in the grammar include:

1. A phonological matrix.
2. Inherent features of a syntactic and semantic sort, including features for the lexical categories given by the base rules: $+N, +V, +Modal,$ and others.
3. Contextual features specifying the frames in which the item can occur.

For every lexical entry E containing a phonological matrix P, a set of inherent features $[+A_1, \alpha_1 A_2, \ldots \alpha_{n-1} A_n]$, and contextual features $[+X_1 - Y_1, +X_2 - Y_2, \ldots, +X_m - Y_m]$, we define a substitution transformation:

SA: 1: $W, X_1, [\quad \triangle] Y_1, Z$
          A_1

      2: $W, X_2, [\quad \triangle] Y_2, Z$
          A_1

          .
          .
          .

      m: $W, X_m, [\quad \triangle] Y_m, Z$
          A_1

          1   2   3   4   5 $\Rightarrow$
          1   2 E 4   5

In plain words, the contextual features provide the set of structural conditions for a transformation that substitutes the lexical entry for the dummy symbol when the symbol is dominated by the lexical category of the entry in question.

For example, in order to fill out the partial P-marker given above, we might find the following entries in our lexicon (where the phonological matrix is given simply as a representation in ordinary English orthography):

Sally, $+N$, $+[\text{——}]$, $+Animate$, $+Human$, ...
          NP

want, $+V$, $+[\text{——}[\text{——}S],]$ ...
          NP

sleep, $+V$, $+[\text{——}]$, ...
          VP

The features for *Sally* provide the basis for this lexical insertion transformation:

SA: $X, [\quad [\quad \triangle]], Y$
          NP N

SC: 1   2   3 $\Rightarrow$
      1         $\begin{bmatrix} \text{Sally} \rfloor 3 \\ +N \\ +[\text{——}] \\ NP \\ +Animate \\ +Human \\ \vdots \end{bmatrix}$

And so on for the others: *want* is permitted to stand in a sentence in which it has a sentential object, and so on. (Since many lexical entries can stand in alternative structures, the contextual features will often be related as *or* choices rather than *and* choices.) If we let $<X>$ stand for the whole lexical entry for an item with the phonological matrix X, we will be able to derive the following base phrase-marker from our grammar:

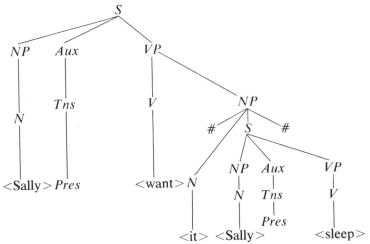

By various transformational rules this structure will yield the sentence *Sally wants to sleep*, and it is thus the deep structure for that sentence. We now turn to a consideration of the transformational component.

6.3 The Transformational Cycle

The theory of grammar I am presenting in this chapter makes several important assumptions about the organization of the transformational rules of grammar. Since the base rules given include the recursive symbol S, and since the structural analysis of every transformation extends over a sentence, the question arises: In a complex base phrase-marker, does it make any difference to which S the rules are assumed to apply at various points in a derivation? The hypothesis we will pursue here is that the rules of the transformational component are **ordered extrinsically** (see p. 44) and that the central set of transformational rules applies cyclically from the most deeply embedded sentences "upward." A further independent assumption is that the transformational rules delete the boundary symbols, #, of embedded sentences (or at least mark them in some way) when the conditions for various transformations dealing with embedded sentences are successfully met. A **surface structure** is then defined as a P-marker derived from a base phrase-marker by the transformational rules applied cyclically and in proper order just in case (if and only if) the P-marker contains no internal sentence boundaries. The operation of the transformations to cull out successful base phrase-markers is referred to as the **filter function** of the transformational rules (T-rules). A base phrase-marker that has such a surface structure is called a **deep structure.**

Suppose we have a base phrase-marker of the following form (the S nodes are subscripted for ease of reference):

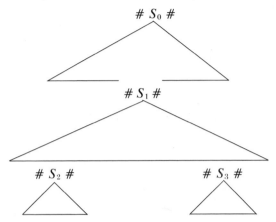

The cyclic hypothesis makes the claim that the correct grammar for the language in question will be one in which the transformations apply in order first to S_2 and S_3 before applying to S_1, and to S_1 before applying to S_0. The order of application for sentences like S_2 and S_3 is left open. Since the structural analysis of a transformation extends only to the extremes of the sentence on which one is cycling, nothing about the shapes of these two sentences can ever have any effect until we have passed both of them to get to the next sentence "up" (S_1).

The **filter-function** hypothesis requires that the rules be set up in such a way that the internal boundaries are deleted at appropriate points, so that the final surface structure for the above base phrase-marker will look like this:

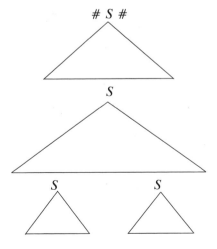

(assuming that nothing essential happens to the remaining structure of the sentence).

Let us now consider the evidence that can be presented for these hypotheses. Let us note first that the cyclic hypothesis is one of a rather limited number of "natural" hypotheses about the organization of a grammar. It states in effect (as Chomsky, 1965, remarks) that the rules for constructing sentences operate in essentially the same way for complex as for simple sentences, with precisely the exception of those rules that deal with constructing complex sentences. Further, the hypothesis makes stronger claims than a number of other hypotheses that might be considered, so that other things being equal we should prefer it as a first hypothesis to these weaker ones. For instance, let us suppose that part of the grammar for each individual language contains a complicated set of "traffic rules" (Lees, 1960) telling us about the order of the transformations, and that no general constraints need be placed on these traffic rules. Under this hypothesis it might be the case that one language had cyclically ordered rules; another had rules in which the rules must operate all the way down on the "oddly" embedded ones, then all the way up on the "evenly" embedded ones; still another language might have completely unordered rules; another might have all the rules mentioning NP's ordered before the rest; and so on. Obviously, the "traffic rules" hypothesis would define a class of grammars that properly includes the class of grammars given by the principle of cyclic ordering. Thus, it represents a weaker hypothesis. We may reject this hypothesis out of hand for the same reason that we rejected the hypothesis about grammars as unrestricted rewriting systems (Chapter 2): it does not sufficiently constrain the class of grammars to approximate those that have been found empirically adequate for given languages.

Obviously, an infinity of possible hypotheses could be entertained about the organization of the rules of a transformational grammar. Thus we can never present absolutely clinching arguments for any given hypothesis. We can, however, consider a number of plausible alternatives and show some evidence that our hypothesis is superior. The form of the argument is as follows: We consider a number of facts about (English) sentences. We show that it is possible to account for these facts according to the hypothesis of ordered cyclic rules; this shows that the hypothesis is **sufficient** to account for the facts. We then show that plausible alternatives will not explain these facts or will lead to other undesirable consequences; we thus try to show that the hypothesis of ordered cyclic rules is **necessary**.

The alternative hypotheses we will consider are two: first, that transformations are not ordered at all (except intrinsically, in the sense that the output from one rule must be present in a P-marker before another rule can apply); second, that the rules are ordered and apply cyclically from the "bottom" up, but that all the applications of each rule must be made before we can advance to another rule. The latter hypothesis we will call the **epicycle** hypothesis. We can schematize the hypotheses thus:

Unordered Rules

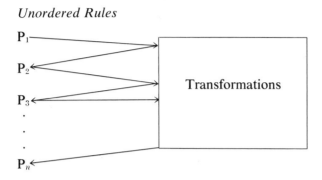

In the diagram, P_1 stands for a base phrase-marker. The transformations are all in a "box." At each step of a derivation we look through all the transformations to see if any are applicable, apply any that we find are applicable and obligatory, apply or not as we wish the optional ones, and then repeat the process until no more obligatory rules are applicable. P_n is then a surface structure if it contains no internal sentence boundaries.

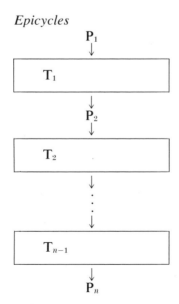

Here we take a base phrase-marker P_1 and apply to it the first T-rule, T_1, cyclically as many times as applicable (again with the proviso that we may choose not to apply it if it is optional). This gives a sequence of P-markers ending with P_2. We repeat the process with P_2 and the second T-rule, and so on. (The epicycle hypothesis was suggested by G. Lakoff and Ross around 1967; for a recent account see Grinder, 1973, and Kimball, 1973.)

Cyclic Hypothesis

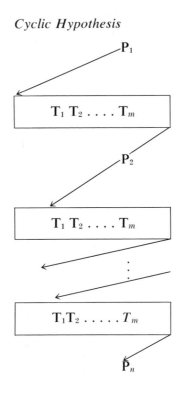

Under the cyclic hypothesis, which we are trying to justify, the entire sequence of transformations is traversed for the most deeply embedded sentences. We then return to the first transformation for the next most deeply embedded sentence, and so on.

Let us first attack the question whether the rules should be ordered at all. Consider the following sentences and nonsentences of English:

1. Go home!
2. You go home!
3. Go home, won't you!
4. Dress yourself!
5. *Dress himself! (imperative interpretation)
6. *Dress you! (imperative interpretation)
7. *She go home!
8. *Elapse! (imperative interpretation)

In Chapter 5 (pp. 99, 101) we considered two of the rules that are involved in the above sentences: Reflexive and Imperative. We can give good evidence that Reflexive requires the presence of two identical *NP*'s in its SA, the second being subject to change into a reflexive. We can also give good evidence that Imperative requires the deletion (optionally, it seems, because of sentences like (2)) of the second-person pronoun *you* (and possibly a modal *will*, in the light of (3)).

Now consider examples like (4), (5), and (6). If we require that Reflexive and Imperative be applied in that order, then we will allow sentences like (4) and correctly block nonsentences like (5) and (6). If Reflexive applies before Imperative, we will still have the first *you* to provide the identity condition for the application of Reflexive, and then Imperative can apply to give sentences like (4). In order to derive (5) we would need an underlying structure like *you dress him* to which we incorrectly applied Reflexive, or we would have to apply Imperative incorrectly to a structure like *he dress himself*. In order to derive (6) we would have to fail to apply the obligatory rule of Reflexive before Imperative. Thus (6) is ungrammatical for the same reason that **you dress you* is ungrammatical. We have shown that we get the correct results if we assume that the two rules are ordered.

Now let us see what the consequences would be of allowing the rules to operate in either order randomly. If we assume that Reflexive has the same form as under the ordered hypothesis, it is obvious that it could never apply after Imperative, since the identity condition would never be met after we had deleted the subject *you* by Imperative. But if Imperative is stated in the usual form, like this:

SA: you, *Pres*, will, *VP*

we will derive sentences like (6). In order to block this result (under the hypothesis of unordered rules) we must change the form either of Imperative or of Reflexive. For example, Imperative might be given like this:

SA: you, *Pres*, will, *V*, *X*, (*NP*), *Y*
      1   2   3   4 5   6   7

where if 6 is second person, then 6 = yourself

But first of all, it is difficult to state this condition so exactly as to block sentences like (6) and allow sentences like these:

Try to persuade Mary to visit $\left\{ \begin{array}{l} \text{you} \\ \text{*yourself} \end{array} \right\}$!

Believe that $\left\{ \begin{array}{l} \text{you} \\ \text{*yourself} \end{array} \right\}$ are saved!

Much worse, the sole effect of complicating the Imperative rule in this ad hoc way is to ensure that we will have only derivations in which the two rules apply in the order we have posited in the original hypothesis. A similar argument can be given against the alternative of changing Reflexive.

Since the two rules we were concerned with in the above argument apply to simple sentences, the operation of the cycle has not entered into the picture at all. What the argument does support is the hypothesis that the transformational rules should be ordered. In order to argue for the cyclic principle, we need to look at complex sentences.

If the cyclic principle is correct, we should be able to find sentences in which a pair of rules must apply in the order *A B*, and other sentences where they must apply in the order *B A*. A number of rules interact in this way.

Consider these sentences and nonsentences:

1. John wants Mary to go home.
2. John wants to go home.
3. John wants him to go home.
4. *John wants himself to go home.

Notice that (3) can only bear the interpretation that the individual referred to by *him* is distinct from John. Taking this fact together with the fact that (4) is ungrammatical, where *himself* must refer to John, we posit a rule called Equi-*NP*-deletion. This rule deletes the subject of an embedded sentence under identity with an *NP* in the next higher sentence. Roughly, the rule might look like this:

Equi-NP-deletion
SA: *X, NP, Y,* [*Comp, NP, Aux, VP*], *Z*
S

1	2	3	4	5	6	7	8 $\Rightarrow$
1	2	3	4	$\emptyset$	6	7	8

where 2 = 5

We need to digress to explain a few features of this rule for later reference. Complement sentences in English take one of three forms:

1. I don't like John's doing that.
2. I don't like for John to do that.
3. I don't like that John does that.

Modern analyses of English have posited three **complementizers,** "*Poss-*ing," "for-to," and "that," respectively, for the sentences above. Choice of complementizers depends largely on the verb. I assume that complementizers are added transformationally (without any particular justification; see Bresnan, 1970, for an opposite view). These complementizers are referred to by *Comp* in the rule of Equi-*NP*-deletion (hereafter referred to as Equi). Under this analysis we must, in fact, restrict the rule above to apply only to cases without *that,* since Equi never operates on *that*-clauses.

Another complication is that we need to add an appropriate condition to the element Y in order to ensure that the correct NP is chosen for the identity condition. Rosenbaum (1967) proposed a general principle requiring that the identity condition be met by the "closest" NP (measured in terms of number of branches). We assume that some such principle is in operation here and that the rule can hence apply also to sentences like *John persuaded Harry to go home,* where the deleting NP is not the subject of the higher sentence, but the object.

Since Equi involves NP's in various positions in a sentence, we might ask how it is related to rules that change the configuration of NP's in sentences. One such rule is Passive (Chapter 5). Consider a sentence in which Passive applies in the embedded sentence:

1. Mary wanted to be interrogated by the police.

According to our above hypothesis about the operation of Equi, this sentence appears to be derived from a structure like this:

2. Mary wanted [for-to Mary be interrogated by the police]
   S

But according to our hypotheses about Passive, this structure in turn derives from a structure essentially like this:

3. Mary wanted [for-to the police interrogate Mary]
   S

If we maintain the same rules that we have posited, we can derive the sentence at hand by applying Passive and then Equi. Notice that by the cyclic hypothesis this is the only order in which the rules can be applied in this particular sentence, since Passive applies in the more deeply embedded of the two sentences and Equi, by its nature, cannot apply until we have gone to the next cycle of rule applications.

But now consider the problem of sentences with verbs like *persuade.* For various reasons we assume that the base structure for such verbs contains an NP object as well as a complement sentence (see Rosenbaum, 1967). For example, one such structure might be essentially this:

4. Bill persuaded Mary [for-to Mary go home]

leading by Equi to

5. Bill persuaded Mary to go home.

But now suppose we apply Passive in the upper sentence; then we have

6. Mary was persuaded by Bill to go home.

We want to know whether in the second cycle Equi should apply before or after Passive. If Equi applies before, then we can obviously derive (6) by a straightforward application of the same rule we have posited. If Equi applies after Passive, then we have to change Equi so that it will apply in one way when Passive has been applied and in another way when Passive has not been applied. But this ad hoc elaboration simply ensures that we will get the same result as if we had applied the rules in the first order.

But now we have two derivations of the sort required for our argument. In the derivation of (1) we have the order Passive-Equi. In the derivation of (6) we have Equi-Passive. And, as the reader can work out for herself, in the derivation of (7) we have the order Passive-Equi-Passive:

7. Mary was persuaded by Bill to be interrogated by the police.

Once again, this ordering follows directly from the assumption that the rules are ordered Equi-Passive and that the rules apply cyclically.

Now let us consider alternative hypotheses, that is, let us try to show that the cyclic ordering hypothesis is necessary (with the qualifications mentioned above on p. 112). Consider first an epicyclic theory. In such a theory the rules will be ordered, but all applications of one rule must precede any applications of the other. There are two possibilities to consider. Assume first that the rules are ordered Passive-Equi. There are independent reasons, mainly semantic, for assuming that the deep structure of (7) is something like this:

8. Bill persuaded Mary [for-to the police interrogate Mary]

After applying Passive throughout, we have

9. Mary be persuaded by Bill [for-to Mary be interrogated by the police]

To apply Equi, we need to revise the rule so that the subject of an embedded sentence can be deleted by the *subject* of the higher sentence (in a structure with a verb like *persuade*) just in case Passive has applied. But once again, this is an ad hoc complication of the rule. That is, we run into the same difficulty with this sentence as we did in assuming the simple order Passive-Equi under the cyclic hypothesis. So let us consider the other possibility, Equi-Passive. Now we have to reformulate Equi so as to apply to the subject of an embedded sentence, or to the object just in case we are prepared to passivize it later on. Otherwise we will be left with results like this:

10. *Bill persuaded Mary for the police to interrogate.

Alternatively, we can make Passive obligatory if we have applied Equi in such a sentence. But we will have to reformulate Passive itself, in either case, since there will no longer be an object to become the subject of the passivized sentence. Notice that the English passive rule can apply only to sentences with objects. We have no sentences like:

11. *Was danced by Mary.
12. *Is interrogated by the police.

Thus, under the theory of epicycles either order seems to fail, since in each case we must revert to unnecessary complications of the rules of Passive and Equi that have the sole effect of ensuring that the rules operate as if they were ordered precisely Equi-Passive and operated in accordance with the cyclic principle.

Now let us consider the other alternative, that the transformational rules are not ordered at all. On this assumption we are free to apply the rules whenever we wish, just so long as the structures in question do indeed satisfy the structural analyses of the transformations in question. Let us note first of all that we have found evidence that two other rules (Imperative and Reflexive) must follow an extrinsic ordering. Assuming the correctness of that argument, we could draw two conclusions: (1) all the rules of the transformational component are ordered (and in addition apply cyclically), or (2) just those two rules are ordered and other rules may or may not be ordered. But it is clearly the stronger hypothesis to assume that all the rules are ordered. Thus, on a priori grounds we should first entertain the assumption that, since we have found some rules to be ordered, all rules must be ordered.

But we can in fact find some evidence that Equi and Passive should not apply randomly. Notice first of all that sentences with *persuade-*type verbs and the complementizer *for-to must* undergo Equi:

13. *John persuaded Mary for Alice to go home.

Now suppose we allow the rules to apply randomly. Then starting with a structure like (8), repeated here,

8. Bill persuaded Mary [for-to the police interrogate Mary]

we could apply Passive twice to get

14. *Mary was persuaded by Bill for Mary to be interrogated by the police.

Since this sentence is ungrammatical, we must either change Equi to allow it to apply here (with all the attendant difficulties and "ad-hoc-icity" noted above) or else allow the theory to mark the sentence as ungrammatical in some new (and ad hoc) way. Notice also that whatever solution we propose must be able to account for the fact that a sentence like (15) cannot have its source in a structure like (16) (under reasonable assumptions about the relation between underlying structures and speakers' interpretations):

15. Mary was persuaded by Bill to go home.
16. Mary was persuaded by Bill [for-to Bill go home]

Whatever the principle is that allows us to find the correct deleting *NP* for Equi (for example, the minimal distance principle of Rosenbaum; see above, p. 117), it will require an ad hoc wrinkle to prevent the first occurrence of *Bill* in structures like (16) from deleting the second one to get incorrect derivations like (16)–(15). And once again, the sole justification for such an extra complication is to make our rules work as if they were conforming to the ordering Equi-Passive and the derivational ordering that follows from the underlying structure we have posited, the simplest formulation of the rules, and the cyclic principle.

Let us look at one more example of an argument for the cycle. One of the rules of English is Raising (it has been known under this name as well as Subject-raising and *It*-replacement). It may be formulated more or less in this way (assuming the *It-S* analysis of complements under *NP;* see p. 107):

Raising
SA: X, [it, [for-to, *NP, Aux, VP*], Y
         NP S
      1 2   3   4   5   6   7   ⇒
      1 4   ∅   ∅   ∅   ∅   7+3+6

(There is a general rule that deletes the *for* of the complementizer when it occurs next to *to*.) The ultimate effect of this rule is to convert structures like the first of each of these pairs into structures like the second of each pair:

It for-to John be crazy seem.
John seems to be crazy.

Someone believe for-to John be crazy.
Someone believes John to be crazy.

Harry's wife expect for-to he fly to the moon.
Harry's wife expects him to fly to the moon.

The effect of the rule on a P-marker can be illustrated thus (for the second pair):

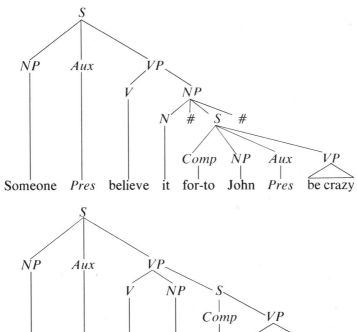

As the diagrams show, Raising has the effect of making a new object where before there was none. Thus, once again the rule may interact with other rules having to do with *NP*'s in ways that may tell us something about the cyclic hypothesis. One such rule is Reflexive. We repeat the rule:

Reflexive
SA: *X, NP, Y, NP,*   *Z*
　　　1　2　3　4　　　5 $\Rightarrow$
　　　1　2　3　4　　　5
　　　　　　 +*Refl*
where 2 = 4, and 2 and 4 are in the same simple sentence

The second condition appears to be necessary to ensure that we do not relate pairs like these by Reflexive:

Mary told John that he could visit Mary.
*Mary told John that he could visit herself.

I want you to tell me all about yourself.
*I want you to tell myself all about yourself.

I talked to the psychiatrist about the fact that I disliked the psychiatrist.
*I talked to the psychiatrist about the fact that I disliked himself.

I saw the man that had robbed me.
*I saw the man that had robbed myself.

The man that robbed me escaped me.
*The man that robbed me escaped myself.

In the above cases there are good independent reasons for assuming that one occurrence of the identical *NP* is in an embedded sentence to which the other one does not belong.

Now suppose we have a sentence in which Raising can apply, but the subject of the embedded sentence is identical both to some object in the embedded sentence and to some preceding *NP* in the sentence into which it is raised. If we assume (1) that the rules are ordered, (2) that Raising precedes Reflexive, (3) that Reflexive and Raising are as stated, and (4) that the rules operate under the cyclic principle, then we should have two reflexives. This prediction is correct, as we can see from sentences like this:

John imagined himself to have killed himself.

The basic structure for this sentence is as follows:

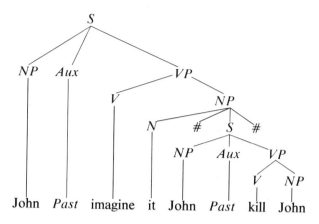

On the first cycle, only Reflexive can apply. On the second cycle, Raising applies first to remove the second *John* from the lower sentence and make it an object in the higher sentence, so that now Reflexive can apply to give the sentence under analysis. Thus we *can* account for the sentence under the assumptions given above. *Must* we account for it in this way?

As a first alternative, consider the epicycle hypothesis. Assume first that Raising precedes Reflexive, as above. Thus we have this structure, to which we must apply some Reflexive rule:

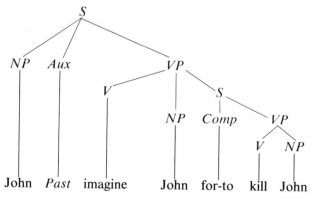

It is first of all clear that we need to allow the rule to operate down into embedded sentences, that is, we cannot maintain the condition we have given above to ensure that the rule operates correctly. Suppose we revise Reflexive so as to apply in the case at hand. But now the relaxed reflexive rule must be constrained so as not to operate in structures like these:

John imagined Mary to have killed John.
*John imagined Mary to have killed himself.

Notice that the statement of the new condition cannot be a very simple matter, since it will have to accommodate structures like these:

John persuaded Mary to visit him (*self).
John promised Mary to shave himself (*him, *herself). [*where* John *is presumed to equal* him]

Now consider the alternative order under the epicycle hypothesis: Reflexive-Raising. Under this hypothesis we must apply Reflexive first to get this structure:

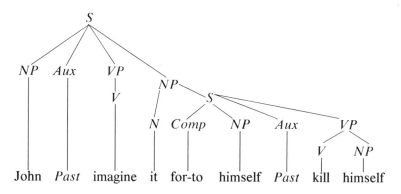

But now we must complicate Reflexive, since we must prevent it from applying to give nonsentences like these:

*John imagined that himself was on a desert island.
*Mary prefers herself's being sent to Rochester.

But the formulation of this revision will have the effect of making the rule operate in just those structures where Raising is going to apply. It is easy to see that the unordered rule hypothesis will run into precisely the kinds of difficulties we have seen with the epicycle hypothesis in this case.

What is common to all the arguments we have considered is: (1) certain rather intricate facts about English sentences follow naturally from the assumption that the rules are ordered and cyclic, and (2) the alternative hypotheses we have considered lead to ad hoc complications that seem merely to make the rules work as if they were cyclically ordered. In each case we have considered, it is necessary to build into one of the pair of rules some conditions or restrictions that have to do with the other rule in question. These unnecessary complications will be greatly compounded in the case of rules that interact with a number of different rules. Thus, Passive has been shown to interact with Equi in a way that provides evidence for the cyclic hypothesis. There are independent arguments of the same sort for the pair Passive-Raising, and for the pair Equi-Raising. If we consider all three rules jointly under either the epicyclic or the unordered rule hypothesis, the complications that we find necessary for each pair will be added together. For example, to the extent that we must build parts of Raising into the Equi rule to make it work correctly, we further complicate the part of the Equi rule that must be amalgamated with Passive to make the latter work right. In the remainder of this book we will assume that the cyclic hypothesis is correct.

6.4 Precyclic and Last-cyclic Rules

The hypothesis that the transformational rules are ordered and cyclic is reasonably well established. The strongest hypothesis that will accommodate facts like those presented in the last section is that all the rules of the transformational component are related in this way. However, there is some indication that this hypothesis is too simple and needs to be relaxed to accommodate the fact that some transformational rules operate in a different way.

Let us notice first that, strictly speaking, some transformations are usually assumed to operate before the transformational cycle: the lexical insertions. We have seen that lexical insertion is essentially a transformational operation. If we assume that a full base phrase-marker is formed before any of the transformations (in the narrower sense) operate, then at least the insertions must be precyclic. If they were cyclic, then we could not add any lexical items for the higher sentences until we had finished applying the cyclic transformations in the lower sentences. Can we find any evidence that this assumption is correct?

There is some evidence against the cyclic lexical insertion hypothesis, as we may call it. David Perlmutter (1968) has shown that some verbs must be constrained so as to appear in frames satisfying various so-called deep-structure constraints that refer to embedded sentences in constructions with the verbs in question. For example, *scream* must occur (in a certain usage) with complements containing a subject different from the subject of *scream,* while *try* must have an identical subject in the complement. These "unlike-subject" and "like-subject" constraints are illustrated in these sentences:

I screamed for Sarah to open the bedroom door.
*I screamed (for myself/me) to open the door.
*I screamed for the door to be opened by me.
I screamed to be allowed to open the door.
I tried to open a pizza parlor in Dubuque.
*I tried for Harry to open a pizza parlor in Dubuque.

But if Passive, Equi, and other cyclic rules have applied on the lower sentences, then we cannot state such constraints in a simple way.

It has been argued that rules other than the lexical insertions must operate on full base P-markers before the cyclic rules begin to operate on the most deeply embedded sentences.

Following the analysis of nominal clauses as consisting of $It + S$, G. Lakoff (manuscript) proposed a rule called S-deletion to account for sentences like this:

The police claimed that Harry was a thief but his wife didn't believe it.

Here *it* can refer to the allegation that Harry is a thief. We can account for this by positing a rule that deletes a second occurrence of a sentence, leaving *it* as a residue. Thus the underlying structure to which S-deletion applies to yield the above sentence is something like this:

The police claimed it that Harry was a thief but his wife didn't believe it that Harry was a thief.

But suppose all transformations work cyclically, as we have argued so far. Then S-deletion can apply in a sentence like the one above only when we have reached the cycle defined by the superordinate sentence formed by the conjunction of the two sentences *I said it that Harry was a thief* and *his wife doesn't believe it that Harry was a thief*. Therefore, any transformational rules that work on the conjuncts of this supersentence must already have applied at the point in the derivation when S-deletion applies. But among these rules are some that might break up sentences that were present in the deep structure, for example, Raising and Passive (which were shown above to be cyclic rules), and if the sentence has been broken apart, how can it form the deleting element for the transformation of S-deletion? For example, this sentence has exactly the same interpretation as the original one:

Harry was claimed by the police to be a thief but his wife didn't believe it.

Unless we endow transformations with some new power, it is impossible to carry out S-deletion on such a structure. Lakoff's solution to the dilemma was to posit a new organization of a grammar that would allow some rules, among them S-deletion, to take place before the cycle. Such precyclic rules may operate on full base phrase-markers before any cyclic rules have operated on them.

It must be admitted that the case for such precyclic rules remains rather weak. Somewhat stronger is the case for constraining certain rules to operate only on the last cycle.

Last-cyclic rules may be ordered among the ordinary cyclic rules. That is to say, it may be that on the last cycle of the derivation a last-cyclic rule may apply, followed by some ordinary cyclic rules. Schematically, we may think of the transformations as organized in this way:

Precyclic rules
Cyclic rules:
$$T_1$$
$$T_2$$
$$.$$
$$.$$
$$^LT_i$$
$$.$$
$$.$$
$$T_j$$
$$.$$
$$^LT_m$$
$$.$$
$$.$$
$$T_n$$

To derive a sentence, we first construct a base phrase-marker, then apply any applicable precyclic rules. We then apply the cyclic rules in the manner indicated before, starting with the most deeply embedded sentence. As we run through the rules, on every cycle except the last we skip any of the rules marked ^LT (the last-cyclic rules). On the final cycle we apply all the rules in order, including the specially marked ones. As we shall see in a moment, the last-cyclic rules may be rules that apply to embedded sentences. In other words, they are not necessarily rules that apply only to highest S's (hence, they are unlike the *root transformations* of Emonds, 1970, which I will mention in Section 9.22). What is peculiar about them is solely the fact that they may not apply until we have reached the last cycle.

Now let us consider an example of a putatively last-cyclic rule. For the argument it is necessary to anticipate some later discussion. Ross (1967a) has formulated a general principle to account for the fact that certain transformations that "move" constituents cannot operate to remove constituents out of sentences embedded in noun phrases. (We will look at a number of examples of such transformational constraints in Section 9.21.) Thus, compare these grammatical and ungrammatical results of the rule called *WH*-movement, which moves questioned constituents to the head of a sentence:

1. Who(m) did John catch under his bed?
2. Who(m) did Sally think John caught under his bed?
3. Who(m) did it seem that John had caught under his bed?
4. *Who did the claim that John caught under his bed horrify his mother?
5. *Who did the claim horrify John's mother that he caught under his bed.
6. Who(m) is it believed that John caught under his bed?
7. *Who is the claim believed that John caught under his bed?

Sentences like (3) and (6) have undergone the Extraposition rule that we discussed in Chapter 5. Sentences (5) and (7), on the other hand, have undergone a rule called Extraposition from *NP*, which appears to differ from ordinary Extraposition. Before this rule applies we have structures like this to deal with:

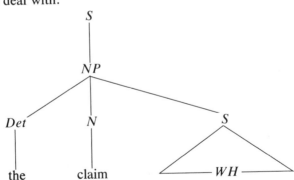

After Extraposition from *NP* we have structures like this:

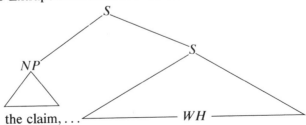

If we want to make use of the principle mentioned above (Ross's so-called complex-noun-phrase constraint) to explain why *WH*-movement should be blocked in sentences like (5) and (7), then we must require that *WH*-movement take place before Extraposition from *NP,* that is, it must operate when the structures are as in (4). But now we run into a difficulty if we think that Extraposition from *NP* is an ordinary cyclic rule. A number of arguments can be given to show that *WH*-movement should operate in such a way as to allow it to reach down into an embedded sentence like (2). For example, in (2) it operates only on the last cycle, not on the cycle for the complement clause of the embedded sentence (*that*) *John caught WH under his bed.* Similarly, in a structure like (8) it operates on the S_1 cycle or perhaps later, not on the S_2 or S_3 cycles (for an opposite view see Chomsky, 1973):

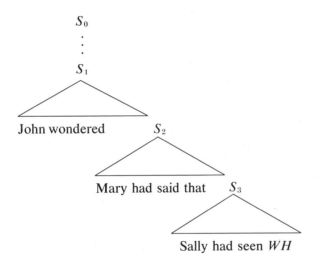

The difficulty mentioned with Extraposition from *NP* is this: no matter how we order it with respect to *WH*-movement, if all rules are cyclic then Extraposition from *NP* may apply on lower cycles than the cycle on which *WH*-movement applies, and it is impossible to maintain the explanation that *WH*-movement is blocked by the complex-*NP* constraint. But if we are allowed to make some rules last-cyclic, we can escape the dilemma. Extraposition from *NP* is a last-cyclic rule (and ordered after *WH*-movement). A number of other last-cyclic rules have been postulated for English and other languages. It would seem that within the standard theory it is necessary to make this addition to the organization of the transformational rules.

6.5 The Semantic Component

The two remaining components of a grammar in the standard theory are the phonological rules and the semantic component. We will say very little about the former (since an extensive literature is available on phonological theory) and not much about the latter. In the standard theory both of these components are interpretive in two senses. First, except for minor variations in the possible alternative pronunciations of a sentence, neither component is creative. By and large, both the semantic interpretation and the phonetic "interpretation" are determined once we have applied the rules of the base, made our lexical choices, and operated the transformational rules. Second, the semantic and the phonological components each accomplish a "translation" of the underlying syntactic structure into a representation in another mode that is language-independent: a phonetic representation in terms of universal parameters and features; a semantic representation in terms of a universal semantic "language." The existence of the phonological component and its basic character are not in doubt, although we are about as far from a satisfactory detailed theory of phonology as we are from a final picture of a syntactic theory. But the basic nature, and indeed the existence, of a semantic component are very much a matter of controversy. We shall first consider what evidence there might be for the existence of an interpretive semantic component in every grammar, and then look at some ideas about its nature.

Under the standard theory the syntactic component of a grammar provides us with a pair of P-markers to form part of the structural description of each sentence generated by the grammar. If we agree that part of the structural description of every sentence is a representation of its meaning, then it is easy to show that there must be some sort of semantic interpretive rules. Let (P_d, P_s) stand for a deep-structure and a surface-structure P-marker. Neither P_d nor P_s is a semantic representation, for, whatever else a semantic representation might be, it must satisfy these two requirements:

1. If two sentences are assigned the same semantic representation, then they must be paraphrases (synonymous).
2. If two sentences are paraphrases, then they must be assigned the same semantic representation.

The surface-structure P_s cannot be a semantic representation, for there are situations that violate both requirements. Against (1), there are ambiguous surface structures. For example, there is no basis for assigning distinct surface structures to the various readings of the string *It's too hot to eat.* Against (2), there are optional transformations like Extraposition that provide distinct surface structures with no concomitant difference in meaning, as in these examples:

It's odd that you have green hair.
That you have green hair is odd.

Can the deep-structure P_d be a semantic representation? Under the standard theory, two sorts of situation seem to militate against this view. First, since deep structures contain lexical items and since there seem to be lexical items that are synonymous in at least some contexts, Requirement 2 is not met by deep structures. For example, the following two sentences have distinct deep structures in the standard theory:

John went to a podiatrist for his chilblains.
John went to a foot-doctor for his chilblains.

Second, since P_d is a P-marker and as such includes a specification of precedence relations, pairs of conjoined sentences like the following ones, which are fully synonymous, will have different deep structures (again, against Requirement 2):

Mary likes Bill and Bill likes Mary.
Bill likes Mary and Mary likes Bill.

Third, if it is possible for two sentences in different languages to be paraphrases of each other, then under standard theory the deep structures for the sentences cannot be semantic interpretations, since they will contain not only the semantically relevant parts of the deep structure but all kinds of other language-particular material, including in particular the lexical items.

Thus it would seem that in the standard theory neither the deep structures nor the surface structures can be identified with the semantic representations of sentences, and that hence the structural description of a sentence must contain (besides phonological and phonetic representations) the triple (P_d, P_s, SR), where SR is some representation distinct from the other two. (Notice that the deep structure does meet Requirement 1 in the standard theory, since deep structures determine semantic representations.)

Another way of seeing the same thing is the following. Deep structures and surface structures are composed of labeled bracketings (trees), phonological matrices, and various other features. Of these others, some are presumably semantic, some not. A minimal semantic interpretive component must at least separate out the semantically relevant parts of these complex objects and ignore others (for instance, syntactic features like gender; phonological matrices).

Having established the existence of the semantic component of a grammar, let us turn to a consideration of its form. The theory of semantics that has been most closely associated with the standard theory is that developed by Jerrold J. Katz and associates (Katz and Fodor, 1963; Katz and Postal, 1964; Katz, 1972). A general assumption about the relation of an interpretive semantic theory to a grammar is that the grammar provides input to the semantic theory in the form of syntactic structural descriptions, and the theory provides a set of semantic interpretations or *readings* for each such syntactic structural description. On the basis of the zero or more readings the theory provides, it is able to assign various semantic properties to the sentence: if it has no readings, it is semantically anomalous; if it has *n* readings, it is *n*-ways ambiguous; if two sentences share a reading, they are synonymous on a reading; if the sentence is true by virtue purely of its form, it is analytic; and so on. (The reader is referred to Katz, 1966 and 1972, and the literature cited there for details.) For our purposes we need to note just three characteristics of the semantic theory as developed by Katz.

First, in this version of semantic theory it is solely the deep structure that is relevant to determining the semantic reading of every sentence. No rules for determining a reading refer to the surface structure or any intermediate structures (or to the phonological structure). As we will see, some linguists have argued that the deep structure is not sufficient to determine all aspects of the meaning of the sentence. It is a corollary of the standard view that no transformational rules may affect the meaning of a sentence.

Second, the rules of semantic interpretation that determine the readings of a syntactic structure (called **projection rules**) operate by progressively amalgamating the deep constituents into larger units. Let us assume that all relevant semantic information is given in the lexical entry for each item.[2] Various projection rules then are stated that have the effect of finding readings for higher and higher constituents of the sentence, discarding those that do not meet certain compatibility requirements of the lexical entries. Thus, the adjective *buxom* contains a specification that it is to apply to the adult female human. If we find a constituent in which the

---

2. Early writings on semantic theory, such as Katz and Fodor (1963), and Katz and Postal (1964), were based on a different theory of grammar, and accordingly are stated in terms of a dictionary that is separate from the grammar. In those writings the first operation of the semantic theory is to find a subpart of a *dictionary* entry that is compatible with the syntactic structure in which the item stands. We assume here that the effect of that first step is carried out by the lexical insertion rule for the entry in question.

projection rules amalgamate this item with items that are specified as human, mature, and female, interpretation continues. If we find a constituent in which this compatibility condition is not met, the constituent (and the sentence) is marked as anomalous. If the item with which *buxom* is combined is not specified for the features in question, or has several readings only one of which is compatible, the semantic theory will make the appropriate assignment. Thus, *my buxom girlfriend* is semantically well formed; *my buxom uncle* and *my buxom cat* are not; *my buxom neighbor* refers unambiguously to a female neighbor, while *that buxom bitch* refers to a human and not a canine. The cycle of application of projection rules is defined by all constituents, not, as with the T-rules of syntax, only by sentences.

The third characteristic of the semantic theory under consideration here is that the result of applying the projection rules to a P-marker is not a P-marker but some other kind of object. The result of applying the first projection rule to the bottommost constituent is a combination of nodes of P-markers and sets of semantic features. Further amalgamations result finally in a set of features organized in some fashion to represent the organization of the meaning of the whole sentence, but not in the form of a P-marker. Again, alternatives are possible. One of the main lines of development I will mention later makes the assumption that semantic interpretations are P-markers, just like other items in a structural description of a sentence.

6.6 Transformational Theory before *Aspects:* A Short Sketch

In this chapter we have looked at a fairly coherent and detailed set of assumptions about the form of a transformational grammar. In later chapters we will look at some further developments in syntactic theory since the period when this so-called standard theory was presented and defended. In this section we look briefly at some ways in which the standard theory departed from earlier assumptions about grammars. I will confine myself to a few remarks about modern transformational theory since about 1957, ignoring historical precedents (see Chomsky, 1966, but also R. Lakoff, 1969, and Aarsleff, 1970).

The idea that a grammar can be conceived of as an explicit set of statements for generating sentences and their structural descriptions originated with Chomsky. As with most such important new ideas, a number of other workers hit on roughly the same idea at roughly the same time (some representative examples are Bar-Hillel, 1954; Harwood, 1955; Hockett, 1954). But the particular way of conceiving of a grammar as a set of iterative rules was developed most clearly and in most depth by Chomsky (see, for example, 1956). The second idea, that there is a particular level of linguistic description comprising transformational rules in a generative grammar, was also conceived by Chomsky (1955, 1957). The notion of transformation in its particular linguistic formulation grew out of work done by Zellig Harris (1952, 1957), but in Harris's work a transformation is basically a relation between sentences, rather than a type of rule embedded in a generative grammar.

The first full theory of transformational grammar was presented in Chomsky's *Syntactic Structures,* albeit in a very preliminary and tentative way as far as details are concerned. This first model of a transformational grammar was developed and extended without basic change in most of the work carried out between the appearance of *Syntactic Structures* and *Aspects* (1965). It underlies such work as Lees (1960) and early papers by Bach, Klima, Lees, Fillmore, and others (see Bach, 1964, and works cited there, as well as papers in Fodor and Katz, 1964).

Let us outline the basic differences between this early model of a transformational grammar and the standard theory. The first major difference is that in *Syntactic Structures* there was no explicit attempt to deal with semantics, nor any attempt to integrate a semantic theory with a syntactic theory. By contrast, it is like the standard theory in that the syntax was conceived of as closely integrated with a phonology in ways that do not differ essentially from the ways in which the standard theory relates phonology and syntax. Just as in the standard theory, the phonological rules (called sometimes morphophonemic rules) were allowed to operate on a full P-marker from the syntax. This represented a major departure from most previous work in phonology, at least in America.

The syntax was divided into two parts, as in the standard theory: a set of phrase-structure rules and a set of transformations, the latter both obligatory and optional. But all the recursiveness of the system was attributed to the transformations. The phrase-structure component consisted of a set of ordered context-sensitive rules defining a finite set of P-markers, the so-called **kernel.** The sentences derived from these structures by obligatory transformations were the **kernel sentences.** They comprised the most basic simple sentences of the language — for example, in grammars of English, the simple active declarative affirmative sentences. All other sentences were derived from the kernel by the application of two kinds of optional transformation: those (like Negative, Question, and Passive) that operate on single P-markers (the **singulary transformations**) and those that operate on pairs of P-markers to form embedded sentences and conjunctions of sentences (the **generalized** or **double-base transformations**). Part of the structural description of every sentence was a so-called T-marker, a structure representing the P-markers of the kernel sentences out of which the sentence was derived and the way in which they were combined and modified by transforma- tions to make up the final derived P-marker (corresponding to the sur- face structure of the standard theory).[3] The lexicon had no special status in this theory. The lexical items were inserted into P-markers by rules exactly like the other rules of the phrase-structure. Thus, among the rules for English would be the rule "$N_x \rightarrow$ boy," where N_x represents some subcategory of nouns. The phrase-structure component was thus a phrase-structure grammar in the strict sense; the elements of the rules were unanalyzed. A number of the major problems in this theory of transformational grammar have been touched on in the preceding chap- ters, where we have tried to motivate various features of the standard theory. Thus, the unanalyzable character of the elements of the rules led to the kinds of cross-classification problems that were touched on in Chap- ter 4 and resolved by the introduction of complex elements in the base. The problem of the ordering of transformational rules was never satis- factorily solved in this theory, but the attempt to solve it led to the postulation of the cycle in the standard theory (see Fillmore, 1963, for an intermediate step).

The first attempt to integrate a semantic theory with this theory of syntax was by Katz and Fodor (1963). Their projection rules were of two basic kinds: rules of amalgamation like those mentioned above (type 1) and a second kind. Since the transformations included rules like Negative and Question, it was necessary to postulate semantic projection rules (type 2) that would indicate the contribution of such transformations to the meaning of the sentence. In Katz and Postal (1964) several such rules were examined, and it was argued that the basic meaning-changing singulary transformations should be reformulated as obligatory rules contingent on the presence of certain elements in the phrase structure. Once this step was made, the only contribution the transformations made to the meaning of a sentence was to combine sentences (in the generalized transformations). With the change of the theory to make all recursion present in the base rules, even this contribution was no longer required, so that it was natural to posit the hypothesis of the standard theory that only the deep structure is relevant to determining the meaning of the sentence (with the consequence that type 2 projection rules were no longer necessary). Although this position has been abandoned by some, as we will see in Chapter 9, the change has not been exactly a reversion

---

3. *Marker* is used here in a special sense, defined by Chomsky and surviving in the term *phrase-marker*. Linguistic theory defined a set of levels: phrase-structure, transformational, phonological, and perhaps others. The grammar associated with each sentence a set of markers for each level, phrase-markers, transformation-markers, phonological markers, and the like, which made up the structural description of the sentence.

to the earlier theory. In most of the cases of determination of the meaning from other sources than deep structure, it has not been particular transformations that have had specific meanings associated with them. Rather, it has been claimed that certain aspects of the meaning of a sentence can be best determined on the basis of the surface structure or some intermediate structure.

Finally, let us sketch some aspects of a version of transformational theory that was presented in Chomsky's *Aspects* as an alternative to one that was basically the same as the standard theory presented here.

In the standard theory, we are allowed to specify just about any kind of limiting context for the substitution transformation associated with lexical items. In the alternative theory of *Aspects,* an attempt was made to limit this freedom and at the same time allow the theory to capture certain generalizations about the deep-structure distribution of lexical items. If we look back at the base rules given above (p. 106), we notice that there are different verbs for just about every combination of items that we develop under the *VP* node. We can capture this generalization in the following way. Let the notation $A \to CS$ (read "complex symbol") mean that the category A is subcategorized into classes corresponding to each of the environments in which it stands that are covered by the immediately dominating node. At the point in the derivation at which this rule applies, we create a complex symbol consisting of the feature specification $+A$ and the feature corresponding to the frame in which the item stands. As a handy label for this feature we can use the frame itself: thus if the item A stands in the environment $[\underset{B}{\quad X-Y}]$ (where B is the node immediately dominating A), then the complex symbol is given the feature specification $[+X-Y]$. Stated once more and more formally:

$A \to CS$ is an abbreviation for all of these rules:
$$A \to [+A, +X_1-Y_1] \,/\, X_1 - Y_1$$
$$A \to [+A, +X_2-Y_2] \,/\, X_2-Y_2$$
$$\vdots$$
$$A \to [+A, +X_n-Y_n] \,/\, X_n-Y_n$$

where $X_i - Y_i\,(1 \le i \le n)$ are all the environments (including perhaps null for either or both X_i, Y_i) within which A may stand such that $X_i A Y_i$ is immediately dominated by some node B.

A rule like that given by the above schema is called a rule of **strict subcategorization.** For example, given the rule developing *NP*'s of our illustrative grammar (p. 106).

$$NP \rightarrow (Det) \ N \ (\# \ S \ \#)$$

we may give a rule for the strict subcategorization of nouns as follows:

$$N \rightarrow CS$$

This schema abbreviates all these rules:

$$N \rightarrow [+N, +Det - \# \ S \ \#] \ / \ Det - \# \ S \ \#$$
$$N \rightarrow [+N, +Det -] \ / \ Det -$$
$$N \rightarrow [+N, + \ - \# \ S \ \#] \ / \ - \# \ S \ \#$$
$$N \rightarrow [+N, + \ -]$$

(The last rule needs no environment, since it is the sole remaining case, where neither *Det* or *# S #* is chosen.) The subcategories of nouns corresponding to these frames are (1) nouns with complements, like *fact, allegation, statement;* (2) common nouns that can take an article; (3) the one abstract noun *it* that we have seen before in our analysis of complement sentences; (4) proper nouns like *Harry* that take no article. Notice that we are building up a complex symbol that already contains some feature specifications. The model of grammar that we are sketching proceeds by continuing to develop these complex symbols by various kinds of rules. Lexical insertion is then accomplished merely by finding a lexical entry that is compatible with the feature specifications of the complex symbol we have developed and amalgamating the entry with that symbol.

The next rule for developing the complex symbol that we need is one that allows us to pick finer classifications of lexical elements. It is possible to show that the rules should first develop nouns and then allow verbs and adjectives to be chosen in terms of the noun features. Some rules allowing us to further specify noun classes might be these:

$$[+N] \rightarrow [\pm Abstract, \pm Count]$$
$$[+N, -Abstract] \rightarrow [\pm Animate]$$
$$[+N, +Animate] \rightarrow [\pm Human]$$

where the notation $\pm X$ means that we may pick either $+$ or $-$ for that feature.

Finally, in order to state generalizations about verbs and adjectives, Chomsky introduced another kind of rule schema, allowing the abbreviation of rules that select verb and adjective features according to the inherent features of the nouns standing in construction with them. An example of such a **selectional rule** for verbs is this:

$[+V] \rightarrow CS \mid \alpha\, Aux\, ((Det)\, \beta)$
where α and β are $+N$ and comprise inherent features

This rule stands for all and only the rules that we get by creating **selectional features** corresponding to the features of the nouns standing in subject and object position for the verb in that derivation: $[+Animate, +N, \ldots]\, Aux - Det\, [+Abstract, +N \ldots]$ and so on. This feature might be associated with verbs like *ponder*, for example.

In *Aspects*, Chomsky offered this alternative theory. Without making any very strong commitment, he chose it as slightly preferable to the model we have called here the standard theory. The main reason for making this choice was that the standard theory is more powerful, and without any indication of the necessity for the extra power the best choice is the more restrictive of the two models. The difference in power has to do with the mechanism by which the two kinds of contextual features are created. In the alternative theory there is a sharp separation between strict subcategorization features and selectional features. Further, the former type is restricted to being defined by environments that are **strictly local** (within the immediately dominating node). In the standard theory there is no such restriction of contextual features. For example, it is possible to give a contextual feature within the standard theory corresponding to this frame: $[+Animate, +N]\, Aux - NP$, that is, a transitive verb that demands an animate subject.

The alternative model has not been followed in this exposition for the following reasons. First, the restrictiveness of the system turns out to be largely illusory. Notice, for example, that although we cannot have a single feature combining the types of environment of strict subcategorization and selectional features, we can provide combinations of features having the same effect. Second, the system makes claims about the relevance of certain features that are simply not borne out. Notice that the definition of the second type of complex-symbol rule forces us to classify verbs not only according to relevant features of their subjects and objects, such as $[\pm Animate]$, but also according to completely irrelevent ones such as their ability to stand with an article $([+Det-])$. Third, as McCawley (1968a) argued, the apparatus of selectional features duplicates the work of semantic projection rules. For example, a theory should not have to account twice for the fact that *surprise* demands an animate object. But if we must choose between the two types of explanations, then we must choose the semantic projection rules, since they allow us to account for selectional facts that are unaccountable under the other theory. Notice that the crucial noun for determining when an object may stand with *surprise* may be buried indefinitely far down, or the selection may depend on an adjective rather than a noun (McCawley, 1968a; Bach, 1968):

The thunder surprised the one that Mary realized Michael
knew was a chimpanzee (*statue).
I surprised the confident one.

Finally, as McCawley (1968b) argued, it is possible to put restrictions on
the standard theory that will reduce its power in more reasonable ways
and at the same time allow the system to capture facts like those just
noted.

In the next chapter we will look at some particular analyses carried
out under the standard theory. In later chapters we will consider further
developments since *Aspects*.

Problems and Questions

1.   Show that a theory that does not use the filter function of transformations to eliminate some base structures from the deep structures is more
restrictive than the standard theory.
2.   Write transformational rules that will add prepositions to the
nominal complements of a verb, such as *look for, wonder about, decide
on*. Discuss problems that arise in trying to formulate rules for such combinations of verbs and prepositions.
3.   Expand the base rules of Section 6.2 to include the possibility of
prepositional phrases for *Time, Location, Manner, Sentence-Adverb*.
4.   Discuss the problems raised for the base rules given in Section 6.2
by such sentences as these:

a) John saw the burglar in the garden at the castle.
   At the castle John saw the burglar in the garden.
   In the garden John saw the burglar at the castle.
b) Unfortunately Mary isn't going home.
   The boys don't not want to go.
   You can go or you can not go.
c) Mary is angry at Bill for leaving her.
d) You just aren't the Horatio that I used to know.
e) She dances in a manner that intrigues everybody.
   *She dances in a manner.
f) ?The square root of two is irrational at three o'clock in Chicago.
g) ?Mary will be there yesterday.
   ?Alley Oop will be there yesterday.
   ?Doctor Wonmug is going to visit Oscar yesterday tomorrow.
h) I called the president at the White House at my house.

5.   Show that the lexical insertion rule as given for the standard theory in Section 6.2 is indeed a transformation in the sense of Chapter 5.

6.   In Section 6.3 we considered three alternative theories about the ordering of transformational rules: cyclic and ordered, epicyclic and ordered, unordered. State several other *general* hypotheses about the ordering of transformations.

7.   Study the argument about ordering using Reflexive and Imperative, and find some other examples of pairs of rules that seem to require an extrinsic ordering.

8.   Find examples of rules that are intrinsically ordered.

9.   For the rules discussed in Section 6.3 in giving arguments for the cycle, discuss an alternative theory under which the transformational rules are ordered cyclically but apply from the highest sentence "down," ending with the most deeply embedded sentences.

10.   Construct an argument for the cycle using the rules Raising and Passive. (For part of the argument it is necessary to consider the fact that sentences with Passive and Reflexive are generally bad: *John was shaved by himself* (with no special stress on himself), and that this can best be accounted for by a restriction that disallows the application of rules like Passive when an *NP* would be "moved" across an identical *NP*—the Crossover principle of Postal (1971); see Section 7.5.)

11.   Construct an argument for the cycle using the rules Raising and Equi. Show first that Equi must be formulated in such a way as to delete an *NP* that is exactly one sentence "down" from the sentence in which the deleting *NP* stands.

12.   Show that in the Reflexive rule as formulated on p. 122, its second condition violates the restrictions on transformations given in Chapter 5.

13.   What arguments could be given against the *S*-deletion argument for precyclic rules?

14.   Show that Equi cannot be a last-cyclic rule. (Hint: use Raising.)

15.   Show the difficulties encountered in allowing Raising and Reflexive to operate in an unordered fashion.

16.   What is wrong with the following argument?

Question-inversion occurs only in the highest sentence as seen in these examples:

Can John go to Bermuda?
I asked if John could go to Bermuda.
Who did Sally sleep with?
Mary asked who Sally slept with.

Therefore, Question-inversion is a last-cyclic rule.

17. What is wrong with the following argument (assume that (1) is correct)?

   1. Extraposition is last-cyclic.
   2. *WH*-movement can move constituents out of a *that*-clause or *for-to* clause only if Extraposition has taken place, as shown by these examples:

      Who is it likely that she saw?
      *Who is that she saw likely?
      Who will it be easy for Sally to marry?
      *Who will for Sally to marry be easy?

   3. Hence *WH*-movement must follow Extraposition.
   4. Therefore (by 1 and 3) *WH*-movement is also last-cyclic.

18. What is wrong with the following reasoning?

   We obviously think of what we say before we decide how to say it. Therefore a theory in which the semantic component is purely interpretive cannot be correct.

19. Show that the deep-structure constraints of Perlmutter are incompatible with the alternative theory presented at the end of Section 6.6.

chapter

7

Syntactic Arguments

7.1 How to Think about Syntax

The reasoning that goes on in linguistics is not different from that in other disciplines. Whenever we attempt to understand some range of phenomena, we must carry out deductions from premises to conclusions, look for crucial evidence, rule out alternative explanations, and so on. There is no recipe for thinking. Nevertheless, certain patterns of argument are so common that looking at a few arguments in detail is worthwhile. At the same time, it is important to see how a pattern of interlocking hypotheses must be built up that can, in the last analysis, only be judged as a coherent whole. In this chapter we will consider a number of interdependent transformations of English, taking care to make clear the steps of the arguments and the interrelationships among our assumptions. Then we will look back at our arguments in an attempt to become familiar with a number of common patterns.

Two distinct kinds of conclusions are sought in linguistics. On the one hand, we may try to show that a particular analysis, rule, or structure is correct for a given language, holding more or less constant a set of assumptions about linguistic theory. On the other hand, we may fix some observations or assumptions about a language and point our arguments toward a conclusion about linguistic theory itself: the form of a grammar, the necessity to include some kind of feature, or the like. So far in this book we have dealt mainly with the second kind of argument. In arguing for various aspects of the general theory, I have presented and mentioned various transformational rules of English. Now we will make these rules themselves the center of our attention and try to establish the existence of the rules, their form, and their interrelationships. We will assume, by and large, that the standard theory as presented in the last chapter is correct.

It may appear as if our reasoning is circular in a vicious sense. We use various rules to argue for aspects of the theory, and then turn around and use the theory to argue for the correctness of the rules. But this impression is based on an incorrect view of the process of scientific reasoning. Reasoning in an empirical science does not proceed in a linear fashion, as I shall stress here. It proceeds on all fronts simultaneously. We are not constructing a pyramid but rather a keystone arch, in which all the pieces must be held up at once.

7.2 *There*-Insertion

Many arguments in English syntax involve the assumption that there is a transformational rule called *There*-insertion (There) that operates in the derivation of sentences like these:

There is a burglar under the bed.
There was discovered yesterday in Washington an immense cloud of fetid gas issuing from the Pentagon.
There is a god.
There appeared a guru walking on the waters of the swimming pool.

Let us list some characteristics of these constructions:
First, the form *there* is distinct from the adverb *there* of sentences like *I saw Charlie there* or *Are you there?* since (1) the former is never stressed while the latter may be, (2) both can appear in the same sentence (*There was someone there.*), (3) they can contrast in the same environment (*There's a vísitor* vs. *Thére's a visitor*), and (4) they mean different things: *there* in sentences like those displayed above is merely a placeholder in a construction (an expletive) denoting existence or allowing delay of the subject, while stressed *there* is a place adverbial (the two have completely different correspondents in related languages like German and French).

Second, the construction is limited to *be* and a rather small class of intransitive verbs like *appear* and *arise*. There are no sentences like the following:

> *There sang a girl.
> *There spied an eagle a young lamb.

Third, we find *be* in this construction not only in its function as the main verb of the predicate, but also as a passive auxiliary and in the progressive (-ing):

> There was a child found in the bulrushes.
> There was found a child in the bulrushes.
> There is a girl running down the street.

Fourth, there are severe restrictions on the noun phrase that occurs after the verb or *be*. Typically, it is indefinite, as in all the examples so far. It usually cannot be a definite pronoun or a proper name:

> *There are they in the closet.
> *There's Sam under a bushel.
> *There's the parrot in a cage.

(I assume that the grammatical sentences of the form *there be Def-NP* have some different source. The two types have different properties; for example, it is possible to begin a discourse out of context with a sentence like *There's a cow in the cornfield,* but not with a sentence like *There's the dog,* with unstressed *there*.)

Fifth, the unstressed *there* of such sentences is apparently limited to the position of the subject of such sentences. Compare the following:

> I see it.
> *I see there.
> I gave it to Bill.
> *I gave there to Bill.

Finally, even though the places where *there* can occur are severely limited, it appears to function as a noun phrase in a number of transformations:

> *Subject-Aux inversion*
> Is John in the kitchen?
> Is there a beer in the fridge?

Raising
I believe him to be a fool.
I believe there to be a burglar under the bed.

Now let us consider some arguments favoring the idea that *there* is introduced transformationally. (Throughout this chapter I will use lower-case letters to label individual arguments, and then refer to them by the name of the transformation and the letter; thus, the following argument will be referred to later as There *a*.)

a) Suppose there is a transformation that takes structures like the following ones and converts them into the sentences with *there:*

a burglar is under the bed
a God is
a guru appeared walking on the water

Let us suppose that the transformation replaces an indefinite noun phrase with *there* and copies the noun phrase after the appropriate verb or *be*. From the formulation of the rule it follows that *there* will appear in just the sorts of environment mentioned above. If, on the other hand, *there* is introduced in the base, we will have to specify in detail just these environments in the sentences in which it occurs. In general, we do not know whether the transformational introduction or the lexical intro-duction is to be preferred. But if *there* is introduced as a noun phrase in the base, it will be the only such lexical item in the grammar of English, and the restrictions we must place on its occurrence will be unique. There are not only no other lexical items that can occur only in the subject posi-tion of a sentence with a particular small class of verbs and an indefinite noun phrase in a later part of the sentence; there are no other lexical items that have this *kind* of restriction on their occurrence.

b) If *there* is not introduced transformationally, we can predict that there will not be any transformations that must be presumed to operate before it is introduced. But there is at least one such transformation, Passive, since the *be* that allows *there* is introduced transformationally. Therefore, *there* is introduced transformationally. Of course, we can escape this conclusion if we change Passive. But we would have to change Passive in a completely ad hoc way, which would have precisely the effect of ensuring that we get the same results as if *there* were intro-duced transformationally (in Section 7.5 we will justify Passive).

Thus, in the following analyses I will assume the existence of a *There*-insertion transformation. But we will also consider the effect on our arguments of denying this assumption.

7.3 Raising

In arguing for the cycle in Section 6.3, we assumed without justification that there is a rule in English converting structures like (1) into structures like (2):

1. I consider for-to Harry *Aux* be a fink.
2. I consider Harry to be a fink.

This rule of subject-raising (Raising) takes the subject of a complement sentence with "for-to" and makes it into the object *NP* of the verb in the next higher sentence. We may consider some assumptions in this account one by one:

I. The derived structure of such sentences has an independent noun phrase, which is a separate constituent from the *to-*infinitival.

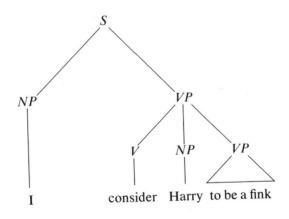

II. In the deep structure of such sentences the *NP* is part of a single constituent with the source of the infinitival *VP*.
III. The larger single constituent is a complement sentence in the deep structure.
IV. The constituent sentence is dominated by *NP* in the deep structure.

Assumptions II, III, IV may be represented thus (we are not particularly concerned with justifying the occurrence of *it* in this P-marker):

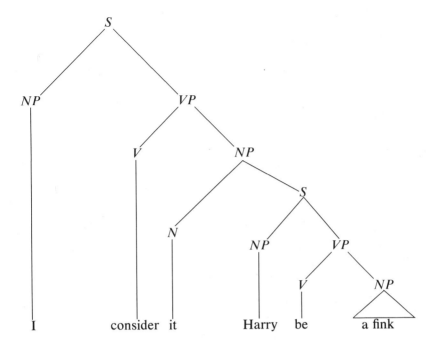

Let us argue first for assumption I. We can conclude that *Harry* in the surface structure representing sentence (2) is an independent constituent by showing similarities between this structure and other structures with independent *NP* objects.

a) There is a construction called *pseudo-cleft* in English. In the clear cases, it applies to single constituents and not sequences of constituents:

3. What I saw was a fish.
4. What hit me was a thunderbolt.
5. What John gave to Sally was a nasty cold.
6. What I believe is that all politicians are sinners.
7. *What John gave was to Sally a nasty cold.

Our hypothesis about the derived structure above is confirmed by looking at pseudo-cleft versions of sentences with Raising. In (3)–(6) what follows *What X be . . .* is a single *NP*. In (7) we have a sequence of constituents, *to Sally* and *a nasty cold,* and the result is ungrammatical. Now compare sentences with verbs like *believe* and *expect*. *NP*'s like *Harry* in (1) can be the single constituent of the construction, but the *NP* together with its following infinitival cannot be:

What I believe to be the greatest danger is governmental power.
*What I consider is Harry to be a fink.

b) With the exception of one marginal construction illustrated as (1) below, object forms of pronouns are used in English only when the pronoun is an independent *NP* in the predicate or is the object of a preposition (sentences 2 and 3), not when the pronoun is the subject of an embedded sentence (4). Here again the questionable case (5) lines up with the independent objects:

1. Him giving a speech really breaks me up.
2. I saw him.
3. Sally walked with him.
4. I said that he (*him) was next.
5. I believe him to be a fink.

To establish assumptions II, III, and IV (as represented in the diagram of the assumed deep structure), we can look first at some differences between sentences with Raising and superficially similar sentences with verbs like *persuade*.

c) A clear difference in the semantic properties of such sentences becomes apparent when we compare versions with active and passive *VP*'s:

1. I persuaded the doctor to examine John.
2. I persuaded John to be examined by the doctor.
3. I expected the doctor to examine John.
4. I expected John to be examined by the doctor.

If there is a difference in deep structures between the two sentence types, we would expect such a difference in semantic interpretation. If there were no structural difference, we would have to make some special statement to account for the semantic difference. Looked at in a slightly different way, if the semantic relations between (3) and (4) matched those between (1) and (2) and their deep structures were different, we would have to make some special rule of semantic interpretation to account for the similarity. With different deep structures, no such special stipulation must be made. Moreover, the difference is consistent with the basic meanings of the respective verbs. *Persuade* necessarily involves three terms: one doing the persuading, one being persuaded, and some state of affairs that is the result of the persuasion. *Expect* is a two-termed relation between someone expecting and what he is expecting. With slightly different constructions we can have sentences that necessarily involve three distinct terms with verbs like *persuade* but not *expect,* while with states of affairs that do not involve distinct entities as actor (like weather verbs) just the opposite is true:

I persuaded Harry that Sally should go.
*I expected Harry for Sally to go.
I expected it to rain.
*I persuaded it to rain.

This difference is consistent with assumptions II and III above.

d) If we can find single lexical items that can occur in both kinds of structures, we can consider this to be evidence for a difference in deep structure. Since the lexical item in question can be characterized by the associated deep structure, it is then unnecessary to set up separate lexical items, or separate types of features, for the same item. Bates (1969) has studied the properties of one such item, the verb (or verbs) *get*. We can find sentences with *get* paralleling both the sentences with *expect* and those with *persuade:*

The medicine man got it to rain.
I got Harry to open the door.

Moreover, single surface structures can have multiple sources and thus show ambiguity:

I got Harry to levitate.

This sentence can mean either that I, a magician, say, arranged things in such a way that Harry levitated, or that I persuaded Harry, a magician, to levitate.

e) Verbs like *expect* and *believe* must be allowed to stand with single sentential complements — in sentences like the following, anyway:

I expect that it will rain.
I believe that you are a first-class idiot.

Our grammar is more general rather than less if we allow such verbs to occur not only with complements in *that,* but with complements in *for-to* as well.

Raising *c* and *d* show that there must be a difference in deep structure between sentences with verbs like *expect* and those with verbs like *persuade.* Raising *e* supports the view that the single deep constituent is a sentence (if the structure with *that* is a sentence). There is relatively little evidence that the constituent sentence is also an *NP* (for some arguments against that view, see Emonds, 1970). But we may mention a few.

f) A number of transformations that apply to single *NP*'s apply to both *that*-clauses and *for-to*-clauses:

Passive (see Section 7.5)
That Sally is pregnant is believed by no one.
For Michael to open the package is preferred by everyone.

Pseudo-cleft (Raising *a*)
What I expect is for Michael to open the package.
What I believe is that Herodotus was Ionian.

Cleft
It's that Harry is sick that I can't believe.
It's for you to mumble that I never expect.

g) Finally, let us consider the possibility that the deep structures for sentences with *expect* are indeed different from sentences with *persuade* (as we have shown), but that some other form than that shown is correct. One such form is the following. Noting the many similarities between sentences like (1) and sentences like (2), some linguists have suggested (Staal, correspondence) that there may be a common source for them:

1. I believe of Henry that he is a fink.
2. I believe Henry to be a fink.

Under this hypothesis, the deep structure of (2) would be something like this:

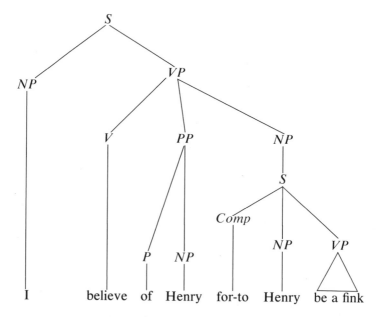

Some transformation like Equi (or Equi itself) would erase the second occurrence of *Henry,* and a special transformation would delete the preposition *of.* Against this view we can give the strong argument that it does not explain how we can have as objects noun phrases that are extremely restricted in their distribution. It will follow from the Raising analysis that we can have such items as the empty subject *it* for weather verbs and the like; (with Passive) we can have as objects parts of idioms like *keep tabs, commit murder, make headway;* and, worst of all for the alternative analysis, we can have an *NP* that is transformationally created, the *there* that we have just shown to be absent in deep structures. Notice that in each case the corresponding sentence with *of NP* is impossible. This difference is predicted by our analysis and the assumption that there is a different source for sentences like (2) above.

> I expect it to rain.
> I expect a murder to be committed.
> I imagined there to be a unicorn in the garden.
> *I expect of it that it will rain.
> *I expect of a murder that it will be committed.
> *I imagined of there that there was a unicorn in the garden.

This last part of this argument is especially strong. If *there* is introduced transformationally, then there is no non-ad-hoc way to account for sentences like the third one without a transformation like Raising.

h) We have justified Raising in terms of sentences like *I believe him to be a fink,* in which the complement sentence originates in the verb phrase of the outer sentence. Let us notice next that we can extend the application of the rule to verbs like *seem, happen,* or *appear* if we allow the rule to operate in subject position also. Let us assume that the deep structure for a sentence with *seem* is something like this:

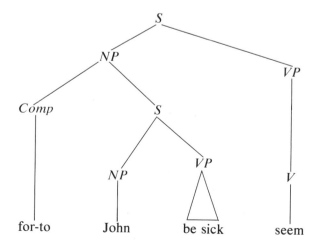

Then the regular application of Raising will yield a structure with *John* in subject position and *to* plus the verb phrase at the end of the sentence: *John seems to be sick*. On the assumption that deep structures determine meaning, the posited analysis for verbs like *seem* is quite reasonable. The logical structure of a sentence like the one above is that a certain state of affairs—John's being sick—has the appearance of reality; in other words, the subject of the underlying predication is not John but his being sick. Moreover, there are other indications that the underlying subject of *seem* is not John. In Section 6.4 we noted that some verbs require an identity between their subject and the subject of the deep-structure complement sentence, for example, *intend*. One would predict that with these verbs the sentences that result from taking a sentence with *seem* as the underlying complement will be odd, and indeed they are:

> John is trying to seem sick.
> Harry intends to happen to be absent.

In both instances we must give an extended meaning to the verbs in order to get an interpretation for the sentence. John can feign sickness; Harry can intend to make it look as if he chanced to be absent. Again, ordinarily we cannot form imperatives with verbs that have sentential subjects. With verbs like *seem* and *happen* the results of applying Imperative are again special:

> Seem sick!
> Happen to be absent!

7.4 Extraposition

In Chapter 5 we assumed with little discussion that there is a transformation of English called Extraposition relating sentences like these:

> It's true that John is ill.
> That John is ill is true.

> It was proved by Mickey that typing causes arthritis.
> That typing causes arthritis was proved by Mickey.

> For you to go to college is crazy.
> It's crazy for you to go to college.

Let us first consider some arguments that there is a transformational relation between sentences like these, leaving open questions about its form, and then consider whether the assumed formulation implicit in the name Extraposition can be justified.

Suppose there were no transformation relating sentences of the form *CSX* and *It XCS* (where C is a complementizer *that* or *for-to*). Then all of the following consequences would result:

a) The semantic projection rules would have to include rules telling us that the pairs of sentences are mutual paraphrases. If there is a transformation relating the two structures, then no such special semantic rules are necessary.

b) For every lexical item that can stand in both types of structures we will have to duplicate contextual features. That is, every such verb or adjective will have to have both the features [It $X - Y S$] and [$S X - Y$], or the like. If the sentence types are transformationally related, then one or the other will suffice.

c) We noted in Section 6.3 that there are three basic types of complementizers in English: *that, for-to,* and *Poss-ing*. For the first two, and marginally at least for the third, we find the kinds of pairing we have been considering:

That John is happy is obvious.
It's obvious that John is happy.

For Mary to go to Europe this summer will be difficult.
It will be difficult for Mary to go Europe this summer.

Your saying that is awful.
It's awful your saying that.

Further, an ungrammatical combination of complementizer and verb will be ungrammatical in either position:

*For John to be happy is obvious.
*It's obvious for John to be happy.

*That Mary will go to Europe this summer will be difficult.
*It will be difficult that Mary will go to Europe this summer.

*Your saying that is true.
*It's true your saying that.

Most analyses of these complement types have assumed (following Rosenbaum, 1967) that a transformational rule, Complementizer-placement, attaches these complementizers to the head of the embedded clause. If this analysis is correct and if we have a rule like Extraposition, we can automatically account for the distributions of the complementizers in both positions of sentences like those just given. If there is no such rule as Extraposition, then we will have to have two rules for complementizer-placement, one for clauses in the subject position and one for clauses in final position. Notice that this argument depends on the assumption that some other rule of grammar will be affected by the analysis in question.

d) A number of further restrictions on characteristics of the sentential complements depend on the particular verb or adjective governing the complement. For example, *know* and *intend* differ in the range of auxiliary elements, moods, and so on that can occur in an associated *that*-clause:

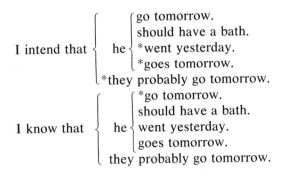

$$
\text{I intend that} \begin{cases} \text{he} \begin{cases} \text{go tomorrow.} \\ \text{should have a bath.} \\ \text{*went yesterday.} \\ \text{*goes tomorrow.} \end{cases} \\ \text{*they probably go tomorrow.} \end{cases}
$$

$$
\text{I know that} \begin{cases} \text{he} \begin{cases} \text{*go tomorrow.} \\ \text{should have a bath.} \\ \text{went yesterday.} \\ \text{goes tomorrow.} \end{cases} \\ \text{they probably go tomorrow.} \end{cases}
$$

These characteristics are, by and large, the same for related sentences with *it . . . S:*

    It is intended that he go tomorrow.
    *It is known that he go tomorrow.

and the like. Such restrictions are accounted for by selectional features on deep structures, by transformational rules, or by some other mechanism. No matter how they are accounted for, the explanations will automatically take care of both types of sentences if we posit a transformational relation between them. If we do not, then independent explanations will be required (but see p. 168 below).

e) Since Klima (1964), it has been assumed that there is a rule deriving some instances of *any* from instances of *some* in the context of negative elements, questions, and so on. Thus, something like the first of the pairs of sentences is assumed to underlie the second:

    I didn't see some books. → I didn't see any books.
    It's doubtful that he has some friends. →
                    It's doubtful that he has any friends.
    I don't believe that he ate something. →
                    I don't believe that he ate anything.

We find the same phenomena in *that*-clauses with and without the presumed operation of Extraposition:

It isn't clear that he killed anyone (<someone).
That he killed anyone (<someone) isn't clear.

If there is no rule like Extraposition relating the two structures, then it will be necessary either to give two *some/any* rules or else to adopt a new kind of rule that works independently of the position of the negative element. Other things being equal, we prefer to remain within the limits of the stricter theory (see Sections 7.76, 9.2). If there is a rule of Extraposition, then we automatically account for the appearance of *any* in one type of structure when we account for it in the other.

f) Consider the following sentence:

It was proved by the D.A. that Maggie was in town.

Under the hypothesis we are attempting to refute, we are allowing structures of the form *it X C S* to be generated independently of structures like *C S X*. In the sentence above, it is possible to have both *it* and *S* in the underlying object position just in case the sentence appears in the passive form. Suppose there is a rule of Passive (for support see next section). If Passive is an optional rule, we will have to make it obligatory in such sentences if we have the configuration *S V it S*. If Passive is an obligatory rule contingent on the presence of some element or configuration in the deep structure, then we must invent a special feature to insure that *it* occurs in the object position with *prove* and a final *S* just in case this passive triggering feature is present in the deep structure. In either case, an ad hoc complication is necessary. (And in either case we can argue that a weakening of the theory is entailed by the type of feature that is necessary.)

g) In the last section (Raising *h*) we argued that the deep structures for sentences like (1) are structures like (2):

1. John seems to be happy.
2. [for-to John be happy] *Pres* seem

Now consider the following:

3. It seems that John is happy.
4. *That John is happy seems.

We can account for (3) and (4) by using the same underlying structure that is necessary for (1), but with a *that*-complementizer. We must now assume that Extraposition is obligatory (or that its converse is blocked) for sentences like (3).

Thus, a number of reasons lead us to believe that there is a transformational relation between the pairs of sentences we have been considering. Let us turn now to some aspects of the form of the rule.

First of all, given that we have established a transformational relation between pairs of sentences like these, which of these forms should be considered closer to the underlying form?

A. That ink tastes awful is true.
B. It is true that ink tastes awful.

(It is also logically possible that some third type of structure underlies both forms.) Let us refer to the hypothesis that the *B* form is derived from the structure underlying the *A* form as Extraposition, and the converse hypothesis (which is defended in Emonds, 1972) as Intraposition. There are a number of arguments for Extraposition.

h) The grammatical function (as subject or object) of the embedded sentences seems to be that which is directly represented in the *A* form rather than the *B* form. Notice these parallels:

1. The statement is true.
  A. That ink tastes awful is true.
  B. It is true that ink tastes awful.
2. Many people hate this decision.
  A. Many people hate for you to go to away.
  B. Many people hate it for you to go away.
3. That claim is believed by almost everyone.
  A. That Australia is arid is believed by almost everyone.
  B. It is believed by almost everyone that Australia is arid.

In (1) the function of *the statement* is that of subject; so also is the function of the *that*-clause in (1 A). In (2 A) the object function of the embedded clause matches that of the *NP* in (2). In (3 A) the *that*-clause is the deep object and superficial subject, just like *that claim* in (3). Notice that these relations are directly represented in the P-markers associated in the derivation with the sentences up until the operation of Extraposition (under the analysis we are defending).

i) The facts about *seem* and similar verbs (Extraposition *g*) also support the Extraposition analysis (more precisely, if our analysis of such verbs given under Raising is correct, then the facts about *seem* support Extraposition). Verbs like *seem, happen,* and *appear* need to be allowed to occur with sentential subjects (with *for-to*) and undergo Raising to yield sentences like these:

John seems to be happy.
Harriet happens to have a big mouth.
The mink appeared to have entered the pond first.

To derive sentences like the following ones by Extraposition, we only need to make our grammar more general by allowing not only sentential subjects with *for-to* but also ones with *that:*

It seems that John is happy.
It happens that Harriet has a big mouth.
It appeared that the mink had entered the pond first.

On the other hand, we need to complicate our analysis by positing totally different underlying structures for such verbs under the assumption that Intraposition is correct.

j) Consider verbs like *prove.* They can occur only in sentences with one or two *that*-clauses or none at all.

Nerode proved the following theorem.
Saint Joan proved that Frenchmen could fight.
That Columbus didn't fall off the edge proved that the earth wasn't flat.
That the dean said so proved my point.

Potentially, any of the *that*-clauses can appear in the form *it . . . S.* Suppose that we adopt the Intraposition analysis. Then it will be necessary to generate structures with exactly the right number of internal *it*'s to match the *S*'s at the end of the sentence in order to prevent generating nonsentences like these:

*Saint Joan proved that Frenchman could fight that the earth is flat.
*Nerode proved the following theorem that the dean said so.

Under the Extraposition analysis this difficulty does not arise, since we associate the *it*'s and *S*'s together in the beginning (or, under a slightly different formulation of Extraposition, we generate an *it* each time we apply the rule).

k) Ross (1967a) has shown that rules of the general type that "move" elements to the right are *bounded* (see Section 9.21), that is, the elements must not be moved beyond the boundaries of the sentence within which the movement takes place. On the other hand, leftward-movement rules may be unbounded. The Intraposition analysis assumes a leftward movement, so that a special stipulation must be made that the rule is bounded. Hence the Extraposition formulation is to be preferred, since its operation falls within the domain of Ross's generalization about rules of this type.

There is one more argument favoring Extraposition over the alternative formulation, but since it depends on some extensions of the theory, I will postpone it to a later chapter (Section 11.6).

7.5 Passive

The Passive transformation is assumed to relate sentences like these:

Heat has destroyed the garden.
The garden has been destroyed by heat.

Castro is writing the agenda for the revolution.
The agenda for the revolution is being written by Castro.

Arguments for the existence of some rule relating actives and passives can be given that depend on paraphrase relations, or on the types of context in which the active and passive forms of verbs can stand (like the arguments Extraposition *a* and *b*). We will concentrate on a few arguments that depend on the interaction of Passive and other rules, as well as one argument that depends on characteristics of the rule that relate to general principles about the applicability of rules.

a) In Section 6.3 (pp. 116–120) we considered the relationship between Passive and Equi. As part of that argument, we rejected a theory in which transformational rules apply "epicyclically" by ruling out both the orders Passive-Equi and Equi-Passive. But the former of these orderings leads to exactly the same results as does the assumption that passive structures are already present in deep structures. Thus, the argument also speaks against the position that both passive and active sentences are basic; that is, it shows that if there is a rule Equi (whose existence can be supported independently of Passive), there must be a transformational rule relating active and passive. (Note that this argument does not in itself decide between a passive transformation and an "active" transformation.)

b) The second argument has to do with structures that become subject to a passive rule as the result of an independently motivated rule for shifting the positions of direct and indirect objects. Assume that double-object verbs like *give* appear in deep structures in configurations like this:

1. John *Aux* give the book to Sally.

From such a structure we can have a passive construction of the form (2) but not (3):

2. The book was given to Sally by John.
3. *Sally was given the book to by John.

However, we do have

4. Sally was given the book by John.

We can account for these grammatical facts by assuming that indirect objects with *to* are subject to shifting and deletion of the *to*, and that Passive can then apply to yield the sentences like (4) above. (Alternatively, we could assume a basic order with the indirect object preceding the direct object and assume that the shift rule worked in the opposite direction.) Moreover, these facts follow automatically from the independently needed shift and *to*-deletion rules and from Passive (Fillmore, 1965). If the passive structures were directly generated in the base, we would have to complicate our grammar. In the first place, we would have to add a new contextual feature to the entries for verbs like *give* to allow them to appear in contexts like (4). And second, for those dialects that have a fourth type of structure like (5) we would have to distinguish ad hoc the deep structures of the type (5) from the type (4):

5. The book was given Sally by John.

Third, for those dialects that do not have sentences of the form (5) additional restrictions would have to be made to disallow them but allow (4).

c) Our next argument shows not only that there is a rule relating passive and active sentences, but also that it should be formulated as a rule deriving passive structures from structures more directly resembling active sentences. The argument is based on a general restriction postulated by Postal (1971), which prohibits the application of a rule that "moves" an *NP* across a coreferential *NP* (see Section 9.21 for a general discussion of such restrictions). We can illustrate this **Crossover Principle** in the following assignments of grammaticality:

1. It is difficult for John to understand Bill.
2. Bill is difficult for John to understand.
3. It is difficult for John to understand himself.
4. *Himself is difficult for John to understand.
5. *John is difficult for him(self) to understand.

6. *He is difficult for John to understand.
7. Portia sold the slave to Claudia.
8. Portia sold Claudia the slave.
9. Portia sold the slave to himself.
10. *Portia sold the slave himself.
11. *Portia sold himself the slave.
12. Caesar sold the slave to himself.
13. Caesar sold the slave himself.
14. Caesar sold himself the slave.

Sentences (1)–(3) illustrate a rule called Tough-movement (Postal, 1971), which takes the object of an embedded complement of a certain class of adjectives (including *tough*) and makes it the subject of a higher sentence by replacing *it*. The Crossover Principle predicts that there will be no way to apply the rule if the object and subject of the embedded clause refer to the same individual. Sentence (3) is impeccable, hence there can be nothing inherently anomalous about the underlying ideas expressed by the structure. But the starred examples (4)–(6) bear out the prediction. Similarly, the sentences (5) and (6) illustrate the *To*-dative movement rule alluded to above. But application of the rule to move *the slave* across a copy of itself (as underlying source for (7)) yields ungrammatical results. Finally, the principle predicts that (12) but not (13) and (14) will be ambiguous as to the identity of *himself*.

Turning back to Passive, we can see that the postulation of a rule that moves two *NP*'s will entail the prediction that passive sentences with coreferential subjects and objects will be ungrammatical. And indeed this seems to be true:

> John shaved himself.
> *Himself was shaved by John.
> *John was shaved by himself.

(It is important to read the examples without special stress on the reflexive pronoun. Sentences with stressed reflexives are not subject to the Crossover restriction, and perhaps have an entirely different source.) If both passives and actives were present in the base, then we would need an entirely different explanation for the ungrammaticality of these examples.

The examples also show something about the directionality of the rule. If the passive form were the underlying one, then we would expect (2) to be more grammatical than (1):

1. Harry shaved himself.

2. Harry was shaved by himself.

Of course, just the opposite is true.

d) We have established both the existence of Passive and the hypothesis that it maps active structures into passive structures. Let us consider an argument against one possible formulation of the rule that has appeared in the literature (Bach, 1967; Hasegawa, 1968). Suppose we assume that the underlying form for a passive sentence like *Sally was being sought by the police* is something like this:

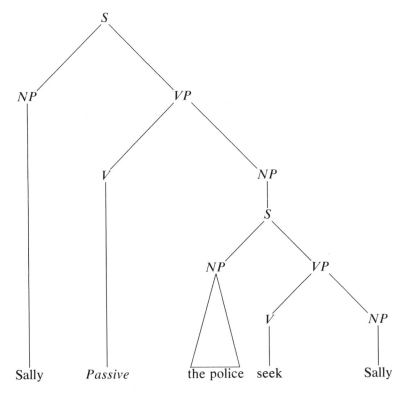

We are interested solely in the assumption that the eventual subject of a passive sentence is generated independently in the base as a subject of a higher sentence. Any such analysis runs into insuperable difficulties because of the existence of passive sentences in which the subject is a highly restricted type of noun phrase. We consider two examples.

There are idioms that consist of a verb and an object noun or noun phrase such that it can only occur in a highly restricted environment: *keep tabs on, make headway, take umbrage,* and the like. Presumably such restrictions are handled by lexical insertion. Either the idiom is introduced as a unit, or the restricted member has associated with it a contextual feature allowing it to appear only in the proper environments. But some such idioms can appear in the passive:

> Tabs were kept on his movements by the F.B.I.
> Considerable headway has already been made in the case.

(These sentences show that there should be a passive transformation, since we would have to complicate the lexical entries for such items ad hoc to allow both the active forms and the passive forms.) But by inter-action with Raising, the proper environment for introducing such items may be removed indefinitely far away from the surface subject:

> Tabs were claimed to have been ordered to be kept on his movements by the F.B.I.
> Considerable headway is said to be believed to be expected to be made in the case.

This means that we literally cannot find the restricting environment for the introduction of such items from the lexicon. Thus, the items will have to be introduced independently of context, and there will have to be some ad hoc method of blocking sentences in which the items appear in the wrong contexts:

> *I hate tabs.
> *Umbrage is lovely.
> *Tabs were claimed to have been ordered to be made on his movements.

Similarly, consider the problem of providing a source for sentences like this one:

> There was believed to have been a fire in the outhouse.

The suggested formulation of Passive would have to find some ad hoc meanings of getting the subject *there* of this sentence into its position as an independent subject of a higher sentence. Notice that *there* is not even present in deep structure (see 7.2).

Combining our arguments, we conclude that there is a passive trans-formation, that it maps active into passive structures, and that no analysis in which the surface subject of the passive sentence is generated inde-pendently can be correct.

7.6 Interrelationships among the Rules

We have justified the existence and form of four transformational rules of English. Let us now consider some aspects of their interrelationships. First of all, let us try to establish their ordering with respect to each other. We will show that they should be ordered as follows:

Raising
Passive
Extraposition There

We can find arguments that Raising precedes Passive, that Raising precedes Extraposition, and that Passive precedes Extraposition and There. Since Extraposition and There apply to distinct types of structures, no direct arguments can be given as to their ordering. (It is possible that their relations to some third rule would show that they too are ordered, but I know of no such rule.)

7.61 Raising—Passive

Since Raising produces structures that are subject to Passive, we can conclude that (in the standard theory) they must apply in that order. For example, given a structure like this:

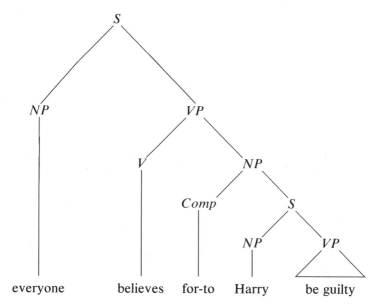

Raising can apply to give this:

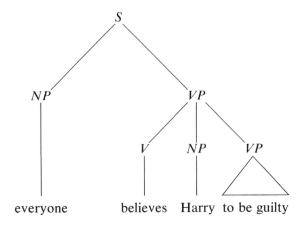

This latter structure is available for Passive, yielding ultimately *Harry is believed by everyone to be guilty*. (This argument and all similar arguments depend crucially on the assumption that the transformational rules are ordered linearly, as Koutsoudas, 1972, has pointed out.)

7.62 Raising — Extraposition

To show that Raising precedes Extraposition, we return to sentences with *happen* and similar verbs. The optionality of Extraposition depends on whether the verb is in absolute final position in its verb phrase.

It happens that John is happy.
*That John is happy happens.

It happens to annoy Harry that John is happy.
That John is happy happens to annoy Harry.

In the assumed analysis, the underlying structure for the last pair of sentences is roughly this:

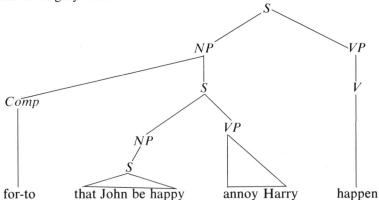

Since the optionality of Extraposition is not determined until we have applied Raising on the last cycle, we can conclude that Raising must precede Extraposition.

7.63 Passive — Extraposition

In the following sentences and nonsentences we can observe a relationship between passive structures and the applicability of Extraposition:

1. It's believed by everyone that Avery is a crook.
2. It's believed that Avery is a crook.
3. That Avery is a crook is believed by everyone.
4. *That Avery is a crook is believed.
5. It is said that spaniels love orange juice.
6. *That spaniels love orange juice is said.
7. Everyone believes that Avery is a crook.
8. *Everyone believes it that Avery is a crook.

Examples (1)–(6) show that in many passive sentences Extraposition is obligatory when there is no agent, otherwise optional. Examples (7) and (8) show that Extraposition must not apply in such sentences unless the sentence is in the passive. Suppose Extraposition precedes Passive; now we must make Passive obligatorily depend on whether or not Extraposition has been applied. If the opposite order is assumed, then we shall have to make Extraposition obligatory in structures like (4) and (6). But notice the similarity between the environments in which Extraposition is obligatory in passive sentences and those in which Raising has occurred.

> It seems that the sun is shining.
> That the sun is shining seems odd.
> *That the sun is shining seems.

In both sets of sentences the determining factor is apparently the presence or absence of something after the main verb of the top sentence (the passivized verb or *seem*). Thus it seems that a uniform explanation (whatever it is) can be provided only on the assumption that both Raising and Passive precede Extraposition.

This argument can be further supported by the fact that Extraposition is a rule of a type (movement across an indefinite context) that is not ordinarily governed by particular lexical items (G. Lakoff, 1970). A lexical item like *rumor* (as a verb) must occur in the passive:

> It was rumored that the Russians had landed on Nantucket.
> *Somebody rumored that the Russians had landed on Nantucket.

To account for these grammatical facts we would have to make Extraposition obligatory (with contingent obligatory application of Passive). But *rumor* must be independently marked as obligatorily subject to Passive for sentences in which it has a nonsentential object:

> This was rumored long ago.
> *They rumored this long ago.

And once Passive is applied, the structure is subject to the same generalization about extraposing subject clauses that we saw in (1)–(6) above.

7.64 Passive — There

The rule There can apply to structures that have undergone Passive (and not to the corresponding active forms):

> There was found an enormous amoeba.
> *There someone found an enormous amoeba. (unstressed *there!*)

There can be formulated in the most general way by referring to *be* (and a small class of intransitive verbs). If There preceded Passive, we would either have to modify There to make it sensitive to the structure underlying Passive or, if Passive is an optional rule, modify Passive so as to make it obligatory in the presence of *there*.

This concludes the presentation of arguments for the existence, form, and interrelationships of the four rules. We now turn to an examination of the types of arguments we have used.

7.7 Some Common Types of Syntactic Arguments

In this section we consider a number of types of arguments that are often used in syntax. I will try to point out the basic assumptions involved in the arguments, and we will consider some fallacious arguments as well.

7.71 Arguments from Native Speakers' Intuitions

Intuitions about the relatedness of sentence types are often adduced as evidence for transformations. We have not used such arguments above, mainly because they are very weak. It is probable that native speakers of English would recognize the relationships among the sets of sentences we have considered and would be able to form the passive for a given active sentence (with a little preliminary practice), extrapose sentences, and so on. But at best such judgments provide necessary but not sufficient evidence for the postulation of a transformation, and this only in clear cases of optional rules, rather than obligatory ones. The reason that such judgments are not sufficient is that they show only that there is some systematic relation between sets of sentences, and the regularity could be the function not only of a transformation but also of a base rule, similarity among lexical features, or semantic redundancy rules. For example, English speakers would probably be just as likely to perceive the relationships in (2), (3), and (4) as in (1):

1. John swatted the fly.
   The fly was swatted by John.

2. Harriet is reading the comics.
   Harriet was reading the comics.

3. Bill sold the boat to Mark.
   Mark bought the boat from Bill.

4. The man ate a duck.
   The men ate ducks.

Yet it is only in (1) that we can give good evidence for a transformational relationship.

Similarly, nothing in linguistic theory tells us that speakers have intuitions about which of two sentences that are assumed to be transformationally related is closer to the basic form. It would be an interesting fact if speakers consistently picked out as "more basic" the active form of an active-passive pair, or if the active were more frequent, easier to process, or the like. But without some supplementary assumptions about speaker performance, judgments, or the like, such data do not constitute evidence for anything about the grammar. (The same remarks apply to questions about the correct form of deep structures.)

7.72 Semantic Arguments

In the standard theory the semantic reading of a sentence is determined by the deep structure. This means that two sentences that are presumed to have the same deep structure must be paraphrases on at least one meaning. Again, this is a necessary but not sufficient condition. Suppose we can find two sentences that are supposed to be related by an optional transformation and are clearly not mutual paraphrases. Then we must draw one of two conclusions: there is no transformation relating the two sentences, or there is some difference other than that produced by the given transformation (that is, the two sentences are not after all directly related by application of an optional transformation to the same deep structure). For example, (2) does not paraphrase (1):

1. Many people didn't see the accident.
2. The accident wasn't seen by many people.

We could use this fact to argue against Passive in the standard theory, or to argue that different deep structures underlie (1) and (2). (Or, as we will see in a later chapter, one can argue that the assumption that meaning is fully determined by deep structure is false.)

A paraphrase argument was used above to support the transformational hypothesis of Extraposition *a*. Since paraphrasability is only a necessary condition for the hypothesis, we must draw on other facts. The paraphrase relation is predicted by the transformational hypothesis. If there is no transformation relating the two types of sentences, then some semantic principle or rule must be drawn upon to account for the paraphrase relation. But we have no advance knowledge whether a transformational or a semantic explanation is to be preferred. Hence, we must ask whether there is independent need for either the transformational or the semantic principle. In this instance we were able to show that there is independent evidence for the necessity of a transformation (for sentences with *seem:* Extraposition *g*. Hence we can derive an argument of the Occam's Razor type for Extraposition (see below, Section 7.7). This argument can be made stronger by showing that the facts cannot be accounted for by various independently needed semantic principles that might be thought to apply to the case at hand. For example, the relation between *it* and its following sentence might be thought to be just an instance of an anaphoric relation, such as is found between pronouns and their antecedents. Since, one might argue, we need to have some semantic principle accounting for such anaphoric relations anyway, we do not need to posit any ad hoc semantic rule for extraposed sentences. But if *it* is a pronoun in such sentences, it is quite unique in its properties. Clear cases of anaphoric pronouns are subject to a restriction that they may not precede their antecedents unless they are in a sentence subordinate to the antecedent (Ross, 1967b; Langacker, 1969). But the *it* of extraposed sentences is subject to no such restriction. This *it* cannot stand in a subordinate sentence preceding its putative antecedent (this is the fact summed up in saying that the rule is bounded; see Extraposition *k*), and *it* cannot be preceded by its antecedent. In other words, it occurs only in the precise position that is excluded for ordinary pronouns:

*He saw John.
*He saw the girl that was with John.
John saw the girl that he was with.
The girl that John was with saw him.

The girl that <u>he</u> was with saw <u>John</u>.
<u>It's</u> odd that <u>Oswald has halitosis</u>.
*The girl who said that <u>it</u> was odd smiled <u>that Oswald has halitosis</u>.

There is one further way in which semantic considerations can enter into arguments about syntactic rules. The standard theory assumes that deep grammatical relations—*Subject-of, Object-of,* and the like—are required for semantic projection rules. Since these relations are defined on the basis of configurations in P-markers, we can argue for particular hypotheses about P-markers, in particular, deep structures, by showing that some condition statable in terms of grammatical relations must be met, or can be met in a better way if we adopt one hypothesis rather than another. In Extraposition *h,* we argued for a version of the transformation in which the nonextraposed sentence was basic by claiming that the necessary grammatical relations are directly represented in this form but not the other. Such an argument has roughly the same force as one based on paraphrase relations. We can argue against the alternative hypothesis by showing that an alternative account of the grammatical relations as exhibited in the sentence must appeal to an ad hoc principle of some sort. (Once again, the appeal to anaphoric relations such as those between pronouns and antecedents runs into the same objections we raised above.)

7.73 Arguments from Co-occurrence Relations

The primary justification for the existence of transformations that was given in early transformational theory (Chomsky, 1957; Harris, 1957) took the following form. A given linguistic item or class of items can occur only in a limited set of environments, say, with particular subclasses of nouns as subjects (or objects, in the case of a verb). If two sets of sentences that show the same network of co-occurrence relations are independently described, then we will have to describe the same set of facts twice. But if there is a transformation deriving one structure from the other (or both from some third source), then we need only state the facts once. For example, we have the same pattern of acceptability in active and passive sentences:

The boy gave the book to the girl.
The book was given to the girl by the boy.
The girl was given the book by the boy.
*The boy gave the girl to the book.
*The girl was given to the book by the boy.
*The book was given the girl by the boy.

*The book gave the girl to the boy.
*The girl was given to the boy by the book.
*The boy was given the girl by the book.

Somewhere in our grammar we must show that *give* in most sentences must occur with animate subjects and indirect objects, but with possibly inanimate direct objects. No matter how we describe this for one of the three forms (one active and two passive), the transformational account will automatically carry over the predictions about the sentences to the other forms. Therefore, there exists a transformation relating the sentences.

This argument is valid only if the transformational hypothesis is the only means available for relating the sets of sentences. In "classical" transformational theory there were only two ways of relating sentences: by transformations or phrase-structure rules. Hence it was sufficient to show that phrase-structure rules could not relate the given set (Section 6.6). But in the standard theory it is possible to avoid the unnecessary duplication of statements about co-occurrence facts by other means than transformations. For example, with selectional features in the lexicon it is possible to give redundancy rules that say in effect "If a lexical item has a feature of the form X, then it also has a feature of the form Y." Does this mean that co-occurrence arguments are no longer relevant to the justification of a transformation? Not at all. It merely means that we must show that a transformational relation is preferable to some other way of handling the facts. For example, we can try to show that a transformation must be posited on the basis of entirely different facts. Then a redundancy rule is unnecessary. Or we can show that the theory would have to be weakened by allowing a new type of redundancy rule (see Section 7.76). Or we might be able to show that the relevant information is not available at the level at which lexical insertion takes place.

A number of the arguments given above depended on such co-occurrence facts, for example Extraposition *b* and *d* (in part at least), and such arguments can be easily found for most transformations.

A good example of an analysis that was necessitated by the earlier theory of Chomsky's *Syntactic Structures* but can no longer be defended on the same grounds in the standard theory is that of the transformational derivation of nominals like *approval* and *abandonment*. In *Syntactic Structures* the only possible explanation for the parallelism among structures like these was in terms of a transformation:

1. John approved of the party.
2. John's approval of the party. . . .

3. . . . the abandonment of the baby by the parents . . .
4. The baby was abandoned by its parents.

Chomsky (1970) points out that in the richer standard theory this conclusion cannot be drawn, since new devices are available to capture the similarities in the distribution of such sets of co-occurring items as those in (1)–(2) and (3)–(4). Thus, the question whether nominals like those in (2) and (3) are transformationally derived must be decided on grounds other than those based on co-occurrence relations. In other words, in the standard theory co-occurrence facts still can be used to argue that two structures must be related in the grammar. But it is necessary to consider further which of several alternative ways of relating structures is correct, since transformational, lexical, and semantic explanations are now available.

7.74 Arguments from Other Rules

Suppose a given structure A is known to be transformationally derived. Then we can give an argument for the transformational derivation of another structure B by showing that it is necessary to allow B to apply to structures of type A. (Examples: There b; Extraposition c, d, e; Passive a, b.)

There are two steps to such an argument: (1) we must show evidence that the A structure is indeed transformationally derived, and (2) we must rule out alternative explanations in order to show that the putative rule deriving B from A should be stated in a way that necessitates that order of application. A frequent mistake is to neglect the latter argument. Let us consider an example of an argument that fails for this reason.

In Passive d we used sentences like the following to show that if Passive is a rule, then it cannot be formulated in such a way that the surface subject of the passive sentence is independently generated in the deep structure:

Tabs were believed to have been kept on him by the F.B.I.
A great deal of headway was said to have been made.
There is believed to be a unicorn among the daisies.

In the account we have given above, these sentences involve Raising as an intermediate step. Can we not therefore argue that such sentences show not only something about the form of Passive, if it exists, but also that it exists? According to the paradigm just given, the structures with Raising are the A structures; the passives are the B structures.

Hence, if Raising is a transformation (and we have argued that it is), Passive must also be a transformation.

But this argument is fallacious, as we can see as soon as we ask why Raising must be assumed to apply before Passive. Suppose there were no Passive. Then the underlying forms for sentences like those above would be something like this:

> [for-to tabs be kept on him by the F.B.I.] was believed.
> [for-to a great deal of headway be made] be said.
> [for-to a unicorn be among the daisies] is believed.

We have already argued (for verbs like *seem*) that Raising must be allowed to apply to structures that are in the subject position. Hence, with no change whatsoever, Raising can apply directly to the above structures to give the sentences needed.

An argument for the transformational derivation of nominals (see end of Section 7.73) can be given on this paradigm. If we can show that Passive must operate in the derivation of examples like *the abandonment of the baby by its parent,* then we can make an argument of the form "If *A* is a transformation, so is *B*." Chomsky (1970), in fact, makes just the opposite kind of argument: If *A* is not transformationally derived, then no transformations can be shown to underlie structures in *A*. This prediction is correct, according to Chomsky, hence the transformational explanation for the derived nominals is to be rejected. To support this argument, then, it must be shown that counterexamples (like the Passive case) are only apparently valid.

Obviously, not every transformational rule can be supported in this way. As I have stressed continually, however, the strength of our hypotheses is a function of the extent to which we can construct an interlocking set of interdependent assumptions to provide explanations for a wide range of phenomena.

7.75 Arguments from the Applicability of General Principles

Several times we have appealed to general principles of some sort in order to support the hypothesis that some rule applies in a certain way, or that a structure has one form rather than another (Extraposition *k;* Passive *c*). In this kind of argument we show that some independently needed general principle, taken together with some hypothesis about the form of a rule or structure, will provide an explanation for various facts. The strength of the argument depends on the strength of the evidence for the principle, independent of the case at hand, and on the extent to which we can rule out alternative *general* explanations. It is not necessary to know exactly what the principle appealed to is. It is enough to be able to show sufficient similarities to other putative instances of the general principle. Then we can assume that whatever the ultimate formulation of the principle is, it will cover the case at hand.

Let us look at one more example. In the last section we noted that Raising could apply just as well to sentences that are already in a passive form as to active sentences. But if the derivation applies in that order, then we would get a different prediction from Postal's Crossover Principle. Since the part of Raising that moves the *to-VP* structure to the end of the higher *VP* is not the movement of an *NP* (and even if it were, it does not cross a coreferential *NP*), the Crossover Principle should not apply, and we should find sentences in which Raising has been applied to a structure of the form below perfectly acceptable:

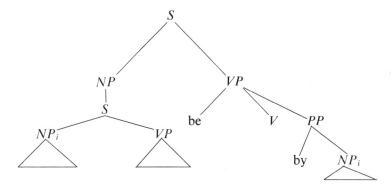

But such sentences are exactly parallel in their acceptability to sentences without Raising. Hence, we can reject the alternative explanation again on the basis of an appeal to a general principle:

*John was believed by himself to be a fink.
*John was shaved by himself.

7.76 Stricter-Theory Arguments

Suppose it is possible to show that of two hypotheses, only one is compatible with general restrictions on the theory of possible grammars, while the other would necessitate a weakening of the theory by the addition of some new type of descriptive device. Then we can argue that the first hypothesis is preferable, other things being equal, since we want to keep our theories as constrained as possible. In Section 9.2 we will consider arguments about the preferability of theories and try to see why this general principle is justified.

The stricter-theory principle was appealed to several times in our arguments above. In There *a* we noted that if *there* is introduced lexically, it will have unique selectional properties. We want to constrain the types of features that are available for lexical items as much as possible. Hence, any extension of the sort necessitated by adding an item like *there* to the lexicon requires a great deal of justification. Other examples of this kind of argument (either explicitly or implicitly appealed to) were Extraposition *e, f, j;* Passive *d.*

Let us consider one more example of the stricter-theory argument that bears upon a general problem of the standard theory. As we have seen, in the standard theory there are several ways in which we can capture generalizations about co-occurrence relations. One major defect of the standard theory as we have presented it is that there are practically no limits on the kinds of features that can be given for lexical items or on the kinds of redundancy rule that can be stated to predict features for items. Compared to the system of lexical features and redundancy rules, the transformational rules are relatively well defined and restricted. This situation makes it possible to give a stricter-theory argument against some of the alternatives to a transformational treatment that might be imagined.

Suppose, for example, that someone proposed that there is no such thing as a passive transformation — that all the co-occurrence facts that can be used to support Passive could just as well be stated by relating sets of features by redundancy rules in the lexicon. We will show that this move would entail a weakening of the theory (see Robson, 1971).

The problem is that we need to predict patterns of co-occurrence in passive sentences on the basis of patterns in the active (or the converse). The question is whether to account for the relationships by a transformation or by a redundancy rule for lexical features. The redundancy rule would require some such form as this: If a lexical item has the feature

$+[X\ Aux - Y]$, where X and Y are nouns

then it also has the feature

$+[Y\ Aux$ be -en $-$ by X $]$

One of the hypotheses about lexical features that was presented by Chomsky (1965) is that the features are unanalyzable units, that is, frame features like those just given are merely convenient mnemonic devices and have no internal structure. But if this hypothesis is correct, then we cannot have such a redundancy rule, as we can see by giving the features some arbitrary designation:

If a lexical item has the feature $+235$, then it also has the feature $+47$.

The trouble is that the first redundancy rule above is not a rule filling in values for features as individual items, but for whole classes of features (hence the symbols X and Y). No generalization about actives and passives can be stated without weakening the theory to allow us to look at the internal structure of a feature, or in other words, without assuming that features are analyzable. Thus the stricter-theory argument forces us in this case (and within the limits of a particular version of the standard theory) to choose the transformational analysis of passive sentences.

An argument of this sort can be countered in two ways. First, we might try to show that the weakening of the theory that is entailed by a particular choice of analysis is necessary on independent grounds. Or we might show that a weakening of the theory in one part can be offset by making tighter restrictions elsewhere. Thus, we might be able to show that without the passive transformation we would be able to limit transformations quite severely. Both of these counterarguments lead us directly into the considerations of Chapter 9, since they both entail changing theories.

In the case we have been considering, it is quite possible that independent reasons can be given for weakening the theory. Thus, we can argue that lexical features must be analyzable in order for us to be able to state implications among types of selectional characteristics that require provision for optional elements (see Chomsky, 1965; G. Lakoff, 1970, for discussions of this point). But it is possible to pursue the matter somewhat further and arrive at another stricter-theory argument against the redundancy-rule theory of passives. One difference between a redundancy rule for passives and a transformation is that the latter but not the former is a mapping of P-markers in a derivation. We have seen that such mappings are subject to general constraints like the Crossover Principle. In order to account for facts like those given under Passive c in the redundancy-rule account, we would have to extend the domain of Crossover to redundancy rules. But there are three objections to this extension. First of all, it is another extension of the theory. Second, we are then faced with the task of showing that the redundancy rules in question are anything other than transformations. And third, a consideration of a relatively clear case that probably does involve a redundancy rule shows that Crossover does not apply (which, if followed out in this case by the proponent of the redundancy approach, would lead to the absurd position that there are two kinds of redundancy rules, those that are just like transformations, and those that are not). Consider verb pairs like *buy* and *sell*. From the semantics of such verbs we would be able to make predictions like this:

If there is a sentence "X sells Y to Z," then there is a sentence "Z buys Y from X."

But if the redundancy rule that captures this fact is subject to Crossover, then (1) should be worse than (2):

1. John sold the shares to himself.
2. John bought the shares from himself.

But the sentences are both perfectly acceptable. Thus, whatever the rule relating the structures with the two kind of verbs is, it is not subject to Crossover (and hence also it is not a transformation).

7.77 One of Your Generalizations Is Missing

Suppose that under one analysis it is necessary to state twice some general fact or set of facts, while under another analysis the facts can be accounted for by a single statement, rule, or principle. Then we can argue for the latter analysis by appealing to what we may call the missing generalization principle. In fact, a number of arguments that we have already discussed come under this general heading. For example, we argued under Extraposition *g* (see also Section 7.72) that the rule is required to account for sentences with *seem,* hence a semantic rule accounting for the paraphrase relation between optional variants involving Extraposition is unnecessary. Put in terms of missing generalizations, we would be missing a generalization if we accounted for the relation between (1) and (2) below by a semantic rule, and between (3) and (4) by a transformation:

1. It is odd that he is in Nome.
2. That he is in Nome is odd.
3. It seems that he is in Nome.
4. *That he is in Nome seems.

The missing-generalization argument is in fact a special case of a more general principle known as Occam's Razor: *Entitia non sunt mulipli-canda praeter necessitatem* (attributed to William of Ockham) — "entities should not be unnecessarily multiplied." Another way of saying the same thing is to say that we seek the simplest explanation compatible with the facts. If an analysis requires two rules or kinds of rules (say redundancy rules and transformations), then we will reject it in favor of an analysis or theory in which only one rule (or kind of rule) is required.

It is impossible to give an exhaustive account of types of arguments. The mark of a good researcher is the extent to which he or she can break out of well-worn modes of thought and come up with new kinds of arguments. For this no recipes can be given. Nevertheless, it is possible to become conscious of commonly used arguments, and it is often useful to run through a number of familiar patterns when attacking a new problem.

Problems and Questions

1. Show that if Passive is ordinary-cyclic in application, so is There.
2. Discuss the effect on the argument of Raising f of relinquishing the claim that there is a transformation There.
3. Construct arguments *against* each of the following; then try to construct counter-counterarguments.

> There a
> Raising b, d, f, h
> Extraposition $b, c, e, f, g, h, j,$
> Passive a, b, d

4. Discuss the problem of the underlying order of direct and indirect objects in the light of sentences (7)–(14) on p. 160.
5. Determine the ordering of the following rules in relation to the four discussed in this chapter and to each other.

> Reflexive
> Equi
> Number-agreement
> Relative-clause

6. For each of the following sets of English sentences and nonsentences, propose and defend a transformation, and show, where possible, how it fits into the system of transformations discussed in this chapter and in Problem 5.

> a) I picked up the chair.
>   I picked the chair up.
>   I picked it up.
>   *I picked up it.
>
> b) John's having gone to Australia disturbs me.
>   The cat's being a mammal surprises me.
>   *The cat is being a mammal.
>
> c) I hate for you to go.
>   I hate to go.
>   *I hate for to go.
>   I am surprised at you.
>   I am surprised that he is here.
>   *I am surprised at that he is here.

d) Who did you see?
   I know who you saw.
   You saw who?
  *I know you saw who.
   Who did John believe that you saw?
   Who is there?

e) I don't believe he is there.
   I believe he isn't there.
   He's not tall.
  *He's tall at all.
   I don't believe he's tall at all.

f) I consider him to be a fool.
   I consider him a fool.
   I expect him to be a fool.
  *I expect him a fool.

7.   What kind of arguments can be given to show that a transformation
does not exist?

chapter

8

The Mathematical Theory of Grammars

8.1 Why Do Mathematical Linguistics?

In the last decade and a half a special branch of mathematics has developed that deals with abstract systems of grammar and their corresponding languages. The field can be pursued for its own sake, but that will not be our concern here. Rather we are interested in two things: first, in showing how the abstract study of grammars can lead to conclusions in empirical linguistics itself; second, in establishing some basic ideas that will be necessary in subsequent chapters.

The reason for using mathematics to study grammars is very simple. To support the validity of a theory or to show·its inadequacy, we need to be able to carry out deductions from premises to conclusions. Very often we can reach important and quite unexpected results by making precise assumptions about a system of grammar, proving that certain consequences follow logically from the assumptions, and then showing that a given theory or characteristic of natural languages enables us to apply the conclusions from the purely abstract system. The motivation for such work was well described by Chomsky (1957, p. 5):

> The search for rigorous formulation in linguistics has a much more serious motivation than mere concern for logical niceties or the desire to purify well-established methods of linguistic analysis. Precisely constructed models for linguistic structure can play an important role, both negative and positive, in the process of discovery itself. By pushing a precise, but inadequate formulation to an unacceptable conclusion, we can often expose the exact source of this inadequacy and, consequently, gain a deeper understanding of the

linguistic data. More positively, a formalized theory may automatically provide solutions for many problems other than those for which it was explicitly designed. Obscure and intuition-bound notions can neither lead to absurd conclusions nor provide new and correct ones, and hence they fail to be useful in two important respects.

Our pattern of argument is as follows:

1. A set of assumptions (primitive terms and axioms) about a system of grammars is made.

2. Results ("theorems") are proved from these axioms.

So far we have a logical structure of this form: "If (*1*), then (*2*)."

3. It is shown that some theory *T* of natural language is essentially like the system of (*1*).

4. Hence, by the same logical steps involved in going from (*1*) to (*2*) we conclude that results proved in (*2*) also apply to *T*.

5. We draw some conclusion about *T:* for example, that it is in principle incapable of being a correct theory of natural language.

Let us consider an elementary theory as an example:

1. A set of terms and definitions of a class of grammars $\mathscr{G}$ (for *grammar, language,* and the like) is given, including in particular the axiom:

   A. For any grammar in $\mathscr{G}$ there is a longest sentence that can be derived from the grammar.

2. From this axiom we are able to prove the following theorem:

   T1. Given a grammar in $\mathscr{G}$, there are no recursive elements in that grammar, where by "recursive element" we mean an element *E* such that we can derive structures properly containing *E* from *E* itself.

3. Consider any theory of grammar in which it is claimed that there is a limit to the length of sentences—not the length of possible utterances but of the sentences "known" by a native speaker. This claim is obviously the same as the assumption *A*.

4. Now we can show that if the theory is not essentially different from the model theory in relevant respects, the theorem *T1* must hold for the system.

5. To the extent that we can give good arguments for theories in which there are recursive elements (see Section 2.2), we can reject the theories that embody assumption *A*.

It is important to notice that we can never *prove* (in the strict sense) results about natural languages. What we can do is pinpoint exactly the conclusions that must follow from various assumptions that we make.

We now turn to two examples of abstract mathematical systems that are related to syntactic theories. The systems stand at two extremes of a hierarchy of types of grammar and language (Section 8.4), and both can be directly related to particular empirical syntactic theories.

8.2 Finite-State Systems

Let us imagine a simple mechanical device that is capable of being in a finite number of **internal states** and can execute two simultaneous operations: (1) move into a new internal state (which might be the same as the one it was just in), (2) print one of a finite set of symbols onto a tape. In its new state it can again switch into another state and print another symbol next to the first. It can never move backward on the tape or replace an already printed symbol by a new one. A particular set of states are designated as **initial states** and another set (not necessarily distinct from the initial states) are called **final states**. Each sequence of symbols that results from starting out in an initial state, moving from state to state and simultaneously printing out symbols according to a finite set of **instructions,** and ending in a final state is a **sentence** generated by the machine. The collection of sentences generated by the machine is a perfectly well defined language. We can represent the machine by listing its set of internal states, designating those which are initial and final, and giving the list of possible transitions, each consisting of a designation for the present state, the next state, and the symbol printed when making that transition. For example, consider the machine with the output symbols a, b, and the single state S, which is both initial and final, and the transitions or instructions:

$(S, S, a) =$ when in state S, go to state S and print a onto the tape
$(S, S, b) =$ when in state S, go to state S and print b onto the tape

This machine defines the language consisting of all possible strings over the alphabet $\{a, b\}$. "Machines" of this sort make up a well-studied type of abstract machine or automaton called **finite automata.** They are often represented by **state diagrams,** in which we let the nodes stand for states and use labeled directed arrows to show the possible transitions and their associated symbols. We may use an ingoing arrow with no source node and an outgoing arrow with no goal node to mark the initial and final states, respectively. Thus the finite automaton just given might be represented thus:

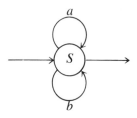

Finite automata can be directly related to rewriting grammars of a particularly restricted sort. Every instruction is a triple (S_i, S_j, a_k). Suppose we interpret the states as the auxiliary symbols of a rewriting grammar and the output symbols as the terminal symbols. Then every such instruction that does not lead to a final state can be given as a rule of a grammar: $S_i \rightarrow S_j a_k$; while those instructions of the given form in which S_j is final can be represented thus: $S_i \rightarrow a_k$. A grammar in which every rule has one of these two forms is called a **finite-state grammar.**[1] Such grammars are equivalent to finite automata. What corresponds to the restriction on finite automata that the symbols be printed one at a time and in the same order is the restriction that the nonterminal symbol S_j always appear to the left of the terminal symbol in rules of the first type. A finite-state grammar defining the above language has the following rules:

$$S \rightarrow Sa$$
$$S \rightarrow Sb$$
$$S \rightarrow a$$
$$S \rightarrow b$$

It is important to realize that in describing finite automata we have used an intuitive picture of a system that can be given a precise mathematical form. When we talk about "machines," "tapes," and the like, we are only using suggestive terminology for what might be a concrete model of the mathematical system itself. For example, we have described the hypothetical machine as a device for printing out symbols on a tape. It would be just as correct to describe it as a machine that "accepts" tapes by looking at inputs and carrying out transitions according to internal state and scanned symbol. The mathematical system that underlies our intuitive picture is absolutely neutral with respect to these two

---

1. Actually, the finite-state grammars given here are a special class called left-linear grammars (named for the position of the single nonterminal element on the right side of every rule). They are exactly equivalent to the symmetrically defined right-linear grammars.

interpretations. (Similarly, the grammars we have been concerned with throughout this book are neutral with respect to the separate problems of "analysis," or acceptance, and "synthesis,' or production.)

When we consider the set of sentences that is defined by a grammar, or automaton, we are considering what is called **weak generative capacity.** The term **strong generative capacity** refers to the set of structural descriptions assigned to its sentences by a grammar. We will concern ourselves here for the time being with weak generative capacity. And we will consider questions about the weak generative capacity of whole classes of grammars and automata. What we have just proved, in effect, is that for every finite automaton defining a language L we can construct a finite-state grammar generating L. We can show similarly that for every finite-state grammar there is a weakly equivalent finite automaton (that is, equivalent in its weak generative capacity). Let there be given a finite state grammar G: we know that it has an initial symbol S. Let the corresponding finite automaton have one initial state S. We know further that the finite-state grammar has only rules of the form: $A \rightarrow B\ c$ or $A \rightarrow a$, where A, B, are auxiliary symbols and a, c represent terminal symbols. Let there be final states B_1, B_2, . . . B_n for all rules of the latter form, and let the instructions of the finite automaton be these for the corresponding rules of the grammar:

(A, B, c)	$A \rightarrow B\ c$
(A, B_i, a)	$A \rightarrow a$

where the B_i are the final states given above for each rule of the second form. Since we can construct a finite automaton for every language defined by a finite state grammar and vice versa, we know that the two systems are weakly equivalent.

A language that can be defined by a finite-state system (that is, a grammar or automaton) is called a **regular** language. A good deal is known about the characteristics of such systems and their associated languages. For example, it can be shown that if L_1 and L_2 are regular languages, then so are the following ones.

Theorem 1. $L_1 \cap L_2$: the intersection of L_1 and L_2, that is, the set of all strings that are both in L_1 and L_2, is a regular language.

Theorem 2. $L_1 \cup L_2$: the union of L_1 and L_2, that is, the set of all strings that are either in L_1 or L_2, is a regular language.

Theorem 3. $L_1 \times L_2$: the concatenate (or Cartesian product) of L_1 and L_2, that is, the set of all strings xy such that x is in L_1 and y is in L_2, is a regular language.

Theorem 4. $\overline{L_1}$: the complement of L_1, that is, the set of all strings over the alphabet of L_1 that are not in L_1, is a regular language.

Theorem 5. $L_1{}^\sim$: the mirror image of L_1, that is, the set of all strings $x = a_1a_2 \ldots a_n$, such that $y = a_na_{n-1} \ldots a_2a_1$ is in L_1, is a regular language.

Let us now consider two further theorems about regular languages. First some definitions. If a grammar has some symbol from which we can derive strings containing instances of that same symbol flanked by non-empty strings of elements, then we say that the grammar is **self-embedding**. Schematically, we can have derivations of this form in the grammar:

$$\ldots A \ldots$$
$$\cdot$$
$$\cdot$$
$$\cdot$$
$$\ldots x A y \ldots$$

For example, this grammar is self-embedding:

$$G_1 \qquad S \rightarrow a\,S$$
$$S \rightarrow S\,b$$
$$S \rightarrow ab$$

From this grammar we can derive the following sequences:

$$S$$
$$aS$$
$$aSb$$
$$aabb$$

Comparing the third and the first lines, we can see that the grammar is self-embedding. Suppose a language has the characteristic that every grammar for the language must be self-embedding. Then, let us say that the language is **essentially self-embedding.** The language just given is not essentially self-embedding, since it can also be defined by the following grammar, which is not self-embedding:

$$G_2 \qquad S \rightarrow S\,b$$
$$S \rightarrow S'\,b$$
$$S' \rightarrow S'\,a$$
$$S' \rightarrow a$$

On the other hand, the language generated by the grammar G_3 is essentially self-embedding:

$$G_3 \qquad S \rightarrow a\,S\,b$$
$$S \rightarrow ab$$

Notice that G_1 is not a finite state grammar, while G_2 is. Further, there is no finite state grammar for the language of G_3, as we shall see. These facts illustrate the first theorem that we will discuss:

Theorem 6. A language is regular if and only if it is not essentially self-embedding.

Proof. Suppose a language is regular. Then every line of the derivations of sentences from its finite state grammar will have one of these two forms:

$$Ax$$
$$x$$

where x consists wholly of terminal symbols, and A is some auxiliary symbol. This follows directly from the definition of a finite state grammar. Thus there is a non-self-embedding grammar for the language. We have proved one half of the theorem: if a language is regular, then it is not essentially self-embedding.

Now consider the other half of the theorem. Suppose that a language is not essentially self-embedding. If the language is finite, then it is regular (it is easy to show that there is a finite automaton to generate any finite set). If it is infinite, it must have some recursive elements. Further, it must be the case that any substrings that we can derive from these recursive elements must have associated with them derivations in which the recursive element appears only on the extreme left or the extreme right of the derivation. For example, suppose A is such an element. Then we will have derivations of substrings like (1) or (2), but not (3), or else, contrary to our assumption, the grammar would be self-embedding:

1. $A\,\ldots$ 2. $\ldots A$ 3. $\ldots A \ldots$

    $\cdot$ $\cdot$ $\cdot$

$A\,x\ldots$ $\ldots x\ \ A$ $\ldots x A\,y\ldots$

Now, every sentence in the language can be partitioned into a sequence of one or more substrings, each associated with a recursive symbol as in (1) or (2). For example, a string might have a partial derivation like this:

$A \ldots$ $\ldots B$ $\ldots C$ $D \ldots$

$\quad \cdot \qquad\qquad\qquad \cdot \qquad\qquad\qquad \cdot \qquad\qquad\qquad \cdot$

$\quad \cdot \qquad\qquad\qquad \cdot \qquad\qquad\qquad \cdot \qquad\qquad\qquad \cdot$

$A \ldots \ldots$ $\ldots \ldots B$ $\ldots \ldots$ $\ldots \ldots C$ $D \ldots \ldots$

$\quad \cdot \qquad\qquad\qquad \cdot \qquad\qquad\qquad \cdot \qquad\qquad\qquad \cdot$

$\quad \cdot \qquad\qquad\qquad \cdot \qquad\qquad\qquad \cdot \qquad\qquad\qquad \cdot$

$\quad x_1 \qquad\qquad\qquad x_2 \qquad\qquad\qquad x_{n-1} \qquad\qquad\qquad x_n$

That is, each sentence is the concatenate of strings from the languages given by the recursive symbols (A, B, C, D, . . .). But each of these sublanguages is regular. For by adding appropriate nonterminal symbols we can generate the sublanguages of type A or D by a finite series of rules of the form $A \rightarrow B \, c$ or $A \rightarrow a$. And for others, we can generate the mirror image of the language by turning the rules around ($B \rightarrow C \, d$ for $B \rightarrow d \, C$); the result is again a regular language, and hence so·is its mirror image (by Theorem 5). But now by Theorem 3 the whole language, being the concatenate of regular languages, is itself regular. Hence if a language is not essentially self-embedding it is regular, and we have completed our proof. The regular languages are exactly those languages for which there exist non-self-embedding grammars.

The content of this theorem can be made clear by thinking of a state diagram for a finite automaton. Corresponding to the recursive symbols of a grammar are nodes associated with loops in the sequence of transitions given in the machine. Because the tape moves in only one direction, the output symbols are printed out linearly by the machine as it goes through its loop. In an essentially self-embedding language, on the other hand, the string must "grow" in two directions. It is simply impossible to represent a self-embedding grammar in a state diagram.

We will not prove the next theorem, but merely state it. First a definition. We say that two strings x and y are in the same **substitution class** in a language L if for arbitrary strings z, w, zxw is in L if and only if zyw is in L. That is, substituting y for x or x for y always preserves the grammaticality of the string. The theorem is this:

> Theorem 7. A language is regular if and only if it has a finite number of substitution classes.

Let us consider a couple of examples to make these concepts familiar. The language consisting of all and only the strings $a^n b^m$ is regular (see G_2 above, p. 184). It has the following substitution classes:

[e]: the empty string

[a]: any string of a's (any time we substitute a string of one or more a's for another, we obtain a string that is in the language if and only if the first one was)

[b]: any string of b's

[ab]: any string of the form $a^n b^m$

[ba]: any string of the form $b^n a^m$ (any time we substitute a string of this form for another, we obtain a string that is not in the language, just as the first one was not)

On the other hand, the language $a^n b^n$, which is not regular, has an infinite number of substitution classes. For example, for each value of n there is a separate substitution class a^n. Substitution of any string of a's of a different length will change the grammaticality of the string.

We have informally considered a number of results that can be proved about regular languages. Let us now relate these results to the empirical study of language. First we will observe that English has characteristics that put it outside the class of regular languages. Then we will consider a simple theory of syntax that is essentially like the theory of finite automata or finite state grammars, and conclude that the theory is inadequate (Chomsky, 1956, 1957).

By Theorem 6, if we can show that a language is essentially self-embedding, we will have proved that it is not regular. If we believe that English has constructions that must be described by using self-embedding elements, then we must conclude that English is not regular. But any English sentence of the following forms exhibits self-embedding:

The man who said that S is here.
John believes that S with all his heart.

By Theorem 7, we can show that English is not regular by showing that it has an infinite number of substitution classes. But this again is easy to demonstrate. Consider sentences like this:

The girl that the boy that the cow chased kissed blushed.

The number of verbs at the end of the sentence must match exactly the number of noun phrases at the head. Such sentences are thus essentially like the sentences of the language $a^n b^n$, and as n changes we have new substitution classes. Thus English is not a regular language. (Another amusing example of a part of English exhibiting an infinite number of substitution classes was given by Bar-Hillel and Shamir, 1960: the forms *missile, anti-missile-missile, anti-anti-missile-missile-*

missile, and in general *anti^n missile^{n+1}*, but not *anti-missile, anti-anti-missile*, ...)

Observe that we are talking about the idealized system that we call the competence of the English speaker. We know that in fact the limits of acceptability are quickly reached in self-embedded sentences. But this fact about utterances follows immediately from the assumption that the speaker or hearer of a language has essentially the characteristics of a finite automaton. By splitting up the problem of characterizing linguistic behavior into a theory of competence and a theory of performance, we are able to achieve a better fit to the facts than if we try to build limitations on embedding and the like into our theory of grammar. For example, we can predict in this way that by changing the performance conditions we can change the limitations on self-embedding (see Section 2.2).

Let us now simply take note of the fact that a theory of syntax proposed in the late 1940s and early 1950s was essentially like the theory of finite automata. In a paper first published in a technical trade journal of the Bell Telephone system, C. E. Shannon described a way of looking at language as a probabilistic or stochastic process. The model given by Shannon is, in the simplest cases, exactly the same as a finite automaton. Consider a finite automaton with one state, which is initial and final, and transitions for each word of English. Such a system is equivalent to what Shannon called a zero-order approximation to English. A first-order approximation to English is given by requiring that the words appear according to their frequency of occurrence in, say, written English (according to their probabilities). A second-order approximation to English is one in which we pay attention to pairs of words. Thus, the first transitions would give the possible first words of English sentences, the next transitions the possible continuations for each of these first words, the next the possible following words for *those* words, and so on. If we add probabilities to the transitions we will have again a finite automaton, but one in which we superimpose a restriction to make the final series of sentences conform to the probabilities. In general, an *n*th-order approximation to English is one in which we take into account possible sequences of *n* words. Shannon gives the following sample of a second-order approximation to written English:

THE HEAD AND ITS FRONTAL ATTACK ON AN ENGLISH WRITER THAT THE CHARACTER OF THIS POINT IS THEREFORE ANOTHER METHOD FOR THE LETTERS THAT THE TIME OF WHOEVER TOLD THE PROBLEM FOR AN UNEXPECTED

As can be seen, each pair of words can stand in a grammatical English sentence, and indeed much longer sequences can be put into English sentences with a little ingenuity.

This picture of the structure of English, together with the mathematical concepts that Shannon developed in **information theory** (see Shannon and Weaver, 1948), were quickly picked up by linguists and considered as possible models of syntactic and phonological structure (see, for example, Hockett, 1955; Gleason, 1955). But as Chomsky showed (1956, 1957), such models must fail, since they are in essence just like finite-state grammars. Increasing the order of approximation does nothing to circumvent the basic problem of the self-embedding structure of natural language, since given self-embedding, we can always find a sentence in which n is exceeded no matter what n we choose for the nth-order approximation. Moreover, the addition of probabilities is irrelevant to describing language competence. Probability means frequency of occurrence. But it is possible for speakers to utter and understand sentences that they have never heard before, that is, sentences with zero probability. On the other hand, since speakers do make mistakes, some sentences that are ungrammatical will have a probability greater than zero. But the inappropriateness of the finite-state model can be seen most dramatically, perhaps, by computing the amount of information that would have to be stored in the brain even if we limited the length of sentences to, say, twenty words. (See Miller and Chomsky, 1963, p. 430, for some statistics on this point.)[2]

8.3 Turing Machines and Unrestricted Rewriting Systems

In the second quarter of this century a number of mathematicians and logicians concerned themselves with the question: What does it mean to say that a process can be carried out in a mechanical fashion? Several different answers were given under a wide variety of formalisms and conceptual schemes, and it turned out that they were all equivalent. In this section I will sketch briefly what is probably the most well-known of such formal systems, the Turing machine (named after its "inventor," the British mathematician A. M. Turing). The finite automata of the last section are the most restricted type of system of any interest. The Turing machines are the most general. After becoming familiar with the basic ideas of Turing machines, we will turn to grammars and show the equivalence of Turing machines and the most powerful type of grammar, the unrestricted rewriting systems. Then we will consider

---

2. For those who wish to explore this topic further, finite automata are studied in Rabin and Scott (1959), which is reprinted together with a number of other papers on abstract machines in Moore (1964). The basic references on finite-state grammars are Chomsky and Miller (1958) and Chomsky (1959). A survey of early mathematical linguistics is given in Chomsky (1963). Two general introductions to mathematical linguistics are Wall (1972) and Partee (forthcoming).

such systems as possible candidates for an empirical theory of syntax, and note some recent results about transformational grammars and their relation to automata.

Suppose you had at your disposal a faithful but unimaginative moron who would do any task you set him, just as long as you were completely explicit in your instructions. For example, suppose you had a long series of numbers to add together. If we could make explicit what was meant by the following parts of the task, then it is plain that no creativity or intelligence would be required but only the ability to follow instructions:

1. Begin by looking at the next set of numbers to add.

2. Take the rightmost digit in the first number and the rightmost digit in the next number; look up their sum and write it down on a special piece of paper ("storage").

3. Take the rightmost digit of the next number, look up the sum of it and the number held in storage, and replace the number held in storage by the new sum.

4. Go back to (3), unless you have reached the end of the set of numbers; if the latter, go to (5).

5. Write down the rightmost digit of the number in storage in a special place.

6. Take the remainder of the number in storage (that is, all but the last digit) and add it to the next to last digit in the first number of the series.

.
.

N. Having exhausted all the numbers, stop.

If we try to pare down mechanical processes like this to ever simpler essentials, we can reduce the mechanical process or "algorithm" to the following: a specification of the current step of our moron, writing down, transferring, or replacing numbers on sheets of paper, looking up sums, and so on, according to an explicit set of instructions. And we can even go further. We can make do with a single strip of tape marked off into squares, which can be scanned only one at a time, if we are allowed any number of squares, a single set of internal states, and a set of instructions telling the recipient to do one of the following things:

1. Move one square to the right or to the left or stay put.

2. Replace the symbol in the currently scanned square with some symbol.

3. Start.

4. Stop.

Since the "tape" is as long as we wish, we can always find new space for storage and computation. Now imagine that we feed a strip of paper to the moron-machine. It is guaranteed to be looking at the initial symbol of a sequence of symbols. If it is in an initial state, it can begin a "computation" by carrying out the first instruction given in its table. It continues until it reaches some final state. We then say that it has computed whatever is now on its tape.

Turing claimed that, when given precise formulation, a machine like the one described above could be reasonably said to provide an explication of presystematic notions like "computable," "algorithmic," "effective procedure," or "mechanically specifiable." Since these are not precise notions, we cannot really prove or refute this claim. But it seems quite reasonable. It is clear that anything that could be done by such a machine is capable of being done in a way that we would agree is "mechanical." For example, it is easy to see how procedures like those above could be programmed on a computer, just as long as we can always add new storage when needed. In the other direction, a very large number of processes of the class that we normally think of as being mechanical can in fact be proved to be within the capacity of such a machine. And finally, Turing machines and a whole series of other formal systems arrived at independently have been proved equivalent. This last result has led to a general claim known as "Church's thesis": If any process can be specified in a series of mechanical, completely explicit steps, then it can be carried out by a Turing machine (or by any of the proven equivalents). This thesis cannot be given a more precise form, since it amounts to an equivalence between precisely defined mathematical systems and a vague, presystematic notion of computability. Church's thesis is often used to simplify proofs. For example, I will show below that any set that can be specified by a transformational grammar can be specified by a Turing machine. Since the operations of a transformational grammar can be given precise formulation, this result follows from Church's thesis.

Let us now look at Turing machines in a little more detail and with a little more precision. A Turing machine is completely described by giving:

1. A finite set of internal states: $\{S_0, S_1, \ldots S_n\}$
2. A finite input-output alphabet: $\{a_0, a_1, a_2, \ldots a_m\}$
3. A designated set of initial states in the set of (1) (let us by convention represent the initial state by S_0)
4. A designated set of final states in the set of (1)
5. A finite set of instructions (we follow the formulation of Davis, 1958, rather than Turing here), each a quadruple of one of the following forms:

a) $S_i\ a_j\ a_k\ S_l$
b) $S_i\ a_j\ R\ S_l$
c) $S_i\ a_j\ L\ S_l$

These instructions are interpreted as follows: When in state S_i scanning symbol a_j, change to state S_l and (a) replace the scanned symbol by a_k, or (b) move one square to the right, or (c) move one square to the left.

Let us assume that a designated member of the alphabet (say #) plays the role of a blank symbol. We can arrange our definitions in such a way that whenever the machine reaches the end of the current expression on its tape, a new instance of # is added. In addition, let every tape expression begin in the form "# x #." This convention has the effect of making the tape infinitely extendable in either direction.

At each point in a computation we can completely describe the machine by giving its current state, the symbol scanned and the remainder of the expression on the tape, for example thus:

xa_jS_iy "the machine is in state S_i scanning a_j and the expression on the tape is xa_jy"

Such a sequence of symbols (of which all but one are in the alphabet, and that one exception is a state) is called an **instantaneous description.** We say that one instantaneous description y **follows from** an instantaneous description x (in symbols, "$x > y$") when one of the following cases holds:

a) $x = za_jS_iw$ $\quad$ $y = za_kS_lw$ $\quad$ and the machine (M) has the instruction $S_ia_ja_kS_l$

b) $x = za_jS_ia_kw$ $\quad$ $y = za_ja_kS_lw$ $\Big\}$ M has
c) $x = za_jS_i$ $\qquad$ $y = za_j\#S_l$ $\Big\}$ $S_i\ a_j\ R\ S_l$

d) $x = za_jS_iw$ $\quad$ $y = zS_ia_jw$ $\Big\}$ M has
e) $x = a_jS_iw$ $\qquad$ $y = \#S_la_jw$ $\Big\}$ $S_i\ a_j\ L\ S_l$

Now we can define such notions as machine "M computes z from w" in terms of sequences of instantaneous descriptions, beginning with the machine in an initial state scanning the leftmost symbol of w and continuing step by step, each step an instance of the relation of "following from," and ending with z in a final state. The close connection between the systems we are considering and formal grammars (where "derivation" is like "computation") should be apparent.

Here is an example of a very simple Turing machine that accepts strings of a's:

1. $S_0\ a\ a\ S_1$

2. $S_1\ a\ R\ S_1$
3. $S_1\ \#\ \#\ S_f$ (where S_f is the one final state)

A computation by this machine is the following:

$a S_0\ a$
$a S_1\ a$ (by 1)
$a a S_1$ (by 2)
$a a \# S_1$ (also by 2. See case (c) above.)
$a a \# S_f$ (by 3)

If the machine encounters anything but a continuous string of a's, it will never reach a final state.

A somewhat more complicated machine defining the language $a^n b^n$ has the following instructions (we will just let numbers represent states $(0 = S_0$, and so on)):

1. $0\ a\ a\ 1$
2. $1\ a\ \#\ 2$
3. $2\ \#\ R\ 2$
4. $2\ a\ R\ 2$
5. $2\ b\ b\ 3$
6. $3\ b\ R\ 3$

7. $3\ \#\ L\ 4$
8. $4\ b\ \#\ 5$
9. $5\ \#\ L\ 6$
10. $6\ b\ L\ 6$
11. $6\ a\ L\ 6$
12. $6\ \#\ R\ 1$

13. $1\ \#\ \#\ f$ (where f is final)

Given an input tape in the language beginning with an a, the machine replaces it by the blank symbol (2), moves to the right until it finds a b, switches to a new state (5), moves to the right until it encounters the end of the string (7), erases one b (8) and moves back to the now initial a, then repeats the process. As the reader can determine, the machine will end in a final state with all a's and b's replaced by blank symbols for strings of the form $a^n b^n$. We can see further that it will reach a final state only for such strings. The strings that are not in the language will fall into the following classes, and we can see for each one that the computation will not terminate in f:

1. The empty string. There is no instruction for the pair $(0, \#)$.
2. Strings in which some b precedes an a. There is no instruction for the pair $(3, a)$, so the computation cannot continue.
3. Strings consisting wholly of b's. There is no instruction for the pair $(0, b)$.
4. Strings consisting wholly of a's. M will continue "forever" going right with instruction (3).

5. Strings of the form $a^n b^m$ where n exceeds m. After all the b's are gone, this reduces to case 4.

6. Strings with more b's than a's. After all the a's are gone, we come to the pair $(1, b)$, for which there is no instruction.

Let us now consider some of the results that have been proved about Turing machines. First of all, let us note that the finite automata can be defined as special cases of Turing machines: those in which every instruction is of the form $(S_i a_j \, R \, S_k)$. Moreover, we have just examined a Turing machine capable of accepting a language that cannot be accepted by a finite automaton (even here we did not use the full power of Turing machines); thus, we know that there are languages that can be defined by the Turing machines but not by finite automata.

A language or set that can be defined by a Turing machine is called **recursively enumerable**. Because Turing machines are the most general formal systems known, to say that a language is recursively enumerable is to say nothing more than that it can be defined by a definite formal system of some sort. The set of all elements that are not in a given set is called its **complement** (see Theorem 4, p. 184). One important result of recursive function theory is that there are recursively enumerable sets whose complements are not recursively enumerable. A recursively enumerable set whose complement is also recursively enumerable is called **recursive**. Thus we have the following hierarchy:

sets that are not recursively enumerable
sets that are recursively enumerable
sets that are recursive

The regular languages, for example, are recursive, since a finite automaton is a very restricted kind of Turing machine, and by Theorem 4 the complement of a regular language is also regular.

Most abstract languages of the sort that one can define in terms of numbers of symbols, dependencies among the symbols, and so on (that is, as far as I can tell, all languages that are set up to illustrate properties of natural languages, plus a good many more) are recursive. To find examples of languages that are recursively enumerable but not recursive it is necessary to go beyond such simple systems. For example, the set of true statements in some system of logic such as the so-called first order predicate logic is nonrecursive but recursively enumerable (if it contains two place predicates or relations, Chomsky, 1963, p. 357).[3]

---

3. The first order predicate logic is a logic built up out of predicates, logical connectives (*and, or, not*), quantifiers (*some, all*), and variables, perhaps also symbols representing particular individuals.

To get languages that are not even recursively enumerable it is necessary to go to some lengths. For example, imagine a language in which each sentence consists of a representation of an arbitrary Turing machine (coded in some way into the terminal symbols of the language) followed by a string x and a string y all meeting the condition that the machine represented will compute y from x. This language can be shown to be not recursively enumerable.[4] Needless to say, such "languages" bear not the slightest resemblance to natural languages.

The difference between recursive sets and recursively enumerable sets can be seen by asking, for each kind of set, whether we can know if a given element (such as a sentence) belongs to the set. In a recursively enumerable set, we are guaranteed that there is a Turing machine that enumerates the members of the set. Thus, if we wait long enough the machine will enumerate the element in question, if it is in the set. But we do not know in advance how long it will take, and for an element not in the set we may never know that it is not in the set. For a recursive set, on the other hand, since we can enumerate both the set and its complement, in a finite length of time we will know whether or not a given element is in the set. An interpretation of this distinction in linguistic terms would be something like this: if a language is a recursive set, then we expect that a speaker of a language will be able to determine whether a given sequence is in his language according to definite rules of his grammar (and within the psychological and physical limits given by a theory of performance). If a language is recursively enumerable but not recursive, then he will have no way of knowing that a given sequence is not in his language. If a language is not even recursively enumerable, then it cannot be described by any definite grammar. We suppose that human languages are recursively enumerable at least (see Chapter 2). If languages are not recursively enumerable, it is difficult to see how they could be learned at all. It seems reasonable to think that they are also recursive. We return to these questions below.

Let us notice before continuing that all languages generated by systems of phrase-structure grammars are recursive. We can show this by using Church's thesis together with an observation about the character of derivations from phrase-structure grammars (see Chomsky, 1959). Since the rules of a phrase-structure grammar yield derivations in which each line is at least as long as the preceding one, we can decide for any given string of symbols whether it is generable from the grammar simply by examining the finitely many derivations of strings of that length from the finitely many rules of the grammar. Thus, there is a definite procedure

---

4. Actually, even this claim will stand only if we make further technical qualifications about the machines in question. Interested readers may consult such works as Davis, 1958.

for determining both the language and its complement. Hence, by a double application of Church's thesis, there is a Turing machine enumerating both the language and its complement, and the language is recursive. On the other hand, there are languages that are recursive but are not generated by phrase-structure grammars. The proof of this statement involves a so-called diagonal argument: suppose we enumerate the set of the complements of all phrase-structure languages according to some definite procedure. We know that this is possible, since we can determine by a definite procedure whether a given string is or is not in the language of a given grammar. The language consisting of the complements of the languages of the grammars in our enumeration cannot itself have a phrase-structure grammar, since we have defined it as containing strings that are excluded from the languages of each of the grammars in our enumeration. Thus it contains some sentence that is not in the language of the first grammar, some sentence that is not in the language of the second grammar, and so on through all phrase-structure grammars.

Now let us consider the connection between certain classes of grammars and Turing machines. In Chapter 2 we described a simple class of grammars called unrestricted rewriting systems. These systems turn out to be essentially identical with a type of formal system called a semi-Thue system (a special kind of Post system) that has been shown to be identical in power to a Turing machine. By Church's thesis we know that no matter what kind of unrestricted rewriting system we set up, since they are definite systems, we will be able to construct a Turing machine that will do whatever the formal system will do. (It would be laborious but quite feasible to show how to construct a Turing machine that would imitate the operation of an unrestricted rewriting system.) Conversely, we can show how to set up an unrestricted rewriting system that will do just what a Turing machine will do. All we need do is note that the instantaneous description of a Turing machine is a sequence of symbols, and show for each type of instruction of a Turing machine how we can form one or more rules for a URS (unrestricted rewriting system):

If the Turing machine has the instruction:	let the URS have the rules:
$S_i a_j a_k S_l$	$a_j S_i \rightarrow a_k S_l$
$S_i a_j \ R \ S_l$	$a_j S_i a_k \rightarrow a_j a_k S_l$ (for all elements a_k in the alphabet of the machine)
$S_i a_j \ L \ S_l$	$a_j S_i \rightarrow S_l a_j$

Now given a Turing machine that accepts a given language, say by mapping it into blanks in a final state, we can construct a URS that accepts the same language by imitating the steps of the mapping process. For example, if we take the Turing machine given above (p. 193) for the language $a^n b^n$, we can construct a corresponding URS as follows:

$$aS_0 \to aS_1$$
$$aS_1 \to \#S_2$$
$$\vdots$$

If we define "accepting" in the same way as with our Turing machine — the URS accepts the language if it maps strings in the language into strings of #'s and ends with the single symbol S_f — then it is clear that the URS does exactly what the corresponding Turing machine does. To convert the system into a grammar we need to do some modifying. Suppose we make a grammar that has the effect of generating an arbitrary string of a's and b's followed by a special symbol C, and a mirror image of the string of a's and b's but with nonterminal symbols A and B in place of a and b, respectively. Now we allow C to play the role of an initial state in a subroutine that maps the strings of A's and B's into #'s just in case the original Turing machine did so with the mirror image of a's and b's (this is obviously possible). Finally, we delete the symbol corresponding to the final state of the Turing machine. We will be left with a string of a's and b's just in case that string is in the language accepted by the Turing machine. Our grammar would begin like this:

$$S \to aSA$$
$$S \to bSB$$
$$S \to C$$

Here would begin the subroutine imitating the reversed Turing machine and ending with the rule corresponding to the last instruction of the machine:

$$\#S_1 \to \#$$

Since all the rules are within the definition of rules of a URS, we know that no matter what Turing machine we choose, we can construct a grammar that generates a string x just in case x is accepted by the machine.

8.4 The Hierarchy of Languages and Rewriting Grammars

This section will briefly summarize what we have discussed about the weak generative capacity of various types of abstract machines and grammars, and mention a few other types of grammars that we have not explicitly discussed in this chapter. An unrestricted rewriting system is defined as a system with rules of the form "$x \to y$" in which we do not place any additional requirements on the form of the rule. Making such further restrictions gives us further classes of grammars, including context-sensitive phrase-structure grammars and context-free phrase-structure grammars (Chapter 3). For languages, grammars, and machines the following hierarchy has been proved to exist:

Type	Grammars	Automata	Languages
0	unrestricted rewriting	Turing machines	recursively enumerable
1			recursive
2	context-sensitive phrase-structure	linear-bounded automata	context-sensitive languages
3	context-free phrase-structure	push-down store automata	context-free languages
4	finite-state	finite automata	regular languages

In each instance, there are languages of Type$_i$ that cannot be generated by grammars or machines of Type$_{i+1}$. (A survey of these results is given in Chomsky, 1963, where the reader may find references to literature dealing with the abstract machines we have not discussed here.)

Where do the natural languages stand in relation to the above hierarchy? We have considered this question at various points in our exposition. In the discussion of finite automata and finite-state grammars, we saw evidence that natural languages are beyond the scope of those systems. In an earlier chapter I argued that the natural languages must be considered at most to be recursively enumerable, and in the last section I argued that they should be considered recursive (see Putnam, 1962). Some linguists have argued that the natural languages are beyond the scope of context-free grammars (Postal, 1964), and this seems to be quite likely.

8.5 The Weak Generative Capacity of Transformational Grammars

The relevance of mathematical studies like those presented so far in this chapter has been limited until the last few years by the fact that all the simple systems studied were known to be inadequate empirically for reasons having to do with strong generative capacity — that is, the ability of a grammar to assign structural descriptions to the sentences it generates—while the mathematical properties of the class of grammars that seemed to offer most hope for an empirically adequate theory were completely unknown. Let us first note two examples of the inadequacy of the rewriting grammars in terms of their strong generative capacity, and then look at some recent steps that have begun to fill in our knowledge about the formal properties of transformational grammars.

An essential property that distinguishes context-sensitive grammars from context-free grammars is that the former, but not the latter, are able to incorporate series of rules whose effect is rearranging elements in a string. Suppose we have a grammar with a rule like this:

$$AB \rightarrow BA$$

By introducing new nonterminal symbols, we can produce the same effect by rules that are—taken one by one—context-sensitive phrase-structure rules:

$$AB \rightarrow \bar{A}B$$
$$\bar{A}B \rightarrow \bar{A}\bar{B}$$
$$\bar{A}\bar{B} \rightarrow B\bar{B}$$
$$B\bar{B} \rightarrow BA$$

where $\bar{A}$ and $\bar{B}$ are new nonterminal symbols. In earlier chapters we have considered numerous examples of sentences that are related formally by a difference in the order of constituents; for example, questions and related declarative sentences, passives and actives, extraposed and nonextraposed sentences. But if we try to relate such sentences by context-sensitive rules like those just given, our grammars will assign the wrong structural analyses to the sentences. In the example just given, for example, a partial phrase-marker associated with those rules would look like this:

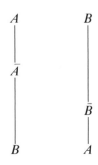

Thus the grammar would assign an analysis in which the A's are of type

B and the *B*'s of type *A*. If we think of the linguistic analogs of such situations, this would be like having a rule inverting noun phrases and verbs, and the grammar would define phrase-markers like the following:

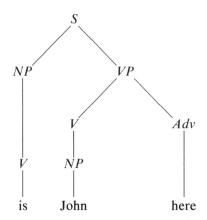

If we want our grammar to relate sentences that are different permutations of the same sets of constituents, and if we want the grammar to preserve the constituency assignments of the phrase-markers, then we must add something like transformational rules to our grammar.

A second inadequacy in the strong generative capacity of rewriting grammars is the fact that the grammars only assign single phrase-markers to given sentences. The only structure assignments that phrase-structure grammars give is the final phrase-marker of the rules. Many examples in earlier chapters show that sentences must be assigned at least two phrase-markers as part of their structural descriptions (for example, deep and surface structures). Once again, if we try to meet this aim we are on the way to defining a type of grammar that is transformational.

In the last few years, formal studies of transformational grammars have established that transformational grammars are extremely powerful systems. In fact, under most of the restrictions that have been suggested by linguists they are exactly equivalent to unrestricted rewriting systems (hence, also Turing machines) in their weak generative capacity. It would take us too far afield to go through a rigorous demonstration of the theorems that have been proved about transformational grammars.[5] But we can present some results and show why it is reasonable that the results are what they are.

First, let us notice the crucial role that is played by rules of deletion

---

5. Most of the proofs are by Stanley Peters and Robert W. Ritchie. See citations in the bibliography of their papers; see also Ginsburg and Partee (1969).

in rewriting grammars. Let us call a grammar in which every rule "$x \rightarrow y$" meets the restriction that y is at least as long as x, a **nonshrinking** grammar. It is possible to show that there is a context-sensitive grammar that will generate any language generable by a nonshrinking grammar (Kuroda, 1964). This amounts to saying that the difference between unrestricted rewriting systems and the more restricted phrase-structure grammars is that it is possible to delete elements by rules of the former but not the latter. Since transformational rules can carry out deletions, it is only necessary to show that the structure of a transformational grammar (the ordering of the transformational rules after all base rules, the cyclic principle, and so forth) does not prevent us from applying deletion rules so that they imitate the effect of an unrestricted rewriting system. As mentioned above, Church's thesis allows us to assume that any language that can be generated by a transformational grammar can be accepted by some Turing machine.

When we define transformational grammars mathematically, it is necessary to make precise certain notions that are vague in the linguistic literature, to make choices where the theory of syntax has left various questions open, and to idealize by simplifying the theory in noncrucial ways. First of all, let us notice that for studies of weak generative power we can dispense with complex elements in syntax and assume that the base of a transformational grammar has simple unanalyzed elements as its basic elements. We can do this because in any given grammar the number of possible combinations of the features that make up the complex elements will have a definite limit, and we can assume that we have as many distinct elements to represent these different combinations as we need. Complex elements are introduced for reasons that have to do with capturing generalizations and so on, and play no essential role in weak generative power. Beyond this, we can make various explicit choices about the type of base that is allowed, and also study the effects of various restrictions on the operation of the transformations.

The first result we will consider is the following. Consider a theory of transformational grammar in which, along with the usual definitions of the operations of transformations, the construction of base phrase-markers from the base rules, and so on, we make the following assumptions:

1. The base is a context-sensitive phrase-structure grammar.
2. The transformations are linearly ordered and apply cyclically.
3. Deletions are restricted to fixed terminal elements, or to constituents identical to constituents that remain elsewhere in the phrase-marker.

Let us call such a system a transformational grammar with a context-sensitive base. Peters and Ritchie have proved that such systems are exactly equivalent to unrestricted rewriting systems in their weak generative capacity. Let us break down the argument into several steps. First we will show that for every URG we can construct a grammar consisting of a set of context-sensitive rules that will generate a language that is just like the language given by the URG, except that it may contain sentences of the form xy, where x is in the original language and y is a string of elements not in the original grammar. If we then delete all instances of this particular terminal symbol, we have the language of the URG. Then we will show that a transformation can carry out the last step, and that hence a transformational grammar can generate any language that can be generated by an unrestricted rewriting system.

Consider an arbitrary recursively enumerable language. It can be generated, as we have seen, by some grammar G in which every rule is of the form "$x \rightarrow y$," with no restrictions on x and y. Let us construct a new grammar G' as follows. For every rule $x \rightarrow y$ of G in which y is as long as x, let G' have the same rule $x \rightarrow y$. For every rule in which y is shorter than x by k symbols, let G' have the rule $x \rightarrow yB^k$, where B is a new nonterminal symbol not in G. In addition, let G' have for every symbol a in the vocabularies of G a rule $Ba \rightarrow aB$. Finally, let G' have the rules (where # is the boundary symbol): $B\# \rightarrow b\#$ and $Bb \rightarrow bb$, where b is a new terminal symbol not in the alphabet of G. Now for every string x derivable from G there will be a derivation in G' of the string xb^i for some $i \geq 0$. This is clear in the case where none of the new rules with B's is involved in a derivation. In case a rule with B is used, then the rules $Ba \rightarrow aB$ will remove the B's so that the derivation can proceed as before on the remainder of the string. We must make the replacement of B by b contingent on the boundary symbol in order to make sure that we do not end up with b's interspersed throughout the terminal strings. For every string xb^i derivable by G' there will be a derivation of x from G. We saw above that for every nonshrinking grammar there is a weakly equivalent context-sensitive grammar. Now we can provide one cyclic transformation.

$$X \quad b$$
$$1 \quad 2 \Rightarrow$$
$$1 \quad \emptyset$$

This rule will map the strings xb^i into x, thus giving exactly the language of G. Thus, with a context-sensitive base, transformational grammars are exactly equivalent in their weak generative power to Turing machines. Peters and Ritchie showed further that the following theorems hold:

For every recursively enumerable language L there is a transformational grammar T generating L (using the filter function of transformations) with any of the following characteristics:

1. the base of T is a context-free grammar;
2. the base of T is a finite-state grammar;
3. the base of T is a fixed grammar with two rules.

These results show that restricting the base does not affect the generative power of a transformational grammar at all. We will consider the linguistic implications of this fact in Chapter 11. The results show further that the power of transformations is such that they can do just about anything. The proof of these theorems involves setting up transformations that are perfectly well-behaved under the linguistic definitions of transformations, but that imitate exactly the operation of a Turing machine. It is not surprising that transformations can do essentially the same thing as the instructions of a Turing machine. What is surprising is that imposing various limitations like the recoverability condition, cyclic operation, and restrictions on the base have no effect whatsoever on the power of the systems.

Let us consider again the linguistic implications of the above mathematical results. In earlier sections of this chapter we saw that finite-state grammars are inadequate as theories because the classes of languages they define do not contain the class of natural languages. In the present section we have seen that transformational grammars of a wide variety of types are equivalent to the most powerful abstract systems known: Turing machines and unrestricted rewriting systems. Thus, transformational grammars are inadequate for just the opposite reasons. They are too powerful and do not sufficiently delimit the class of natural languages.

Another way of looking at these conclusions is the following one (from Peters and Ritchie, forthcoming): If we compare existing partial grammars for natural languages with the full class of systems given by the standard theory (and derivative theories), we can see that only a small fraction of the possible kinds of rules is in fact used. For example, it is perfectly possible to write a transformation that will take an NP occurring at the head of a sentence, and add three copies of the NP to the end of the sentence, each one followed by a copy of the second NP in the sentence; that is, a rule that would carry structures like (1) into structures like (2):

1. John loves Mary.
2. John loves Mary John Mary John Mary John Mary.

And it is possible to give a transformation with seventeen terms that imitates the operation of a Turing machine (Peters and Ritchie, forthcoming). Further, all known transformational grammars for natural languages meet certain formal conditions that would make the languages described by them recursive (Peters and Ritchie, 1973). Thus, it is apparent that the standard theory projects a much too large class of possible natural languages. In subsequent chapters we shall bear in mind these defects of the standard theory and, in Chapter 11, consider some attempts to render it a closer approximation to a correct theory of natural languages.

Problems and Questions

1.   Construct state diagrams and write grammars for the following regular languages:

a) $a^n b^m c^i$ $(n, m, i \geq 1)$
b) $a^n bc^m$ $(n, m \geq 0)$
c) $ab^n c$ $(n \geq 0)$

2.   Prove Theorem 2 on p. 183.
3.   Which of the following are not regular languages?

a) $a^n bc^n$ $(0 \leq n \leq 5,000)$
b) $a^n b^m c^i$ $(n = m$ or $n = i)$
c) $a^n b^{2n} c^{3n}$
d) $a^n b^m$ $(n \neq m)$

4.   Prove that for every language defined by a nonshrinking grammar (that is, a grammar where every rule $x \to y$ meets the condition that y is at least as long as x) there is a context-sensitive phrase-structure grammar that defines the same language (see p. 201).
5.   Construct Turing machines that will carry out the following mappings:

a) $a^n b^m \to b^m a^n$
b) $a^n \to a^{2n}$
c) $x \to x^\sim$ (where x is an arbitrary string of a's and b's and $x^\sim$ is its mirror image)
d) $x \to 0$ (where x is any string of the form $a^n b^n$ $(n \geq 1)$ and y is any
   $y \to 1$ other string of a's and b's)

6. Write the least powerful grammar (in terms of the hierarchy of p. 198) for each of the following languages ($n, m \geq 1$)

a) $a^n b^m c^n$
b) $a^n b^m a^n b^m$
c) $a^n b^m a^m b^n$
d) xx^- (x a string in a,b)
e) xx (x a string in a,b)
f) x, where x is a string of a's and b's such that the number of a's is exactly the same as the number of b's

7. Show that every finite language has a finite-state grammar.

8. In arguing that English is not a regular language (pp. 187–189), we tacitly assumed that by exhibiting subclasses of sentences or words in English that could not be described by a finite automaton or finite-state grammar, we could conclude that English itself was not describable by one of these equivalent theories. Show that this assumption was legitimate by applying Theorem 1 (p. 183).

9

Revisions in Transformational Theory

9.1 A Change of Emphasis

So far in this book I have attempted to give a coherent presentation of the standard theory of transformational syntax, a slightly modified version of a theory presented by Chomsky (1965). The presentation has been deliberately pedagogical so that an attentive reader with no previous extended work in linguistics could follow the development. In the remaining three chapters, the style and content of the book will be rather different. In the present chapter we shall consider a number of developments in syntactic and semantic theory since *Aspects*. The presentation will take on the character of a survey and critique, but our treatment will be quite selective. The reader is urged to consult the works referred to on his own. In the previous chapter we ended with a hint at some difficulties of the standard theory. In the following chapters we will take up this critique in more detail and consider one attempt to circumvent the problems of the standard theory, ending with some programmatic remarks about an approach that seems to offer promise for fruitful future research. In line with the change in our emphasis, I will forgo the pedagogical device of giving problems at the end of each chapter. A good deal of the following material represents an expansion and further development of ideas presented in several recent papers by Peters (1970) and Bach (1970, 1971a, 1971b, 1974).

9.2 Comparing Theories

In Section 7.76 we touched on arguments using the following paradigm: Given two theories that cover the same range of data, we will choose that theory that makes stronger assumptions. In the following discussions we lean heavily on this principle. Hence it will be worthwhile to justify this principle, and also to note some necessary preconditions for invoking it.

The central task of linguistic theory is to answer this question: What is the nature of human language? The question can be viewed as an attempt to delimit exactly the class of human languages and to state what makes them different from other systems: systems of signals among other species than man, arbitrary programs for a general-purpose computer, logical and mathematical systems, and the like.

Let us say that a theory T_1 is **stricter** than a theory T_2 if every consequence of T_1 implies every consequence of T_2 but the converse is not true. Now it is obvious that T_1 will delimit a narrower range of possible facts than will T_2 (see Section 4.5 for an example of this reasoning). On a priori grounds we will choose T_1 as a preferable theory. The reasons for this are several. T_1 tells us more about the object of our considerations (say, language), than does T_2. This means that it will be easier to falsify T_1 by finding new instances of features of language showing that T_1 is wrong, and (as the philosopher of science Karl Popper, 1959, has stressed) falsifiability is a virtue rather than a defect in constructing scientific theories. Because of the nature of human knowledge, we can never know that a theory is correct. But if it is easy to find consequences of a theory that can show that it is wrong, and if we find that new facts do not contradict the consequences of our theory, we can place some measure of confidence in the correctness of the theory. Consider the extreme case of a completely empty theory that does not make any claims at all about its subject matter. Since there is no way to show that it is false, there is no reason for us to think that it might be correct, either.

Here is a simple example. Suppose a necessary consequence of one theory is that the moon is made of green cheese, and another theory predicts simply that it is made of some solid substance. It is easier to show that the first theory is wrong than that the second is wrong. Hence, on a priori grounds, the first theory is better. By testing it we can find out more than we can by testing the second theory. Of course, as this example shows, when we begin to construct a theory we rule out an infinite number of very strict theories because we have good reasons to believe that they are wrong—but not because they make specific claims.

Again, consider the mathematical models we discussed in the last chapter. A theory that languages are recursively enumerable makes no claims beyond the one that languages are definite systems of some sort. A theory that languages are regular makes more claims and is easier to refute. In this instance it is possible to refute the latter theory, and that technically is a virtue of the theory. But these two theories are both preferable to a theory such as that of Hockett (1968) that denies that languages are definite systems at all.

In order to make a stricter theory argument valid, a good deal of preliminary work must be done. First of all, it must be the case that the theories are comparable. If T_1 makes assumptions that T_2 does not make and vice versa, then it is impossible to compare the theories according to relative strictness. Second, the theories must be explicit enough in their essentials that we can really tell how they are related in terms of strictness of assumptions. And finally, to be worth considering they must both be relatively strict. As we shall see, several of the competing revisions of transformational theory fail in all three respects when we try to compare them.

With these remarks in mind, we can turn to some revisions and additions to transformational theory. It will be convenient to divide them into two groups: those that represent a tightening of the theory by making stricter assumptions, and those that represent a weakening of the theory.

9.21 Restrictions on the Operation of Transformations

From the outset of work on transformational syntax, it was evident that many rules must have various specific restrictions on their operation in order to prevent them from generating ungrammatical sentences. A perusal of transformational analyses of particular languages will show that, in addition to a structure index and a set of elementary transformations, many rules contain "conditions" of various sorts. We seek to delimit the class of possible transformations as closely as possible. But the addition of ad hoc restrictions runs directly counter to this general aim. Suppose we find that many transformations obey the same restrictions. Then we can strengthen our theory by disallowing as many ad hoc conditions as possible and replacing them by general restrictions on whole classes of transformations. In this way, we not only constrain our theory in a desirable way but also discover general facts about language. We have already considered several such general restrictions: the conditions on recoverability of deletions (Section 5.4) and Postal's Crossover Principle. The most extensive work on restricting transformations has been done by John Ross (1967a). Here we will consider a number of Ross's general restrictions on a class of "movement" transformations.

Consider two rules of English. There is a rule that positions an interrogative word at the head of a question, giving pairs like the following ones (the underlying structure is given first):

John *Past* see who.
Who did John see?

Mary is living where.
Where is Mary living?

Another rule positions a relative pronoun at the head of its clause:

The man [Mary loves the man] is here.
The man who Mary loves is here.

The house [John lives in the house] is on 53rd Street.
The house in which John lives is on 53rd Street.

We do not need to state these rules explicitly here, but we can see that in each case the rule takes some element and moves it to the head of the sentence. But if we state the rules in the most general way — and the rules are intended to be completely explicit and applicable without assuming any other knowledge on the part of the speaker — then we can project not only an infinite number of grammatical results like those above but also ungrammatical ones like these:

1. John saw the girl that was living with who.
    *Who did John see the girl that was living with?

    I know the man that is living where.
    *Where do I know the man that is living?

    The man [Mary hates the girl that is living with the man] is here.
    *The man who Mary hates the girl that is living with is here.

    The house [I am acquainted with the man that is living in the house] is on 53rd Street.
    *The house in which I am acquainted with the man that is living is on 53rd Street.

2. John believes the claim that the man is living with who.
    *Who does John believe the claim that the man is living with?

    The house [I resent the allegation that John lives in the house] is on 53rd Street.
    *The house that I resent the allegation that John lives in is on 53rd Street.

3. Mary lives in New York and where.
    *Where does Mary live in New York and?

    The man [Mary loves the man and his brother] is here.
    *The man who(m) Mary loves and his brother is here.

    John hates his mother and loves who.
    *Who(m) does John hate his mother and love?

4. That Harry lives where is obvious.
    *Where is that Harry lives obvious?

    The man [that Mary loves the man is unlikely] is here.
    *The man who that Mary loves is unlikely is here.

To account for these restrictions, Ross posited three general constraints on a class of "movement" transformations. Let us define a movement transformation as one with a structural change of one of the following forms:

$$\ldots X, A, Y \ldots \qquad\qquad \ldots X, A, Y \ldots$$
$$1 \quad 2 \quad 3 \Rightarrow \qquad\qquad 1 \quad 2 \quad 3 \Rightarrow$$
$$2 \ 1 \ \emptyset \ 3 \qquad\qquad 1 \ \emptyset \ 3 \ 2$$

Sets (1) and (2) illustrate the **Complex Noun-Phrase Constraint:**

No transformation may move an element out of a sentence *S* in a structure of the following form:

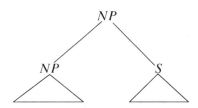

In the first set the structure is a relative clause; in the second it is a complement to a noun like *claim, fact, statement.*
    Set (3) illustrates the **Coordinate Structure Constraint:**

No transformation may move an element out of a structure that is part of a coordinate structure, that is, a structure of the form:

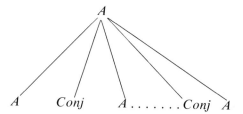

The sentences in set (4) illustrate the **Sentential Subject Constraint:**

> No transformation can move an element out of a sentence that is dominated by an *NP* that is in turn dominated by *S* (that is, in most cases, the subject of a sentence).[1]

We have already mentioned one more of Ross's restrictions, the Bounding restriction (see Section 7.4, Extraposition *k*). There is a rule of English called Extraposition-from-*NP*. Its operation can be seen in pairs like these:

> The package that arrived from New York is huge.
> The package is huge that arrived from New York.

> John met a girl that he had not seen for several years in the subway.
> John met a girl in the subway that he had not seen for several years.

It has been argued (Ross 1967a; Bach, 1971a; see Section 6.4) that this rule must be a last-cyclic rule. It can be stated somewhat like this:

$$X, [NP, S] Y$$
$$1 \quad 2 \quad 3 \quad 4 \Rightarrow$$
$$1 \quad 2 \quad \emptyset \quad 4+3$$

Yet if we apply the rule blindly we can produce ungrammatical results like these:

> The man that saw the girl that was in the subway sneezed.
> *The man that saw the girl sneezed that was in the subway.

> That the girl that he had not seen for several years had a smashed liver was news to John.
> *That the girl had a smashed liver was news to John that he had not seen for several years.

The Bounding restriction rules out movement of an element beyond the

---

1. For a more precise statement of several of the above constraints, together with many examples and discussion of alternative treatments, the reader should consult Ross (1967a).

boundaries of the next sentence "up." Some rules are not bounded (strictly, upward-bounded), for example, *WH*-movement and Topicalization:

> Who did Sally claim that Harold knew?
> Mary, I don't believe you have ever met.

If these constructions were bounded, then we should be able to construct, at most, sentences like these:

> Sally claimed who did Harold know.
> I don't believe Mary you have ever met.

Ross made an interesting observation (see Extraposition *k* in Section 7.4). Apparently all rightward movements are bounded, but leftward movements may or may not be. An example of a leftward movement rule that is bounded is one type of adverb movement:

> I know that he was here yesterday.
> I know that yesterday he was here.
> *Yesterday I know that he was here.

Another possible bounded rule is one that takes a directional adverb to the head of its sentence:

> Away ran Henry.
> Away I believe ran Henry.

Although the specific details of Ross's constraints may be called into question (and some particular analyses invoking them have been; see, for example, Kiparsky and Kiparsky, 1970), the general approach seems quite hopeful. The constraints were offered as general constraints on all transformational grammars. Some recent research indicates that they may not hold for all languages, from which we could conclude either that the constraints are specific to English or that they need to be reformulated so that they can follow from some other general facts about English and other languages. It seems to me that the latter approach is the more promising. It is clear that they are not semantic constraints, at least under our current understanding of semantic structures, since it is possible to have quite meaningful structures expressing the same underlying forms with different constructions. Thus, in some dialects of "real" English (nonliterary, conversational English as it is heard on the street) there are perfectly well formed sentences in which a pronoun is retained in the relative clause:

The man that Mary knows the girl that is living with him is a bastard.

Further discussion of general questions about relative clauses will appear in Sections 11.2 and 11.51; see also Bach (1965). For more on restrictions of the sort posited by Ross, see especially Chomsky (1973).

9.22 Some Further Restrictions on Grammars

If we consider the number of fairly well motivated transformations that have been posited for natural languages and compare it with the number of possible transformations that are countenanced by the formal definition of a transformation presented in Chapter 5, one interesting fact emerges. Very few of the transformations that are theoretically possible have actually been found to exist. This fact has led a number of linguists to seek general restrictions that might account for the small number of actual choices that natural languages seem to make. (Of course it must be remembered that the well-studied constructions of natural languages form a very small proportion of the actual possibilities known to exist, and further, that the number of languages that have been studied in depth is still quite small.)

Joseph Emonds (1970, 1972) has developed a theory predicting that — with the exception of a class of **root** transformations that deal with structures directly dominated by the highest S in a phrase-marker — no transformation may result in a type of structure that is not given in the base rules. An example of this is the Passive transformation. The base rules that have been traditionally assumed for English develop structures of the form

NP Aux V Prepositional-Phrase

The output of the passive transformation is not some wildly different structure (such as *V NP by NP*), but rather another structure of exactly the above form: *NP Aux V by NP*. On the other hand, the root transformation of *Subject-Aux* inversion does produce questions that depart from the standard form of the base structures: *Aux NP V X*.

Emonds's theory entails a considerable amount of rethinking of the basic assumptions underlying the analyses of English that have been carried out under the standard theory. This is not the place to attempt an exposition of these revisions (I have already mentioned one in connection with my arguments for the standard analysis of Extraposition, Section 7.4). For details the reader should look at Emonds (1970, 1972). One crucial point about Emonds's theory that needs to be examined is that it makes very weak claims unless we can also support stringent restrictions on the types of base structure allowed. We will return to some predictions of Emonds's theory in Chapter 11 (Section 11.52), when we come to consider some problems about establishing base structures.

Another problem is that it must be ensured that the root transformations do not give back the power that has been excluded from the structure-preserving transformations. The main difference between constraints of the type exemplified by Ross's work and the theory of structure-preserving transformations is that the former represents mainly a tightening of the theory without changing its basic nature, while Emonds's work entails a more wholesale revision. My remarks above about the comparability of systems should be borne in mind. Too many open questions exist about the total systems suggested by the various writers we are considering to permit comparisons of the strictness of the systems relative to each other and the standard theory. One other important consideration has been stressed by Chomsky (1970). We must remember the difference between a total theory of grammars and various realizations of that theory.

9.3 Weakenings of the Theory

Section 6.4 mentioned Perlmutter's work on deep-structure constraints. The theory of deep-structure constraints represents a weakening of one of the versions of transformational theory given in *Aspects* (see Section 6.6). In that theory, the only selectional restrictions allowed are those that refer to the features of the lexical items in the same simple sentence as the item in question. A deep-structure constraint such as the "unlike subject" constraint on verbs like *scream,* on the other hand, must refer to the subject of a sentence that is a complement to the verb in question. The issue is beclouded by the fact that the properties of the semantic theory — if any — associated with the grammar will play a crucial role in trying to assess the relative strengths of the various theories to be compared.

Perlmutter (1970, 1971) also has dealt with a series of phenomena that appear to show the necessity for surface-structure constraints as well, that is, filters or checks that need to be placed on the grammar but that cannot or should not be handled by placing restrictions on particular transformations. The paradigm case is one in which several different transformations can lead to a result that must be blocked. Perlmutter's basic arguments stem from facts of Spanish clitic pronouns (a convenient source for the arguments and data is Perlmutter, 1970). An especially strong case can be made if we can show that some intermediate structure must be allowed to be developed, such that it would result in an ungrammatical sentence but can be "saved" by the operation of some optional transformation that removes the illicit sequence from the final form of the sentence. Here are some examples from various sources. In each case, we give an ungrammatical full sentence, followed by a grammatical sentence that results from the operation of an optional deletion rule:

> *Mary went to the movie with Ishmael and someone, but I don't know who Mary went to the movie with Ishmael and.
> Mary went to the movie with Ishmael and someone, but I don't know who(m). (Ross, 1969)

> *John didn't see any friends at all, but Harry saw some friends at all.
> John didn't see any friends at all, but Harry did. (Baker, 1970)

> *They're stopping flagellating themselves.
> Flagellating themselves they're stopping.
> They were busy flagellating themselves but now they're stopping. (Ross, 1972)

Arguments of this sort require strong evidence that the "exonerating" transformations do indeed exist, or that it is impossible or undesirable to place the restriction in question on some transformation. It should also be borne in mind that the additions to the theory weaken it only if all other things are equal. Indeed, Perlmutter explicitly considers the question of restricting transformations in some way such that the total theory would not necessarily be weaker than the original theory without surface-structure constraints. On the other side, it should be mentioned that the standard theory (with its various devices for blocking surface structures) can almost always be allowed to accommodate an analysis without surface-structure constraints. For example, Perlmutter's "templates" for allowed sequences of clitic pronouns could be handled by generating them directly in the base with a sentence boundary, and then allowing them and the sentence boundary to be deleted just in case none of the ungrammatical sequences were present in the final surface structure.

In 1965 G. Lakoff's Indiana thesis (subsequently published in largely unchanged form as G. Lakoff, 1970a) was circulated. In it he considered the major problem of exceptions to transformations. The device he worked out was a system of marking lexical items for their behavior with respect to various transformations. Some had to meet the structural description of a transformation, some could not meet one, some had to be blocked from application of the rule, and so on. The devices he added extended the power of a grammar (although he did consider some restrictions, for example, the restriction that no transformation may mention a particular lexical item).[2]

---

2. For details and many interesting analyses that led directly into the so-called generative semantic point of view, which we will consider below (Section 9.6), the reader should consult the original work. For an example of a grammar of a non-Indo-European language using Lakoff's framework, and a good summary of its major points, see Carrell (1970).

In the cases we have considered (and we have made only a small selection) it should be borne in mind that the writers were not innovating for the sake of novelty. In each instance there were major problems that could not be handled in a natural way within the standard theory.

One final weakening should be mentioned. As presented in Chapter 5, the terms of the structure index of a transformation could include not only categories of the base but also references to the feature composition of items. This in itself represents a weakening of the original theory of transformational grammars, since it is possible to do almost any kind of special coding by means of features. This point will be of importance when we come to look at some recent claims about transformation-like operations that are non-Markovian in character, in other words, that require knowledge of something beyond the immediate form of a P-marker.

9.4 Transformations Plus and Minus

In Chapter 8 we noted the extreme power of transformations. Given the formal definition of a transformation, there are any number of "crazy" rules that could be formulated and that any linguist with a little experience would know to be impossible. For example, the formal definition of transformations allows a rule of the following form:

$$X, NP, Aux, V, NP, Prep, NP, Adverb, Y$$
$$1 \quad 2 \quad 3 \quad 4 \quad 5 \quad 6 \quad 7 \quad 8 \quad 9 \Rightarrow$$
$$6 \quad 3 \quad 8 \quad 7 \quad 4 \quad 1 \quad 5 \quad 2 \quad 9$$

No linguist would ever think of looking for such a rule. If he did find one and could really justify it, it would (and should) constitute a major shake-up in linguistic thinking. But quite aside from implausible rules like this, many rules that are logically possible, and do not even seem to be particularly implausible, seem not to occur in natural languages. For example, there seems to be good evidence for some kind of a subject-raising rule in English (Section 7.3), but as far as I know no language exhibits a rule that would be quite similar in its formal nature, namely, taking the subject of a higher sentence and making it the object of a complement sentence.

Theories like those of Emonds represent attempts to account for these enormous gaps in the actual choice of transformations that occur in natural languages. In Chapter 11 I will present a substantive theory of transformations that attempts to meet this issue in a rather different way. The point to be made here is that the definition of *transformation* is too wide, since it allows all sorts of rules that are never encountered in actual linguistic work. Since the central aim of linguistics is to delimit exactly the set of possible languages, this must be considered a major defect.

On the other hand, there seem to be linguistic phenomena that require rules going beyond the formal restrictions on transformations. One that we have looked at is Reflexive. Recall that one of the restrictions on transformations is that they require only Boolean conditions (that is, statements using *and, or,* and *not*) on their structural analyses. But the condition that seems to be required for reflexivization goes beyond this restriction. For Reflexive to work properly, it is necessary to state one of the following equivalent conditions:

NP_1 and NP_2 (the reflexivizing and reflexivized NP) must be part of all the same sentences (in structures dominated by all the same S nodes).

NP_1 and NP_2 must command each other (an element A is said to **command** an element B if B is part of structure dominated by the first S above A, Langacker, 1969).

There is no S such that S dominates a structure containing NP_1 but not NP_2.

As the first and third of these conditions make clear, quantification must be used over elements of the P-marker; in other words, the transformations require more than Boolean conditions.

In defining transformations, we also stipulated that the number of terms in the structure index must be a fixed finite number. Yet there seem to be processes in natural languages that are best stated in terms of an indefinite number of terms, so that the rule for such a process is actually a schema for an infinite number of rules. One such rule is Gapping (Ross, 1970a). Consider these pairs:

John ordered meat, and Bill ordered fish.
John ordered meat; and Bill, fish.

Mary went to New York, Harry went to Washington, and Sally went to Waukegan.
Mary went to New York; Harry, to Washington; and Sally, to Waukegan.

Mary ate a turnip, Sharon cooked a steak, and Bill ate a parsnip.
*Mary ate a turnip; Sharon cooked a steak and Bill, a parsnip (*for a paraphrase of the preceding sentence).

Ross proposed a rule that has essentially this form:

SD: *NP, V, X,   NP,   V,   X*
       1   2 3 3n+1 3n+2 3n+3 ⇒
       1   2 3 3n+1   ∅   3n+3
   Conditions: 2 = 3n+2, 1 ≠ 3n+1, 3 ≠ 3n+3
            n = 1, 2, 3, . . .
            heavy stress on all but the verbs

The rule is actually even more complicated to state than this, but the important thing to note is that it has an infinite number of terms in its structure index and cannot be stated as a transformation in the strict sense. Coordinate structures in general seem to be the typical cases that demand rule schemata rather than strict transformations. Suppose we wish to derive a structure like *B* from a structure like *A:*

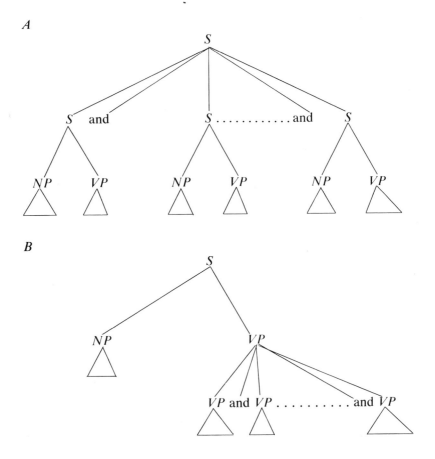

It seems likely that, instead of carrying out an intricate series of "regular" transformations, we should be able — at one step — to check the identity conditions on the elements and produce the new structure in one kind of rule. The purpose of linguistics is to find the kinds of rules that languages seem to demand, rather than to fit them into a preconceived formalism. (Examples of such treatments of coordinate structures may be found in Gleitman, 1969, and Schane, 1966.)

In both the case of non-Boolean conditions and that of indefinite numbers of terms in the structure index of a transformation, it is desirable to search for general conditions capable of limiting the type of rule that would be allowed to violate the restriction in question. A general characteristic of linguistic theory at present — and this is true of phonology as well as syntax and semantics — is that we probably have a much too simplistic picture of the structure of a grammar. As we develop more knowledge about all aspects of language, we can expect that our picture will become much more complex.

In the case of coordinate structures, a rather obvious characteristic of the types of constructions may be relevant. Many linguists (see Section 11.3) have suggested limiting the number of different base categories that should be available to a grammar, for example, to three: *S, NP, V.* Obviously, just about any semantic content can be stated in terms of elements like these. Suppose, in particular, that conjunctions are considered a type of verb. They differ from all other verbs in that they can take an indefinite number of arguments or *NP*'s, *S*'s or the like. Given that transformations often involve verbs, we would be able to look at a transformation and tell whether it is a schema for an infinite number of rules or just one, merely by noting whether the verb involved is of the type that requires a fixed number of possible complements or an indefinite number. This amounts to saying that infinite rule schemata are limited to coordinate structures.

9.5 Abstract Elements

Consider two theories of syntax that differ as to the relationship between surface (say, phonologically manifested) elements and the underlying formatives associated with them. The first theory, which we may call *concrete,* requires that every underlying formative have a corresponding bit of phonological material associated with it (a **morph**) unless it can be shown that some formatives disappear in the environment of other phonologically manifested formatives. But in no case would a formative be manifested everywhere as ∅ (that is, there are "zero morphs" but no "zero morphemes").

The second theory, which we may call *abstract,* does not contain any such condition; it may happen that some underlying formatives never have a phonological reflex.

So-called concrete theories fall roughly within the range of the types of syntactic theories that were being sought by structural linguists at about the time when Chomsky's *Syntactic Structures* (1957) appeared (see Bach, 1965a, for the general background, and Hill, 1958; Bloch and Trager, 1942; Joos, 1957, for examples).

From this point of view, all versions of transformational theory are abstract. The freedom to set up hypothetical underlying forms, which might disappear without a trace in the surface structures, represented a great step forward, mainly because it offered what appears to be a truer recognition of the complex and possibly quite indirect relationship between underlying and surface forms and because it recognized frankly the abstract nature of all linguistic elements. After all, if a phoneme is an abstract element (as was already clearly recognized, although within a rather different framework and with different conclusions, in Twaddell, 1935), then we can turn from the relatively uninteresting question of whether linguistic theory should admit abstract elements (which, like every other science, it does) to the question of just what sorts of abstract linguistic elements there are.

Concrete theories are obviously stricter than abstract theories (in the temporary special sense we have given the terms *concrete* and *abstract*). Therefore, it is incumbent upon us to look for restrictions on setting up abstract underlying formatives that do not appear in surface structures. A general answer to this need for restrictions has not yet appeared, and perhaps we can only deal with individual cases as such. Let us, however, look at two analyses in which relatively great use has been made of the ability to set up abstract underlying "zero" elements.

Katz and Postal (1964) attempted to show that many transformations, originally formulated as meaning-changing optional transformations, should be "triggered" obligatorily by certain abstract elements in underlying structures. The reanalysis was part of a program to find syntactic justification for the position that the semantic content of a sentence is determined solely by the underlying structure of a sentence. More precisely, Katz and Postal defended a thesis that went part way toward the semantic hypothesis of the standard theory by claiming that the only contribution of transformations to the semantic reading of a sentence is to compound the semantic readings of sentences in transformations that embed or compound sentence structures. In other words, their claim was that there are no meaning-changing "singular" (see above, p. 134) transformations. One example of such a reanalysis was that of the imperative.

The underlying structure for imperative sentences was claimed by Katz and Postal to be something like this:

Imp you will *VP*

Various kinds of evidence were offered for this analysis. For example, sentences like the following one are ambiguous:

You will go home.

The sentence can be a prediction or a command. If underlying structures (of simple sentences) determine meaning, then there must be a difference between the underlying structures for the two different sentences amalgamated in the above. But since this was just an instance of the general hypothesis they defended, it was necessary to give other arguments in terms of selectional restrictions and the like (as in Section 7.73) in order not to beg the general question.

The element *Imp*, which disappears in the operation of the imperative transformation, is an abstract element (as we have used the term). But an unrestricted use of such abstract elements is undesirable. Some attention is paid to this problem in Katz and Postal (1964), mainly by way of positing a universal fixed set of underlying abstract elements such as *Imp* and *Q* (for questions).

Our second example comes from the period during which the complex nature of syntactic elements, as discussed in Chapter 4, made its way into linguistic theory. Beginning with G. Lakoff (1970a (1965)) and continuing through much work along the "generative-semantic" line, it has been proposed that instead of unanalyzable and totally unique elements such as *Imp*, the underlying structures of many (if not all) sentences contain various abstract elements, particularly verbs, that are complexes of features (like other formatives) but are deleted in the course of the derivation of a sentence. To take up the imperative example again, we might posit a source for (2) in some underlying structure such as (1), where the complex abstract elements are represented in bold letters:

1. **I order** you [you will go home]
2. Go home!

Arguments for such analyses fall into several classes. First of all, we may be able to show that independently needed transformations will do part of the work of deriving (2) from (1). In this example, one might be able to show that Equi would delete the *you* that we saw to be necessary for Imperative (Sections 5.4 and 6.3). Second, we can show that many facts about sentences with overt verbs of commanding and so on are paralleled by facts about simple imperatives. Then we can argue that *if* the former facts are accounted for in our grammar, by positing abstract underlying structures like (1) we can explain properties of the resultant simple structures in the same way. The *if*-clause is essential. Suppose we can show that some other theory, say a theory of language use or "speech acts" (Searle 1969), exists apart from grammars or as a separate component; then the facts can be accounted for in a uniform way there and we do not need the abstract elements.[3] But, as an inescapable consequence of such analyses, there must be transformations that delete the abstract elements. (In the next section we will mention what appears to be a very strict theory that countenances no deletion transformations whatsoever, and see that the necessary extra apparatus in the form of special rules of interpretation gives back with one hand what is taken away by the other.) Many interesting facts have been uncovered and many interesting analyses proposed with the use of such abstract elements, but in one way or another they represent a weakening in practice, if not in principle, of the standard theory.[4]

9.6 The Relationship between Semantics and Syntax

In this section we will examine in much too brief a way what has probably been the most debated development in syntax since *Aspects:* the controversy between **interpretive** and **generative** semanticists.

We must first face a terminological problem. The position called "interpretive" is one in which various rules of semantic interpretation are posited as parts of a grammar. In this sense, the standard theory is interpretive. But the particular theory we are dealing with claims that besides the projection rules that operate on the deep structures, there are other rules of interpretation that depend on surface structures, or intermediate structures, or even several at once. This view has been called the "extended standard theory" by Chomsky in recent publications (1972a; see also 1971). It seems to me that this term begs a historical question. The opposing theory of "generative" semantics could equally be considered an "extended standard theory." On the other hand, other terms — "surfacism" and the like — that have been suggested are misleading or

---

3. For a semiserious *reductio ad absurdum* argument tending in the latter direction, see Bach (1971c).

4. Sources besides those mentioned for study of the question of "abstract verbs" are especially R. Lakoff (1968) and Ross (1970b).

rhetorically objectionable. The issues are clear enough (even though, as we shall see, probably undecidable at present). I use the term "interpretive semantics" both narrowly and broadly. In the present and following chapters, and unless specifically stipulated otherwise, I will use *interpretive* to refer to Chomsky's "extended standard theory" and mean a theory claiming that there is a special set of interpretive semantic rules, in particular, rules that depend on more than just information represented in the deep structures (as in the classical theory of Katz, 1966). When we wish to refer to a theory claiming that deep structures alone determine the semantic reading of sentences by means of rules of interpretation, I will call it the standard interpretive theory (on the analogy of the standard syntactic theory).

It would take many more pages than I am willing to devote to it to untangle the many specific claims and counterclaims that have been made in the controversy and to follow the many variations that have occurred in the course of the last few years. I therefore issue a disclaimer at this point and urge the reader who is so inclined to read the recent writings of such authors as G. Lakoff, R. Lakoff, McCawley, Postal, and Ross, and works referred to by them, for the "generativist" view. For the interpretivist view, one may consult the recent writings of Chomsky, Jackendoff (especially 1972), Akmajian, Dougherty, Hasegawa, and others (a good summary is given in Partee, 1971).

Instead, I will focus on a few aspects of the controversy and provide a general critique of the framework of discussion. The conclusions will be that many new facts have been uncovered by the discussion, but that no sufficiently precise and complete theory has been presented in enough detail to allow even a tentative judgment. I will also argue that for these and other reasons the conflict is actually unresolvable. Even though I do not claim to give a complete picture of either side of the controversy (and indeed none has been given), I believe my critique is general enough to establish that the conclusions will hold even if the missing details are filled in.

We will concentrate on two issues: Are there rules of interpretation that depend on more than deep structures? Is there a level of deep structures distinct from semantic representations? The interpretive theory answers both questions in the affirmative; the generative-semantic theory answers them both negatively.

9.61 Rules of Interpretation

Consider sentences (1) and (2), the forms of which we have claimed to be related by Passive:

1. John didn't date many girls.
2. Many girls weren't dated by John.

In ordinary interpretations, these sentences mean something like the following:

1a. It is not true that John dated many girls.
2a. It is not true of many girls that John dated them.

A proponent of an interpretive theory of negation and quantifiers like *many* (see, for example, Jackendoff, 1972) would argue that it is incorrect to block the application of Passive to such structures as the one underlying (1), and perhaps also incorrect to make it obligatory for the structures underlying sentences like (2), or to posit different deep structures that would then by some other rules result in just the right correspondences of meanings and surface structures. Rather, he would claim, a general principle involving order from left to right in *surface structures* determines the possible readings. Thus, the semantic interpretation is contingent only in part on the deep structure. The deep structures determine only the collocations of predicates and arguments that enter into the final interpretation, while other parts of the interpretation, such as those involving scopes of quantifiers, relations between pronouns and antecedents, and negation of all or part of a sentence, are dependent on surface structures or even on intermediate structures. (And some of the interpretive rules must apply cyclically; see Jackendoff, 1972.)

Proponents of generative semantics, on the other hand, would claim that the sentences do indeed have different deeper representations and that rules and principles that are in part, at least, independently needed will explain the difference. For example, G. Lakoff (1970d, 1971) has argued that the deep structure of the respective sentences is something like this:

1b. *Neg* the girls [John dated the girls] be many
2b. the girls [*Neg* John dated the girls] be many

In support of the interpretive position, we can argue that supposedly optional transformations like a rule of Topicalization or Question-movement can restore the missing interpretations when the relative positions of negative elements and quantifiers are changed again:

1c. Many girls John didn't date.
1d. How many girls didn't John date?

In support of the generativist position, we can point to sentences that presumably have very much the same form as the underlying structures we have posited and do show the expected interpretations:

The girls that John didn't date were many.
The girls that weren't dated by John were many.

I claim that the problem of decision here is one of theory. Each theory makes use of a number of additions to grammatical theory: for the interpretivists, special rules of interpretation of relatively unrestricted form and with unlimited possibilities for interaction with other parts of the grammar; for the generativists, special kinds of abstract underlying structure, ad hoc transformations, and constraints on derivations of practically unlimited power (see Section 9.7). In other words, I believe we are in a theoretical impasse that can be stated in the form of a thesis:

Generative and interpretive semantic-syntactic theories are strongly equivalent.

In other words, whatever facts, predictions, structural assignments, and the like we choose, given a description in one theory we can find one that covers the same facts, makes the same predictions, and assigns the same structural descriptions in the other. I cannot show this, because the necessary precise theory construction has been done for neither theory. But it can be shown to be reasonable from the fact that both theories appear to be weaker than the standard theory (in the sense of Section 9.2) and from some mathematical results that will be presented in Chapter 11. Until the necessary theoretical sharpening and tightening has been done, the great masses of papers that have appeared and been circulated in the controversy are merely presentations of interesting data, which must someday be measured against a yet-to-be-constructed theory.

9.62 Deep Structures = Semantic Interpretations?

Throughout this book we have considered many examples showing that there must be a level of representation on which we can show the difference between sentences with similar or identical surface structures and the similarity between sentences with sharply different surface structures. In the standard theory, the structural description of a sentence includes at least three elements: a surface structure, a deep structure, and a semantic reading. A very natural question, then, is: Are not the deeper similarities among sentences sufficiently represented in the semantic reading of a sentence? In fact, are not deep structures the same as semantic readings? Beginning with an unpublished note by Ross and Lakoff in 1967, and partly independently, a number of linguists arrived at some variant of the conclusion that something like the deepest syntactic representation of a sentence is actually the same as its semantic representation. This conclusion is closely tied to a topic of Chapter 11, the Universal Base Hypothesis. There we will see that this question itself, if taken in conjunction with some reasonable hypotheses about the universality of semantic representations, is unresolvable within present theory; and we will look at some revisions of the theory that render the question answerable. Here we focus on several selected topics and arguments, with the understanding that the discussion is incomplete. Once again, the reader is referred to works of the generative semanticists like those mentioned above. I also mention some specific papers below.[5] Before turning to these specific questions, we need to clear away a little underbrush.

The question of the identity of deep structures and semantic representations (or put differently, "Do deep structures exist?" the title of the unpublished note mentioned above by Ross and Lakoff) must not be confused with the question whether there is a semantic "component" in a grammar or grammar-cum-general-theory. It seems to me that the latter question must be answered affirmatively by anyone who reflects on the matter. First of all, a description of a linguistic system in its entirety must have "rules of semantic interpretation" of the sort posited by logicians, stating the condition under which certain sentences are true, false, analytic, contradictory, and so on. For example, consider these results of such semantic rules:

1. The sentence *The moon is blue* is true if and only if the moon is blue. (Carnap, 1939)
2. A widower is a man.
3. A widower is a fine woman.

(1) is a typical, if rough, example of a rule giving the truth conditions for a sentence. (2) is analytic because the predicate expressed by *widower* contains the predicates expressed by *man,* and (3) is contradictory because it affirms of some object that it both does and does not have some property (Katz, 1966). Second, there must be some rules that tell us how to relate

5. Papers that deal specifically with the question of the identity between so-called deep structures and semantic representations are, besides the note of Ross and Lakoff, Chomsky (1972); McCawley (1968a), especially the "Postscript"; Bach (1968).

sentences. For example, sentences may **entail** other sentences, as (1) does (2):

1. My neighbor Henry is an artist.
2. Some person is an artist.

In other words, (1) may be true or false (assuming we know the identity of Henry and so on), but if (1) is true then so is (2). Some sentences are logically equivalent to others, for example these:

The canteloupe is a fruit and the carrot is a vegetable.
The carrot is a vegetable and the canteloupe is a fruit.

(McCawley, 1968a). Many of the other possible relations between sentences are semantic in character, and there must be a semantic component of some sort to give us this information, since such information forms part of what a speaker knows about his or her language.

Moreover, we cannot assume that all the entailments, equivalences, and the like are part of the semantic representation (deep structure) of a sentence. It is simple to show this in the case of entailments. Whatever else basic representations may be, they are, in present linguistic theories, finitely long objects. But we can show that a sentence can have an infinite number of entailments. Thus, (1) above entails not only (2) but also these sentences:

Henry is not someone who is not an artist.
Henry is not an abstract object.

Since an infinite number of structures could fit the place of *abstract object* in the last sentence — for example, *the number 1, the number 2, ...* — (1) entails an infinite number of sentences (see Cohen, 1971), and not all the entailments of a sentence can be represented directly in the finite basic structure. Hence there must be a semantic component that derives information about the semantic content of a sentence and relates it to other sentences. The question we are concerned with is not the existence of rules of entailment, truth conditions, equivalence, and so on, but rather: What is the nature of the objects that enter into these rules and are related by them? In particular, are they to be identified with the deep structures of the standard theory? Let us focus our attention on two questions that can be untangled from the network of assumptions and claims that have been made around this question.

First, let us ask the question: Are semantic representations phrase-markers? In the standard theory (with the concomitant semantic theory of Katz), they are not. In the generative semantic view, they are.

To say that semantic representations can be phrase-markers is to say very little (Chomsky, 1972), since just about any imaginable system of logic, or language, can be represented in the form of labeled directed trees defined in terms of three relations: the labeling relation, the dominance relation, and the precedence (left-to-right) relations. Thus, the important question is not whether semantic representations *can* take the form of phrase-markers, but whether they *should* take this form (again, we must move from sufficiency toward necessity).

Several types of arguments can be given to support the view that semantic representations (let us continue to call them by the neutral term *basic structures*) are indeed of the same formal nature as phrase-markers.

First, by a stricter-theory argument we can say that we need to countenance phrase-markers anyway (Section 3.6) and that a theory asserting that all syntactic-semantic representations are phrase-markers is stricter than one asserting that only some are.

Second, at the level of lexical representation we need to have the left-to-right part of the phrase-marker hypothesis anyway (*top* $\neq$ *pot*). Hence it is more parsimonious to consider this relation to hold between lexical elements as well as within them.

Further, conjunctions of sentences show the same properties as do (ordered) discourses (this argument is due to David Dowty in a class presentation at the University of Texas at Austin). For example, we impose the same temporality interpretations on the pair (1) as on the pair (2):

1. Sally got married and she got pregnant.
   Sally got pregnant and she got married.

2. Sally got married. She got pregnant.
   Sally got pregnant. She got married.

Thus, we see that at the outer and inner limits of the level of sentences, precedence relations play a role in linguistic representations. Since precedence relations are part of the definition of a phrase-marker, we can support this part of the phrase-marker hypothesis.

Third, questions of scope of negations and the like can be stated naturally in terms of the dominance relations among various elements, and "binding" relations among items like antecedents and their pronouns in terms of precedence relations. Hence we have very natural machinery for expressing part of what we know to be necessary in giving the semantic representation of a sentence. To be convincing, however, this argument must be bolstered by showing that the semantic representations are determined (solely) by the basic representations. Further, many equivalent systems can do the same necessary jobs, so that it is difficult to decide among them. In other words, we run again into the theoretical impasse that we reached in Section 9.61.

Fourth, the input to a rule of semantic interpretation is a phrase-marker. If we can show that the output should also be a phrase-marker, we can support the position that the ultimate semantic representations are also phrase-markers. Suppose that there is a rule relating the structures underlying sentences like (1) to those underlying sentences like (2):

1. John went swimming but Mary didn't want him to go swimming.
2. John went swimming but Mary didn't want him to.

What is the nature of the rule? If it is a semantic rule of interpretation, then it interprets (1) as (2) and we assume that the input of the rule is a phrase-marker. What is its output? By considering sentences in which the rule would have to apply twice in succession, we can conclude that the output must also be a phrase-marker:

3. John wanted to go swimming but Mary didn't want him to.

Let us assume that (3) is interpreted as (4):

4. John wanted to go swimming but Mary didn't want him to want to go swimming.

For reasons of parsimony and generality we can argue that the same rule must be invoked to relate (4) to (3) as was used to relate (1) to (2). Therefore, there is an intermediate step of this form:

5. John wanted to go swimming but Mary didn't want him to want to.

But then (5), which is the output of the rule, must also be the input to the rule, and the rule must both operate on and produce a phrase-marker. Examples like these (Grinder and Postal, 1971; Lakoff, 1970c) have been used to support a narrower position than the one facing us, namely: the so-called rules of interpretation that relate sentences of the forms cited are garden-variety transformational deletions. Some linguists have argued that there are no deletions, that no lexical material is lost in the course of a derivation. But examples like those above seem to show that, whatever the nature of the rules of semantic interpretation, they fall within the general definition of transformations as rules that relate phrase-markers. Once this is admitted, we can return to the details of finding out what kinds of transformations they are and how they are related; that is, we turn from a terminological to a substantive question. The conclusion we can draw for our present purposes is that some putative rules of interpretation share the phrase-marker-relating properties of transformations, and hence support the general position that semantic representations are phrase-markers.

With the usual qualification—namely, that the theories under discussion are not susceptible to complete comparison—we conclude tentatively that part of the thesis of the generativists, that semantic representations are phrase-markers, can be supported. Because of the many unknowns we must be tentative. And if our general thesis (p. 225); is correct, one reason for qualification is that careful theory construction is still needed before we can either show the truth of our thesis of the equivalence of generative and interpretive theories, or derive some crucial consequences that would allow us to decide between them on empirical grounds. Let us now turn to a brief consideration of a second major question.

Is there a single level of deep structure, intermediate between semantic representations and surface structures, with the properties of the deep structures of the standard theory? Two essential propositions of the standard theory are these:

    I. Aside perhaps from grammatical formatives introduced by transformations, the entire lexical content of the sentence is present in the deep structure.

    II. No transformations (in the usual sense) precede the operation of lexical insertion.

We will consider two kinds of arguments that have been offered against I and II. Both rest on a general argument of the Occam's Razor type. If we can do what we need to do (show similarities and differences among surface structures) by means of semantic representations, then the burden of proof falls on those who claim that there exists a third kind of entity besides the surface structure and the semantic representation (remote or basic structure).

The first argument is modeled on a well-known argument used by Halle (1959) in phonological theory to show that there is no level of phonological representation corresponding exactly to the phonemic representation of then-current structuralist phonology. The form of argument is that of the Missing Generalization. Consider a language with the stops /p t k b d/ as basic phonological units and a rule, say, that assimilates the voicing of a stop to that of an immediately following stop. (This example is modeled on Modern Dutch, while Halle's example was Russian; such situations have been shown to exist in many languages.) The rule of assimilation will have the following results:

Underlying form:	bt	bd	kt	kd
Result of rule:	pt	bd	kt	gd

Standard ("taxonomic") structuralist theory (see Chomsky, 1964, for discussion and references) would require that there be two rules for one process: one replacing stops of one sort by their voiced or voiceless counterpart phonemes in a particular environment, the other choosing the voiced or voiceless "allophone" or conditioned variant of the phoneme /k/ under exactly the same conditions. In other words, in order to keep a representation that would correspond to the taxonomic representation, we would have to have a representation intermediate to the two above, in which the clusters are represented as follows:

Taxonomic representation:	pt	bd	kt	kd

If we drop one of the requirements of the taxonomic representation ("biuniqueness"; see Chomsky, 1964) we can capture the generalization in a single rule.

Now consider the following example from syntax (given in Bach, 1968). The following two sentences are ambiguous in the same way:

1. John is looking for a secretary who knows Mongolian.
2. John is trying to find a secretary who knows Mongolian.

Both can have either of these two interpretations:

There is a secretary who knows Mongolian that John is trying to find.

John is trying to find a secretary who meets the requirement of knowing Mongolian.

If the thesis of the last section, that semantic representations are phrase-markers, is accepted, then we can argue for a representation of the different interpretations in terms of the position of the quantifier or indefinite noun phrase with respect to the various sentences involved. But in the theory of deep structures incorporating Proposition I, at the deep-structure level the requisite sentence node is missing in (1), although present in (2):

1.

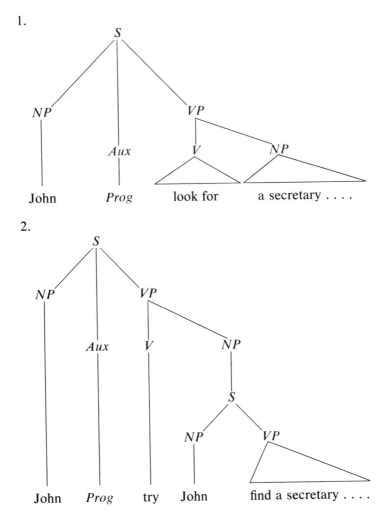

2.

Thus, it is impossible to state the principle or principles governing the different interpretations uniformly for the two cases. On the other hand, if (1) has an underlying structure like that of (2) the generalization can be stated. However, we have violated Proposition I, since the lexical item *look for* has been split into several parts.[6]

---

6. In Bach (1968) I argued for an intermediate position, in which all but the phonological representation was present in the deep structure, and the theory was allowed to associate lexical items not just with single nodes in a phrase-marker but with whole chunks of them. McCawley (1968a) presents a similar argument in terms of the derivation of sentences with *respectively*.

Many analyses from the generativist point of view have been presented that violate Proposition II, in that certain transformations such as Predicate-Raising (McCawley, 1971) may precede lexical insertion. The strongest case against the proposition could be made if we could show that some transformations, which apply in clear cases to what everyone agrees to be a syntactic structure, must be assumed to operate before the insertion of certain lexical items. The clearest case has been made by Postal (1970a). Postal argues from the many similarities between sentences like (1) and (2) below that the underlying representation of (1) must be like that of (2), and that therefore some of the transformational operations and their associated restrictions must both precede and follow lexical insertion (contrary to Proposition II):

1. Harry reminds me of a rhesus monkey.
2. It strikes me that Harry and a rhesus monkey are alike.

A good deal of the ensuing discussion of Postal's analysis of *remind* turns on the question of the grammaticality and interpretation of examples like this (Kimball, 1970; Bolinger, 1971):

? Harry reminds John of himself.
? Harry reminds himself of a rhesus monkey.

Apparently, speakers' reactions to such sentences are not uniform (even after we have cleared away all the possible disturbing factors, possibilities of varying meanings for *remind* and so on, that are noted by Postal). The situation is typical of much recent discussion in this respect. The crucial examples for deciding between theories are of such an indeterminate status that it is impossible to interpret them as evidence. In earlier work on transformational grammar, Chomsky (1957) took the position that we should decide among theories on the basis of the clear cases, and let our decisions lead us to answers about the unclear cases. But in the framework of the generativist-interpretivist debate the only thing that has become clear is that the crucial cases are precisely the unclear ones. This fact leads us to one of the final conclusions in this book (Section 11.6). We need to look to new *kinds* of data to help determine our theories. One new kind is the very fact that some cases are clearer than others, and indeed some linguists have begun to use such data to help decide which of several analyses to choose. If one analysis leads us to think that some class of sentences should fall neatly into two categories of grammaticalness, and another allows us to predict just which cases will be unclear (perhaps by the mediation of some other hypotheses) or tells us where we may expect speaker variation of various kinds,[7] then we have a basis for choice.

9.7 Derivational Constraints

The standard theory makes these assumptions about derivations from a grammar (ignoring the role of the cycle):

I. Part of the derivation of a sentence is a sequence D of phrase-markers: $P_1, P_2, \ldots, P_n$, where P_1 is a deep structure and P_n is a surface structure.

II. In order to check whether D is indeed a proper derivation from a grammar, it is only necessary to look at pairs of phrase-markers in the sequence D that are immediately adjacent (P_i, P_{i+1}) and note whether they satisfy some transformation.

In other words, the primary rule of the transformational part of a grammar is a rule relating pairs of adjacent phrase-markers in the derivational sequence. There are no rules that must operate on or relate pairs not immediately adjacent, or that might have to relate more than two phrase-markers. This assumption has been challenged by G. Lakoff and others in a number of papers (most accessible is G. Lakoff, 1970b). G. Lakoff claims that "ordinary" transformations of the sort that we have been discussing are only special cases of a much more general kind of "global rule" or, as he later calls it, "derivational constraint," which does not meet Condition II. Let us consider a simple example, by which we can also show the difficulties involved in resolving the theoretical questions.

In Chapter 7 we considered in some detail the standard analysis of the transformation There and its interaction with Passive and Raising. Now consider the following sentences:

There were believed to be two unicorns in the garden.
There was believed to be a unicorn in the garden.

As these examples show, the verb in the topmost sentence, in which *there* finally appears as subject, must agree in number with a noun phrase that is the subject of the embedded sentence. The number agreement cannot take place cyclically because we have not reached the relevant

---

7. Examples of such extensions of the range of data to include speaker variations are Carden (1970) and Elliott, Legum, and Thompson (1969).

verb on the first cycle involving the verb of the embedded sentence; and when we reach the relevant sentence, we would have to be able to *find* the right *NP* in a sentence that may be (as we saw in Section 7.5) indefinitely far away. One might then propose a derivational constraint that would state precisely what we have just stated informally. That such a "rule" would violate the conditions for a transformation can be clearly seen from the language of the formulation: the verb that at *this* point of the derivation has *there* as its subject must agree with the *NP* that *was* the subject of the relevant embedded sentence at an earlier point of the derivation.

This example remains weak unless we are able to show that other analyses of the relevant structures are to be ruled out or that we cannot or should not get around the problem in various ad hoc ways. For example, it would be possible to mark *there* for number as part of the There transformation. Then we would have the necessary information at the right point of the derivation. Or we could reformulate There so that it can apply across an indefinite number of intervening verbs, carrying structures like the first of the following ones directly into structures like the second (on the "top" cycle):

someone *Tns* be believed to be imagined. ... to be *X*

there   *Tns* be believed to be imagined. ... to be someone *X*

This example shows the difficulty of the question. It is at present possible to do almost anything in any of the various competing "theories," so that arguments for the necessity of new, more powerful devices are virtually impossible. Once again we are driven back to the general conclusion that more theoretical tightening must be done before we can even ask questions about derivational constraints.[8]

9.8 Conclusions

In this chapter I have given a review and critique of some developments in syntactic theory since *Aspects*. I have chosen topics especially relevant to the development of ideas in this book. A great deal of syntactic work that I have not even mentioned has been done both on general and

---

8. A number of recent articles, for example, Casagrande (1970) and G. Lakoff (1970b), have presented arguments for derivational constraints. A recent critique of Lakoff (1970b) is Baker and Brame (1972). More recently G. Lakoff and others have argued that certain facts must be handled by "transderivational" constraints, that is, "rules" that make reference to several derivations, not just to phrase-markers at various points in a single derivation.

special topics. Therefore, the reader who wishes to fill in missing details should consult the recent volumes and issues of such journals as *Language, Linguistic Inquiry, Papers in Linguistics, The Journal of Linguistics, Foundations of Language,* and the annual publications of the Chicago Linguistic Society, as well as the collections of preliminary reports and working papers of a semipublished or privately circulated nature that are to be found in the departmental libraries and offices of major linguistics departments.

One general conclusion has emerged again and again in the latter portions of this chapter. Many questions cannot be raised because of the necessity for preliminary theoretical work that will narrow down the extremely broad existing restrictions on possible grammars. In Chapter 11 we will consider some mathematical results showing a fortiori that the questions are unanswerable for systems at least as powerful as the standard theory.

10

Explanations in Linguistics

10.1 Procedure

The notion of explanation has loomed large in general discussions of linguistic theory in the last several decades. In this chapter I will first take up some notions deriving from a consideration of goals for linguistic theory and then put the discussion of various levels of success in linguistics into the context of a more general account of explanatory hypotheses.

10.2 Levels of Adequacy in Linguistics

In Chomsky (1964, p. 62), as well as in various other writings, three levels of adequacy are defined: observational, descriptive, and explanatory. A grammar is said to be **observationally adequate** if it "presents the observed primary data correctly." By "primary data" is meant examples of actual utterances. If we are thinking of a linguist constructing a grammar, we may take the primary data to be a corpus of transcribed utterances. Since any listing of the data (even if abbreviated and organized in some way) would constitute an observationally adequate grammar, this level holds little interest. In particular, such a grammar would provide no way of predicting what further utterances might be possible in the language.[1]

---

1. Sometimes the term is used in an extended sense to relate to what we have called weak generative capacity (Section 8.2). A grammar is observationally adequate in this sense if it correctly predicts what is and what is not a grammatical sentence in a language. See, for example, Prideaux (1970). On the notions we are considering here, see especially Chomsky (1964); Chomsky and Halle (1965); Householder (1965); Chomsky (1965) and (1972b: Lecture 2). A good deal of this chapter is adapted from Bach, 1974.

There is an intentional ambiguity in such discussions of primary data, grammar construction, and the like. On the one hand, we may be thinking of the acquisition of a language by the child (or other learner). In this instance, the primary data are the utterances from which the child learns his language, and the grammar is his internalized competence. On the other hand, we may think of the problem in terms of a linguist constructing a grammar, as above. This ambiguity is legitimate only within the context of a theory that makes some psychological claims about the set of grammars given by the theory. On this account, linguistic theory attempts to reconstruct explicitly what the child does by virtue of his innate linguistic abilities, and thus the theory embodies a set of hypotheses about the linguistic abilities of the human mind. We return to this point below.

A grammar is said to reach the level of **descriptive** adequacy if it gives "a correct account of the linguistic intuitions of the native speaker" (Chomsky, 1964, p. 63). In another place (Chomsky, 1965, p. 24) the following explanation is given:

> A grammar can be regarded as a theory of a language: it is *descriptively adequate* to the extent that it correctly describes the intrinsic competence of the idealized native speaker. The structural descriptions assigned to sentences by the grammar, the distinctions that it makes between well-formed and deviant, and so on, must, for descriptive adequacy, correspond to the linguistic intuition of the native speaker (whether or not he is immediately aware of this) in a substantial and significant class of crucial cases.

As Peters (1970) has remarked, two quite distinct notions may be involved in this latter characterization. On the one hand, a descriptively adequate grammar provides sets of structural descriptions that correspond to intuitions of a native speaker. But on the other hand, if the grammar "correctly describes the intrinsic competence of the idealized native speaker" something more is demanded, a correspondence not just to the derivable structural descriptions but to the rules themselves.

To make this difference clear, let us consider two grammars of English, both of which relate sentences like the following ones transformationally and assign them the same sets of semantic interpretations, deep phrase markers, and surface structures:

John saw Sally yesterday.
Sally was seen by John yesterday.

Suppose one grammar relates the sentences by a single passive transformation of the sort discussed above (Sections 5.3, 7.5), while the other grammar contains two distinct transformations, each carrying out a part of the structural change (Chomsky, 1970, argues for such a reformulation).

If we attribute some kind of psychological reality to the rules of the grammar, then the two accounts would be making different claims about the competence of the idealized speaker of English, but not about the sets of structural descriptions corresponding to the speaker's intuitions (unless we want to make a claim that speakers have intuitions about rules, which seems to have no basis).

The terms *observational* and *descriptive adequacy* apply primarily to grammars, but both can be applied secondarily to general (meta-) theories about grammars. A general theory is descriptively adequate if it defines a class of grammars that can be shown in principle to meet whatever criteria we take to constitute descriptive adequacy for grammars. Since just about any way of organizing data would meet the level of observational adequacy, this term is rarely used for general theories (except in the extended sense of the footnote on p. 237).

We can show that a particular analysis (that is, partial grammar) is descriptively inadequate by showing that it does not correctly characterize intuitions about acceptability, ambiguity, paraphrase relations, and the like. For instance, a grammar of English that failed to show the differences in the way the following sentences are interpreted would be descriptively inadequate:

The student is anxious to understand.
The student is hard to understand.

We have already noted that certain theories of grammar are descriptively inadequate. For example, since finite-state grammars cannot in principle describe self-embedded structures, no finite-state grammar for English can be descriptively adequate (Section 8.2). Similarly, since phrase-structure grammars provide only a single representation of the structure of each sentence, a general theory embodying only such grammars as descriptive devices cannot be descriptively adequate.

In contrast to the two terms so far considered, which apply primarily to grammars and only secondarily to general theories, the third term can be applied only to general theories. A theory is said to reach the level of **explanatory adequacy** if and only if it provides some principled basis for selecting descriptively adequate grammars over grammars that are not (or less) descriptively adequate. Such a theory would be explanatory in the sense that it would answer the question: Why do speakers of a language have the grammars that they have?

Defined in this way, the notion of explanatory adequacy only makes sense in the context of a theory that makes the assumption noted above, that the linguist is providing an account of a psychologically real grammar in the speaker's head. We can schematize the problem as follows:

The box can be thought of as representing either a language acquirer or an explanatorily adequate theory.

Both descriptive adequacy and explanatory adequacy are goals to be aimed for. No one has yet succeeded in finding even one descriptively adequate grammar for a language, nor in proposing any general theory that is explanatorily adequate. On the other hand, various proposals for grammars and theories have been shown to be inadequate in one or another sense. This state of affairs is not surprising when we reflect that in a sense both terms mean "correct" or "true" (with respect to answers to various questions). Notice further that "explanatory adequacy" is being used in a very special sense, not to be equated with a more general notion of explanation (Section 10.4). Essentially, what is expressed in the term is a decision to consider a certain problem, namely, language acquisition, a proper part of what is to be explained by linguistic theory. We could just as well take some other question involving language, for example, "How do people create poetry?" and define as explanatorily adequate only these theories about language that provide some hypothesis about poetic creation. The term has played more of a role in the debate over goals and methods of linguistic inquiry than within linguistic theory itself (although some of the particular proposals about theory that have arisen from the discussion have been central in linguistic theory).

10.3 Explanatory Adequacy

For the time being, let us take as given that the question of language acquisition is a necessary concern of linguistics and that we should seek explanatory theories in this sense. We can separate out two subquestions in attempting to understand how people acquire their linguistic competence: (1) What is the class of grammars from which grammars for particular languages are chosen? (2) Given such a class of possible grammars, how does the child select the grammar (or a grammar) appropriate to his language? In the first instance, we consider absolute limitations on the form or content of grammars. In the second instance, we deal with the problem of selection among those possible grammars.

10.31 Absolute Hypotheses

We have considered in this book a number of theories about linguistic competence. Although none of these theories is in any sense complete, we can still draw some tentative conclusions about various classes of grammars. The theories that seem to offer the greatest promise are those incorporating some kind of a base component specifying an infinite set of underlying or basic structures, plus a different component or set of transformational rules or something like such rules (for example, derivational constraints or various kinds of interpretive rules). Taken together, the various parts of a grammar define an infinite set of well-formed derivations, which serve to pair semantic interpretations and phonetic representations. To the extent that we can justify such theories of grammars over others (such as phrase-structure grammars), we have partially met the requirements of explanatory adequacy.

In addition to the formal specification of types of rules, we found it necessary to place further constraints of various kinds on the operation of the rules. In Section 5.4, we argued for the recoverability condition partly on the basis of the descriptive adequacy of grammars incorporating the condition. Grammars obeying the constraint were shown to be better able to account for judgments of grammaticality, interpretations of sentences, and so on, than grammars violating the constraint. In this instance, the constraint on grammars does not actually lead to the correct analysis of imperatives, reflexives, and so on, but only rules out an infinite number of incorrect analyses, such as those in which we might derive the sentences on the right from the structures underlying the sentences on the left:

Harry never did shut up.	Shut up!
John shaved the first customer that entered his shop.	John shaved himself.

Arguments for or against some restriction on the class of grammars available to the child can be quite complex and indirect. Let us take up an extended example.

One of the ways in which two grammars may differ in the theory presented in Chapter 6 is in the statement of the cyclicity characteristics of particular transformations: some are cyclic, others may be last-cyclic. Presumably, within such a theory the child must notice, at a certain stage of his or her language acquisition, certain crucial sentences that tell him or her whether some rule or other is cyclic or last-cyclic. It would be desirable to find some general way to predict the cyclicity of rules. Let us now consider a general constraint that might be imposed on grammars that would require that certain rules apply cyclically.

In Chapter 8 we cited some mathematical studies showing that transformational grammars are equivalent in weak generative capacity to Turing machines. In some more recent work, Peters and Ritchie (1973) have studied the effect of placing various restrictions on the operation of transformational rules. Recall that in the standard model a well-formed surface structure has to meet the condition that it contain no internal sentence boundaries. This filtering property is used to ensure that embedded sentences appear in the proper contexts and undergo whatever obligatory rules must apply to them. A stronger restriction on grammars would be to require that at the end of every cycle i all internal sentence boundaries have been removed from S_i, the sentence defining that cycle. Grammars meeting this constraint are called **local-filtering** grammars. Peters and Ritchie (1973) have proved that local-filtering grammars are essentially less powerful than ordinary filtering grammars. Some formal languages that can be defined by ordinary filtering grammars cannot be defined by local-filtering grammars. The local-filtering constraint is of linguistic interest because it distinguishes between possible analyses in just the cyclicity properties of rules that we have been considering.

Consider two rules involving embedded sentences: Equi and Raising (Sections 6.3, 7.3). As we have seen, there are convincing arguments that both rules are cyclic in the ordinary sense. Within the theory of Chapter 6, this is an arbitrary property of the rule. But in a grammar meeting the local-filtering constraint the rules must be cyclic (under the assumption that the rules are involved in the removal of internal sentence boundaries).

To see this, consider a sentence involving the obligatory application of Equi:

1. John tried to go to Acapulco.

The underlying structure of this sentence is something like this:

John *Past* try # [for-to John go to Acapulco] #
                 S

There are no sentences with *try* in which Equi does not apply:

*John tried for Sally to go to Acapulco.

Now suppose we erase the internal sentence boundaries when we apply Equi. Consider a sentence in which (1) is embedded one sentence down:

2. Harry said that John tried to go to Acapulco.

The underlying structure for (2) is roughly this:

3. #[Harry said #[that John tried
S_0 S_1

#[John go to Acapulco]#]#]#
S_2

If Equi did not apply until the last cycle, then at the end of the S_1 cycle it could not yet have applied and S_1 would still contain internal sentence boundaries. Hence, in a local-filtering grammar the regular cyclic character of Equi is necessary.

Further, the NP that controls the operation of deleting the NP in the embedded sentence must be present in the first sentence "above" the complement sentence, or else we would pass through a cycle without removing sentence boundaries. This result again seems to be correct (Postal, 1970b). Notice that (4) is unambiguous as to the identity of the underlying subject of *visit,* while (5) is ungrammatical:

4. John wanted Mary to want to visit Sally.
5. *John wanted Mary to try to visit himself.

It follows further, from the local-filtering constraint and the assumption that applications of rules like Equi are involved in the removal of sentence boundaries, that any application of Equi (or similar rules; see Grinder on "Super-Equi," 1970) in which the deleting NP is more than one level of embedding away from the deleted NP must be optional. This result also seems to be correct.

Similar arguments apply to Raising. In its obligatory applications, at least, the rule must be cyclic and it must raise the NP in question just one level "up."

The tentative conclusions we have reached suggest that the local-filtering constraint (or some equivalent condition, or a more general condition from which it might follow) should be added to the definition of "possible grammar for a natural language." The justification of the hypothesis arises when we consider the independent evidence that rules like Equi and Raising are indeed cyclic and have the "adjacency" property that they seem to have. It might be thought that properties like cyclicity have nothing to do with descriptive adequacy, since we are talking about rather abstract features of grammars, but the decisions rest ultimately on intuitions about grammaticality, interpretations of sentences, and so on.

Besides formal constraints on grammars like those we have just considered, it is necessary to impose constraints on the content of grammars. I will take up the question of such substantive constraints in the next chapter. For now, let us merely note that the distinction between formal and substantive constraints is not absolute. Some formal constraints depend on substantive assumptions about the content of grammars. For example, suppose we wish to investigate the hypothesis that transformational rules are cyclically ordered in the grammars of all natural languages. Since the definition of the cycle requires reference to the category S (at least; see Chomsky, 1970, for discussion of other possibly cyclic categories), without the assumption that the grammar of every language contains the category S the cyclic hypothesis would have no predictive power.

10.32 Evaluation Procedures

So far we have said nothing about explanatory adequacy that could not be paralleled in any other discipline. Consider a chemical-physical analogy. A theory of atomic and molecular structure that derives the properties of individual elements and compounds from the laws of interaction of elementary particles has more explanatory power than one that assumes the elements and compounds to be arbitrarily different. The postulation of universals of form and substance in natural languages is exactly like the postulation of an underlying structure for chemical substances.

But the chemical analogy is only partly appropriate. One of the facts about human language that needs to be explained is that any individual's language competence is determined only in part by a general theory of possible grammars. The particulars of his competence — that is, the particular language that he learns — are determined by the linguistic environment. The natural child of parents who speak Tagalog or Chinese, if displaced into a totally English-speaking environment, will learn English, not Tagalog or Chinese. It is thus part of the concern of linguistics to understand how a child comes to know his particular language. Linguistics, like other sciences about socially transmitted behavior, has a double dimension that is lacking in sciences like chemistry. We do not have to account for how chemical elements acquire their properties in infancy. We do have to account for how users of natural languages acquire their knowledge. Linguistics must deal with theories about particular languages and at the same time provide a theory about those theories.

It is because of this two-level nature of language that linguists have been led to consider explanatory hypotheses that make use of some kind of selection procedure. There are various ways of conceiving of the problem (on the following discussion see especially Chomsky, 1957, and Peters, 1972).

Approaches to the selection problem have differed primarily in the richness of the hypotheses defining the class of possible grammars, that is, in the kinds of absolute restrictions on grammars that we considered in the last section. Clearly, the difficulty of solving the selection problem decreases to the extent that we are able to narrow down the class of grammars made available to the language-acquirer. We can see this by considering two extreme views (both obviously false). Suppose no restrictions are placed on the class of possible grammars. Then everything about the nature of language must be explained by a solution to the selection problem. At the other extreme, suppose that there is exactly one grammar in the class of possible grammars. Then nothing need be explained by a selection procedure.

At the time when Chomsky's work first became known, some linguists conceived of the selection procedure in terms of a set of procedures of segmentation and classification that could be applied to any corpus of utterances and that would result in a grammar for the language of the corpus (this view was codified in Harris, 1951). Assumptions about the form of grammars were extremely weak. It was assumed merely that linguistic theory provided a set of formal categories such as phoneme, morpheme, and morpheme-class. It was one of the major achievements of Chomsky and his coworkers to turn attention toward a richer specification of the class of grammars and to restate the problem of selecting a grammar in a weaker form. Rather than demand a mechanical discovery procedure for grammars, Chomsky suggested that an **evaluation procedure** of some sort might be provided, so that the problem of selection could be seen as a problem of comparing grammars made available by the general theory of language and choosing one over the other in terms of some measure or other. The problem was conceived of as one of constructing hypotheses that would mark one grammar as more highly valued than another according to some formal measure. Construction of such an **evaluation metric** (or **simplicity metric**) was to be tested by various sorts of evidence as to whether the suggested measures did lead to correct grammars in some sense. Such hypotheses are specific empirical hypotheses *within* linguistic theory, and quite distinct from the notion of simplicity that plays a role in a general philosophy of science.

What sorts of evidence can be given for the correctness of various hypotheses about an evaluation metric? As suggested above in our initial definition of explanatory adequacy, one kind of evidence has to do with descriptive adequacy. That is, given an evaluation metric E and two grammars G_1 and G_2 (both compatible with the general specification of a class of possible grammars), E should select G_1 over G_2 if G_1 is more descriptively adequate than G_2.

Most discussions of an evaluation metric in such terms have dealt with phonology. Thus, one of the intuitions that native speakers have about their language is that some sequences of sounds are possible (even though nonexistent), while others are not. A phonological theory and an evaluation metric should be constructed in such a way that we can account for the differences in our reactions to nonexistent words like *blick* and *bnick,* the former possible in English, the latter not (Chomsky, 1964; Halle, 1962). Or, to take an example from Sapir (1925): the phone /ŋ/ (velar nasal) has a different status in English than either /n/ or /m/. According to Sapir, speakers of English perceive the velar nasal as being "really" a sequence of phonemes. Thus the fact that no English words begin with /ŋ/ is simply a reflection of the same constraints that rule out words beginning with /nd/, /mp/, and so on. Our general theory and its evaluation metric should force us to this analysis. Note that it is always necessary to consider both form and content of the theory and the evaluation metric.

Let us consider one example from syntax. Suppose we wish to analyze sentences like these:

1. Mary wants John to go to work.
2. Mary wants to go to work.

Within a transformational theory, there are two choices open to us. Both types of sentences could be directly given in the base rules, or we might allow only the type represented by (1) to be directly generated by base rules and assume that (2) is derived from an underlying structure, in which there is a second occurrence of *Mary,* by the operation of a transformation like Equi. It is clear that the transformational account is the simpler of these two choices, since at the cost of a very general rule of deletion (which is needed for a whole range of other sentences with verbs like *persuade,* adjectives like *ready,* phrases like *big enough* or *too hot,* and so on) we need not say anything at all about the restrictions on the type of (1) (that is, that everything *except* an *NP* equivalent to the subject of the whole sentence can stand in the position of *John*). That this account is supported by considerations of descriptive adequacy can be seen simply by noting that every speaker of English knows he must interpret (2) in such a way that it is *Mary's* going to work that is involved.

This example is instructive in showing that the options given to us by the general theory are essential in considering hypotheses about evaluation. In a theory that includes various kinds of rules of semantic interpretation, a richer lexicon, redundancy rules, and so on, we must consider other possibilities. Thus, some recent analyses of English within an extended interpretive theory (such as Jackendoff, 1972) have argued that (1) and (2) would indeed be directly generated (more or less as given above) in the base and that rules of interpretation rather than transformations are the proper way to account for the descriptive facts. Since we do not know in advance how to compare simplicity in various components of a grammar, a more complicated evaluation metric must be constructed, in which we try out various possibilities for weighting different parts of the grammar. In this case, we might argue that the metric should be constructed in such a way as to favor a transformational account over an interpretive account, since the transformational rule of Equi can be shown to interact with other transformations like Passive in a way that an interpretive rule could not. An interpretive rule would have to be complicated to take care of sentences like this:

Mary wants to be considered for the job.

Notice that, by definition, it is meaningless to use an evaluation metric to compare analyses from different general theories. We can, however, compare two theories, each with its own evaluation metric, to show that one theory but not the other leads us to select descriptively adequate grammars over descriptively inadequate ones. The following example (from Chomsky, 1955) will serve to show the form of such arguments. Suppose we have two theories: *P,* a theory of phrase-structure grammar, and *T,* a theory of transformational grammar, each with an evaluation metric based on counting occurrences of symbols in rules. We want to analyze sentences like these:

1. Eating strawberries is fun.
2. I like eating strawberries.
3. John is eating strawberries.

Because of sentences like these,

4. Tennis is fun.
5. I like the werewolf.

we would want to assign the structure *NP* to *eating strawberries* in (1) and (2). Because of sentences like (6):

6. Myrtle is a turtle.

we would want to provide for structures like *NP be NP* in our grammars. In the phrase-structure grammar of *P,* the simplest grammar would assign this structure also to (3), since in this way we could eliminate a rule that would generate such sentences directly and separately. Under *T,* on the other hand, a grammar that derived such phrases with *V-ing* as in (1) or (2) transformationally would probably be simpler than one that generated them directly in the base. If all these assumptions are correct, then we can argue for the explanatory adequacy of *T* over *P* by pointing out that the structure *NP be V-ing X* is ambiguous:

7. Felicity is eating strawberries.

In fact, (3) is ambiguous in just this way (one reading is absurd and presumably false for anyone named John: *The person we both identify as John is identical with the activity of eating strawberries*). It should be emphasized that this argument does not depend on the claim that two different analyses *cannot* be assigned to sentences like (7) in *P*, a claim which is obviously false. Rather, what is claimed is that the simplest grammar would be descriptively adequate under *T* but not under *P*.

Since evaluation metrics are specific hypotheses within linguistics, we can support the correctness of an analysis only indirectly by appeal to a metric. The paradigm of reasoning here is as follows: Suppose we have managed to provide evidence for some version of an evaluation metric by showing that it leads to correct analyses in a number of clear cases. Then we may consider a new instance and see that the metric would lead us to choose one analysis over another. We may provisionally accept that analysis as correct. The strength of our confidence is directly dependent on the extent to which we have independent reason to think that the metric is correct. What we are doing, in effect, is testing the metric (and the theory in which it is embedded) by a prediction that we will find no evidence that the more highly valued grammar is incorrect (and in the best case, that we will actually find independent evidence that it is descriptively adequate). Only in this way can we escape circularity.

It is difficult to go much beyond this very general and vague kind of discussion at the moment. Most of the attempts to support one or another proposal for a metric have concerned very general issues, such as the question of weighing complexities in different parts of the grammar (Chomsky, 1970, for example), or the adoption of various proposed abbreviative notations. Before taking up notations, let us take a look at a different sort of evidence that has been offered for various aspects of an evaluation measure.

Up till now, I have followed Chomsky's account, in which explanatory adequacy and evaluation procedures are presented in terms of leading to descriptively adequate grammars, that is, grammars that correctly characterize the native speaker's intuitions. Quite often, however, justification for various proposals is given not on the basis of native speakers' intuitions but rather in terms of expectations of linguists. In such discussions, appeal is made to notions like "linguistically significant generalization," "natural class," and "more general rules." Here we are not dealing with speakers' intuitions but rather with intuitions of the "native speaker of linguistics" (*gratia* Charles Cairns).

An example of this mode of reasoning is to be found in Halle's argument for the use of features in phonology (1962). Halle considers the relative generality of rules fronting (specifying articulation with the tongue farther forward) /a/ in the following environments: (1) before a high front vowel (/i/), (2) before any front vowel (/i e æ/), (3) before /i/, /p/, /z/. According to the intuitions of most linguists, (2) is the most general of these environments, the class of front vowels is a natural class, and so on. If we require that relative degree of generality be reflected in the symbolism that we use for our rules, so that more general rules require fewer symbols, then, Halle argues, we must choose a theory of phonology in which the fundamental units are not phonemes but rather the features of which these phonemes are composed.

Abbreviative notations of the sort we have been assuming (see Section 3.4) are essential parts of an evaluation metric. The theory of possible elements and rules and the abbreviative notations must be chosen in such a way that the right predictions about descriptive adequacy and linguistically significant generalizations can be made.

Consider, for example, agreement rules in syntax. Suppose we have a language (like Latin) in which attributive adjectives agree with the nouns that they modify in gender, number, and case:

filium bonum 'good son' (masculine, singular, accusative)
agricolae boni 'good farmers' (masculine, plural, nominative)

and so on. We can show, first, that if a theory of generative grammar does not use complex elements in syntax (see Chapter 4) it has no natural means for expressing such agreements. The best we can do is to use abstract elements like *Accusative, Feminine, Plural,* and then spell them out in the form of the appropriate endings. As Chomsky (1965, pp. 170ff.) showed, this leads to an arbitrary choice of the ordering of these elements, and in addition we must complicate our rules for other parts of the syntax unnecessarily to allow for the presence or absence of these elements. But if we adopt a feature analysis in which these abstract elements are thought of as properties of complex symbols, we can avoid these problems. Further, if we think of the features themselves as bipartite, that is, consisting of a feature and a specification of the feature for two or more values (1-*Gender,* 2-*Gender,* 3-*Gender;* ± *Plural;* 1-*Case,* 2-*Case,* and so on), as for phonological features, we are in a position to adopt an abbreviation using variables over these feature specifications to state rules of agreement:

$$Adjective \rightarrow \begin{bmatrix} \alpha\ Number \\ \beta\ Gender \\ \gamma\ Case \end{bmatrix} \quad [\underline{\quad\quad} X \begin{bmatrix} +Noun \\ \alpha\ Number \\ \beta\ Gender \\ \gamma\ Case \end{bmatrix} \ ]$$

If we can support the contention that such a form is the correct way to state an agreement rule, we can support at one and the same time a theory making the particular decisions about features and abbreviations that we have used and an analysis of a language in which the hypothetical elements like gender, number, and case are as presupposed above.

But how exactly do we go about supporting the contention that such a rule is correct? In other words, how do we know that our intuitions as linguists about what is and what is not a linguistically significant generalization are correct? As far as I can see, there are two possible ways to go. One way is to take the stronger position on descriptive adequacy that was mentioned above, in which we assume that descriptive adequacy includes some account of the actual rules or generalizations that make up the grammar of the native speaker (and not just the structural descriptions that the grammar assigns to his sentences). The other way is to seek some external justification or explanation for the rules that we posit. In the first instance, we might test our ideas by looking at facts about language acquisition or language history (see Kiparsky, 1968). In the second instance, we move into the fit between our linguistic theories and other theories about language use, phonetics (in the case of phonology), and so on. We return to these points below.

But in any case it can be shown fairly easily that purely formal definitions of notions like those we are considering are insufficient (though perhaps necessary). Consider first the notion of "natural class." In phonology a natural class is held to be a class that can be specified by fewer feature specifications than any of its individual members. In the example above, the set of front vowels is a natural class by this definition, whereas the set consisting of /p i z/ is not. But many classes of segments that would be natural classes under this definition do not seem to fit our requirements for expressing linguistically significant generalizations. For example, the set of segments that can be specified as [+continuant] in English includes all vowels and all spirants, but it is doubtful that this is really a natural class in any linguistically relevant sense. Similarly, a rule that fronts vowels before all front vowels is a more "general" rule than one that fronts vowels before /i/ (that is, a high front vowel). But if we try to justify this characterization in terms of our expectations for the presence of such rules in natural languages, we find that the universal form of such an "umlauting" rule is one in which the segment /i/ occurs in the following environment, rather than the more general class of front vowels — or the even more general classes (in the sense of requiring fewer specifications of features) of all vowels or all segments. (This example is from unpublished work of Charles Cairns.)

We run into parallel problems in syntax. Is a rule that applies to verbs less general than a rule that applies to verbs and adjectives? What are the concepts that go into our understanding of such categories as noun and verb in the first place (parallel to the question: what are the universal features that make up the substance of phonological theories)? In the face of such questions many linguists have concluded (rightly, I believe) that a great deal of work needs to be done in specifying more narrowly the content of linguistic rules. I will take up this question of substantive universals in the final chapter.

10.4 Explanation in General

How do the notions that we have been examining fit into a more general account of the nature of explanation? This is not the place to enter into an extended discussion of the nature of scientific explanation (see Bach, 1974, for some remarks), but one aspect of scientific explanation is relevant to an understanding of the more special use of the term *explanatory* that we have been examining.

The general notion of explanation seems to be a relative one. That is, there is no absolute sense in which some hypothesis or theory can be said to have given a final explanation. Explanations arise out of the questions that we ask, and it seems to be part of the nature of human knowledge that answers to questions lead to new questions. At the very least, we are always led to ask how our theory about some problem area, like language, fits into theories about other problem areas, or into a more general scheme covering both our original area of concern and some broader area of which it is a part. This is true no less of linguistics than of other fields.

For example, there is a sense in which we can say that a single de-scriptively adequate grammar explains facts about a language. But then we are led to ask why or how this grammar itself is to be explained (for example, how a speaker of the language acquires this grammar), and then we seek explanations either in absolute terms or in terms of an evalua-tion measure or other selection procedure, that is, we seek an explana-torily adequate theory in Chomsky's sense (see Chomsky, 1972b, Lec-ture 2).

But now suppose we find a theory of language that meets this test of explanatory adequacy (not an imminent danger, to be sure). Then we are immediately faced with a new problem: Why this theory rather than some other theory? And we turn to the problem of fitting the theory into a more general theory of human psychology or of testing the mesh between this theory and theories about other aspects of language, such as language history, language acquisition, and language use. In doing so we might be led to modify our original theory. This is just another way of saying that theories must be tested and justified externally as well as internally. It might very well turn out to be the case that some parts of the theory can be justified or tested only in this external way; that the kinds of data we look at within linguistics are insufficient to allow us to choose among many alternative theories, all compatible with the facts.

But it does not follow from this relative character of explanation that we must follow a step-by-step procedure in our research. Indeed, if we followed this requirement in attempting to understand the world we would never get anywhere, since we can never feel confident that we have satisfactorily explained any phenomenon, no matter how narrow. It is sometimes said that we need to understand competence before we can seriously deal with questions of performance (as in Chomsky, 1964, p. 52). I think that this position is misguided. It is misguided first of all because we might wait forever before beginning to untangle problems of performance. But it is misguided above all because until we try out various theories about both competence and performance we have no idea whether a certain range of facts is a matter of competence or performance. Langendoen and Bever (1973) show in a concrete case that what might be thought at first to be a matter of grammar, that is, competence, is in fact a matter of a theory of conversation or interpretive strategies.

This point can be made not only with respect to linguistics (narrowly conceived) vis-à-vis other disciplines like psychology, but within linguistics itself. We have assumed throughout this book that the question whether a certain phenomenon is a matter of syntactic theory is self-evident. But this fiction (which may be excused on grounds of pedagogical necessity) must be recognized as a fiction. Without some ideas about what an adequate theory of semantics might look like, as well as an adequate theory of language use, we simply have no idea whether a particular judgment of acceptability, say, is to be accounted for in a syntactic way.

11

Universal Grammar

11.1 Orientation

There is a sense in which universal grammar means just the same as general linguistic theory. Every general hypothesis we have considered so far may be taken as a hypothesis about universal grammar. But at various points, especially in the previous chapter, I have argued that purely formal theories of grammar are insufficient. In the present chapter we will take up a number of questions about the content of grammars, that is, universals of a substantive nature. Since work of this sort is in its infancy (within the context of generative grammar), much, if not all, of what I say here must be taken as very speculative. The intent of the chapter is not to present results but to suggest some lines of research that might be followed in the future.

We will first consider some very general facts that point toward a rich substantive theory of universal syntax, whatever it may turn out to be in detail. Then we will discuss problems about universal aspects of the base, substantive constraints on transformations, and, finally, some possible explanations for the form and substance of transformations.

11.2 Evidence for Substantive Universals in Syntax

The aspects of language that are most directly available to our observation are meanings and sounds. If we think about the logically and physically possible systems of sounds and meanings and then turn to the actual facts of phonetics and semantics in natural languages, we find overwhelming evidence that there are many constraints of a substantive nature.

In phonetics we find that the stock of linguistically relevant distinctions for all languages can be exhaustively described using a quite small number of universal distinctive features. The phonetic realizations of these features vary a good deal from language to language, but again within quite definite limits. Further, the phonological rules that can be justified for particular languages seem to obey heavy substantive constraints.

It might appear that the possible meanings that morphemes and other linguistic elements may have are unlimited. But here again, it seems that there are specific universal constraints.

Some semantic universals are so basic that it is easy to overlook them. For example, every language seems to have a basic category for names of individuals, and there seem to be definite limits on the kinds of "thing" that can receive such individual or proper names. Thus, a "language" like that of the philosopher W. V. O. Quine, in which proper names are eliminated in favor of individual "predicates" (sentences containing *Pegasus* are analyzed into sentences containing the formula *x pegasizes*), seems highly unnatural to a linguist (see Quine, 1961). Of course, the way in which names are formed, the role that naming plays in particular cultures, and so on, may vary a good deal.

Many textbooks in linguistics and anthropology use color terms as an example of "linguistic relativity," the thesis that there are no limits on the number of ways in which the world of human experience is categorized in language. The color spectrum has no "natural" segmentation into different colors. But a recent study by Berlin and Kay (1969) casts considerable doubt on the thesis that color categorization is arbitrary. Berlin and Kay found that, although languages did indeed differ in their systems of basic color terms, there was a very systematic way in which they differed. They were able to establish the following implicational hierarchy (p. 4):

$$
\begin{bmatrix} \text{white} \\ \text{black} \end{bmatrix} \leftarrow [\text{red}] \leftarrow \begin{bmatrix} \text{green} \\ \text{yellow} \end{bmatrix} \leftarrow [\text{blue}] \leftarrow [\text{brown}] \leftarrow \begin{bmatrix} \text{purple} \\ \text{pink} \\ \text{orange} \\ \text{gray} \end{bmatrix}
$$

What the schema means is this: If a language has two color terms, they will always be white and black; if a third term, it will be red; if there are four, they will be the three so far plus green or yellow (and the next will always be the other of these two), and so on. Even more significantly, striking agreement was found across languages as to the identification of "true red" and so on. In fact, agreement on such "foci" was found to vary no more among speakers of totally different languages than among speakers of the same language. We may call this result the "congruence of intra- and interlinguistic diversity."

Returning to phonetics, we find something like this same congruence. Many sounds that seem highly exotic to the beginning student of phonetics who happens to be a native speaker of English actually show up in paralinguistic behavior, language acquisition, and dialect and idiolect variation among speakers of English. Many languages systematically use implosive voiced stops, clicks, and glottalized ejective sounds. But some speakers of American English use imploded stops in words like *boy* [ɓɔy] and glottalized ejectives as the final consonants of such words as *cake* [kɛyk'], especially in emphatic pronunciations. And we are all familiar with the marginal but quite regular use of clicks in giving commands to horses, expressing disapproval (*tsk, tsk*), and so on.

Given these similarities across languages in meanings and sounds, it would not be surprising to find strong resemblances in grammatical systems as well. And indeed there are pervasive similarities in syntax, even in quite specific and "surface" facts. Later in this chapter we will take up the problem of accounting for these similarities. Here let us simply look at a few examples.

Certain sentence types occur in all languages. All languages have ways of expressing commands, asking and answering questions, and making statements (with varying degrees of qualification). Such resemblances (which are as much pragmatic and semantic as syntactic) are undoubtedly to be accounted for on the basis of universals of human communication. But the ways in which these basic "speech acts" (Searle, 1969) are expressed are not arbitrarily different.

Typically, commands use special forms of the verb or sentence structures that are shorter than the forms or structures for declarative sentences (except where the desire, probably another universal, to express politeness or soften a command provides longer forms). In Turkish, second-person forms of the verb require an ending for declarative sentences, but the bare verb stem is used for commands: *git* 'go!' (Swift, 1963). In Swahili, declarative sentences require a person marker on the verb, but again the bare verb stem is used for the imperative: *piga* 'beat!' (Ashton, 1944). In English and German, where most sentences require a pronominal subject if there is no overt *NP* subject, the pronoun is dropped in the simplest form of the command: *komm* 'come!'

Now, there is obviously no logical necessity for imperatives to be formed in this way. It might be the case that imperatives were formed in arbitrarily different ways in different languages, or that imperatives were formed in similar ways, but only by adding some element. To the extent that the observation just made is correct, it constitutes a fact to be described in an account of universal grammar.

The ways in which questions are formed are again quite similar across languages. Let us consider so-called word-questions first, that is, sentences illustrated by these English examples:

Why is Harriet so angry?
Who called the police?
Where did Henry buy that beautiful banjo?

Quite generally, the actual morphological forms that are used for such interrogatives are connected to indefinite *NP*'s and pronouns, either in their actual makeup or in the environments in which they can stand. For the latter kind of connection, compare these English sentences and non-sentences (see Chomsky, 1964):

Someone else came to the party.
Who else came to the party?
*The man else came to the party.

The plumber, I saw him yesterday.
*A plumber, I saw him yesterday.
*Who, I saw him yesterday?

Similarly, in Japanese, the *theme* of a sentence is marked by *wa,* translating in many contexts as definite in corresponding English sentences. Interrogatives cannot occur with *wa:*

Ie wa mimasita.	'(unspecified subject) saw the house'
Ie o mimasita.	'(unspecified subject) saw a house'
Nani o mimasita ka?	'What did (unspecified subject) see?'
*Nani wa mimasita ka?	

For the first, morphological connection, Japanese examples will again serve: *dare, nani* mean 'who, what'; *dare ka, nani ka* mean 'somebody, something'; and so on. We find the same kind of connection in many unrelated languages.

Beyond this morphological and contextual connection, however, the number of possible syntactic constructions associated with interrogative-word questions is strikingly small. Many languages require movement of the question word to the head of the clause, whether indirect questions like the English examples above or indirect questions like these:

I asked who wanted to go to the beach.
I don't know who I like better, Tweedledum or Tweedledee.

Moreover, the existence of such a Question-movement rule seems to be strongly correlated with the word-order type of the language (according to the position of the verb; more on this below).

Yes-no questions again take quite restricted forms: use of a question-particle (like the *ka* of the Japanese examples above), use of a special intonation, or a shift of the normal order from subject-first to verb-first, as in English.

Many facts of this sort have been noticed and recorded by researchers (most notably in recent times by Joseph H. Greenberg and his co-workers; see especially Greenberg, 1963). These cross-linguistic generalizations and interconnections can be quite specific. Thus, many languages have nominalized constructions that are either transformationally derived from, or closely connected to, full sentences. Quite typically, the *NP* that would represent the subject in the corresponding sentence is marked by whatever case or preposition is used in the language to indicate possession:

Harriet refused to be drafted.
Harriet's refusal to be drafted didn't surprise me.
I wasn't fazed by Harriet's refusing to be drafted.

We noted above the congruence of intralinguistic and interlinguistic variation in semantics and phonetics. Something like that fact exists in syntax also. When a language has a variety of sorts of constructions, whether free variants or obligatory constructions used in particular circumstances, we find that the variants conform pretty much to what we find in other languages and are not just arbitrary. Let us look at two areas of syntax: relative clauses and the word-order of basic constituents.

We may define (for present purposes) a relative clause as a sentence or remnant of a sentence that is used to modify a noun or noun phrase. The most usual types of English relative clause (unreduced) are these:

1. the man who(m) John saw in the basement
2. the man that John saw in the basement
3. the man John saw in the basement

We may schematize these three types as follows, with *WH* standing for a relative pronoun, *That* standing for an invariable relative particle or complementizer, and ø standing for the absence of a noun phrase in the clause itself:

1. *NP WH . . . ∅ . . .*
2. *NP That . . . ∅ . . .*
3. *NP . . . ∅ . . .*

Each of these three types occurs in many other languages. If we look at constructions in English derived from relative clauses, we find their counterparts elsewhere, too. A recent study of relative clauses in various languages (Schwartz, 1971) lists, in addition to the three types above, the following forms:

4. *NP That . . . Pro . . .*
5. *NP That WH . . . Pro . . .*
6. *. . . ∅ . . . NP*
7. *. . . Pro . . . NP*

(where *Pro* refers to a resumptive pronoun coreferential to the head of the clause). There are no relative clause structures like (5) and (7) in (present-day) English, but there are types like (4) in at least some dialects of English:

That's a movie that you cry when you see it.

And under special circumstances types like (6) occur (including attributive adjectives):

the rapidly approaching train

Thus, of seven different structures listed by Schwartz, five occur as variants of one or another sort in English, and none of the English types is restricted to English. This suggests that there are only a limited number of ways in which relative clauses and related structures can be formed in natural languages. A theory of universal grammar must account for this in some way.

Consider next a language that exhibits regular variation in the word order of basic constituents. In Modern German there are three types of patterns, as illustrated in these sentences:

1. Kommt Hans morgen?   'Is Hans coming tomorrow?'
2. Hans kommt morgen.   'Hans is coming tomorrow'
3. (Ich weiss, dass) Hans   '(I know that) Hans is coming
   morgen kommt.   tomorrow'

In yes-no questions (and some other types of clauses) the verb is in initial position; in main declarative sentences and *WH*-questions the verb is in second position; in subordinate clauses the verb is in final position. What is striking about this variation is that it conforms exactly to the three basic order types that were shown by Greenberg (1963) to have such far-reaching typological consequences.

In this section I have tried to offer some suggestive evidence for the view that syntactic theory must include some strong restrictions of a substantive sort on the content of grammars. In subsequent sections we will consider some ways in which facts like these might be accounted for in a general theory of syntax.

11.3 Universal Aspects of the Base

Since about 1965, linguists have speculated about the possibility that the base rules of all languages are identical or closely similar. In this section we will take up several hypotheses revolving around universals of the base.

In early transformational studies of various unrelated and related languages, it turned out that the deep or basic structures (or their counterparts in the *Syntactic Structures* model, the underlying phrase-markers for kernel sentences) were much more alike than the surface structures. The deep structures were held to be most closely associated with the meanings of sentences and, at least in the view of many linguists, it seemed that the meanings of sentences were more nearly similar across languages than their surface structures. This last observation (or belief) is closely associated with the hypothesis that all languages are equally "complete" (Hill, 1958): the expressive power of every language is adequate to whatever task is set it. With time and patience and the possibility of paraphrase, one can translate from any language into any other.

Given these findings and beliefs, it was natural that many linguists were led to enunciate various hypotheses about the universality of various aspects of the base. We can look at two principal arguments for setting forth such hypotheses.

First, it is necessary to propose specific hypotheses about such matters to avoid the trap of building our own presuppositions into our theories. How can we know that the similarities across languages in their deep structures are not just artifacts, the result of importing ideas about underlying structures from one language to another, like the much-maligned attempts of grammarians of previous centuries to fit every language to the mold of Latin? As far as I can see, there is only one way to avoid this trap, and that is to take such assumptions explicitly as hypotheses and to consider evidence for or against them.

Second, if we could establish the correctness of one or another general hypothesis about the universality of deep structures, we would have gone a long way toward accounting for the mysterious fact that learners of languages behave as if they learn or know deep structures without ever apprehending them experientially. Surface structures are "abstract" enough; deep structures are hopelessly so for any theory of language acquisition that depends on a simple account of learning from experience.

Thus, whether they turn out to be correct or not, there are good reasons for investigating specific hypotheses about universals of the base.

Base components of transformational grammars are made up of three sorts of elements: categories like *NP, V, S;* rules for constructing phrase-markers using these categories; lexicons that give specific members of classes and categories established by the rules. We take up each type in turn.

Many accounts of transformational grammar enunciate the hypothesis that there is a universal set of deep grammatical relations or functions: *Subject-of, Object-of,* and so on (Chomsky, 1965 and elsewhere). Since these functions are defined by specific categories and their configurations in deep phrase-markers, such hypotheses require both that there are certain universal categories and that there are quite specific limitations on the base rules of various languages.

Thus, *Subject-of* (as defined by Chomsky, 1965) is that relation holding between an *NP* and the sentence that immediately dominates it:

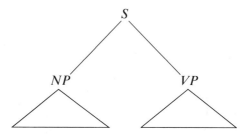

Such a notion cannot be defined for every language unless every language has the categories *NP* and *S*. Similarly, the relation *Object-of* requires the elements *VP* and *NP*.

But beyond the requirement that certain categories be present in the deep structures of every language, this view says nothing about the totality of possible categories. Typically, transformational grammars use not only such "universal" categories as *S* and *NP* but also elements like *Aux* or *Determiner,* which seem to have a much more language-dependent character.

One attractive hypothesis about base categories is that the categories are all universal (either in the sense that they must be present in every language, or in the weaker sense that there is a finite and small set of possible categories of which some may be absent in one language or another). Some studies relating to this question are G. Lakoff (1970a), where it is argued that verbs and adjectives share many characteristics and should be represented by a single category, and Bach (1968), where similar arguments are advanced for the thesis that nouns, verbs, and adjectives are to be represented (in English) as a single deep category (see also Lyons, 1966, for a similar view). Fillmore (1968), from a different point of view about the nature of underlying representations, argues that there is a single universal set of semantic relations holding between verbs and their arguments, which he calls *Cases*. Most of these discussions have been carried out under the standard assumption that the categories of the base are unanalyzed elements (see Section 4.5). A number of writers, for a variety of reasons, have put forward the view that this assumption is incorrect and that the categories themselves should be considered complexes of features (McCawley, 1968a; Chomsky, 1970; Dougherty, 1971).

The main problem with such discussions is that we do not know enough about the bases for the categories or the features that might underlie them. The relevant considerations are of two sorts: semantic and syntactic. Semantically, we can ask about the use of categories in stating semantic rules about truth conditions, entailments, and so on. It is only in the last several years that serious work on the formal semantics of natural languages has been undertaken (largely by philosophers; see, for example, Fillmore and Langendoen, 1971; Steinberg and Jakobovits, 1971; Davidson and Harman, 1972). It is to be expected that further work along these lines will shed light on the question of base categories, but only if there is an explicit attempt to integrate hypotheses about semantics and hypotheses about syntax. Syntactically, we can ask about the behavior of various categories under transformations (on this, more below).

Let us consider next the question of universal constraints on the base rules. Once again, the theory of underlying grammatical relations has implications for the base rules that we postulate. If *Subject* is a necessary deep relation in every grammar and if it is defined as suggested above, then every language must have some rule of the form:

$$S \rightarrow X \; NP \; Y$$

where either X or Y is nonnull and neither contains NP. Similarly, *Object* requires the category VP and a rule

$$VP \rightarrow X \; NP \; Y$$

If we take these two claims together, then languages can have only the following types of underlying structures (for transitive verb structures):

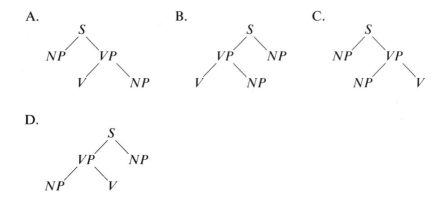

In terms of Greenberg's classification, these types represent

A. *S V O*   B. *V O S*   C. *S O V*   D. *O V S*

at the underlying level. Two other logical possibilities are missing:

E. *V S O*   F. *O S V*

The vast majority of languages fall into the three types A, C, E at the surface level. Since type E is not in the set allowed by Chomsky's theory, we could falsify that theory by showing that some language of type E (*V S O*) had that structure in its underlying system as well. Some linguists have questioned the existence of a *VP* category in underlying structure, and some have argued that *S O V* languages have no *VP* node (Muraki, 1971; Hankamer, 1971). We will return to these questions below in connection with the question of universal transformations, since it is impossible to make any strong claims about underlying structures unless the possible transformations are limited in what they can do to rearrange constituents.

Little is known about universal aspects of the lexicon. Since it is precisely in the linking of particular sequences of sounds with particular meanings that languages are more or less arbitrary, one might think that nothing could be claimed in this area. But at least in the area of redundancy rules for syntactic-semantic features it seems that many regularities are language-independent. If a language has a feature *Animate*, then it seems as if the rule that redundantly specifies this feature for human nouns would be present in the language. Similarly, there seem to be constraints of a substantive nature in the area of the assignment of particular meanings to particular lexical categories. Once again, as with the question of the basic categories themselves, we probably have to wait for a better understanding of semantics and its relation to syntax before much can be learned in this area.

Hypotheses about universals of the base would appear to be interesting and important hypotheses about the nature of human language. But some mathematical studies of the last several years show that the strongest possible hypothesis — the idea that the base rules of every language are literally the same (the Universal Base Hypothesis) — cannot at present be disconfirmed (hence corroborated) by any empirical evidence of the sort usually considered by linguists. This is so because it is possible to construct a universal base that will form the basis for a transformational grammar meeting any of the usual tests for descriptive adequacy.

11.4 The Peters-Ritchie Results on Limiting the Base

In Section 8.5 we sketched the proofs given by Peters and Ritchie that a formalization of transformational grammars along the lines of Chomsky (1965) yields a set of grammars that are equivalent in weak generative capacity to unrestricted rewriting systems (hence Turing machines). This result remains true whether the base is a context-sensitive grammar, a context-free grammar, or a finite-state grammar. In fact, the result is true even if the base is a fixed finite-state grammar (with two rules!). Thus, the following result is logically true, given the structure of a transformational grammar:

I. There is a fixed (universal) base B such that every recursively enumerable language can be generated by a transformational grammar with B as its base.

If we make the plausible assumption that natural languages are at most recursively enumerable (that is, are definite systems describable by any imaginable grammar; see Sections 2.6, 8.4, 8.5), II will follow from I:

II. For any natural language L there is a grammar for L with a universal base.

Translated into linguistic terms, this result means that we can never find any evidence from judgments about the grammaticality of sentences to show that the assumption of a universal base is wrong. There are, in fact, an infinite number of universal bases meeting the requirements of Theorem II.

But what about the other parts of descriptive adequacy? In Peters and Ritchie (1970) the following conjecture was made. If we mean by descriptive adequacy the assignment to sentences of the correct degrees of ambiguity, paraphrase relations, coreference relations, and the like (that is, the sorts of properties traditionally used in syntactic work along with grammaticality for judging grammars), and if we make extremely weak assumptions about the functions distributing these properties over sentences, III is true:

III. For every natural language, there is a descriptively adequate grammar with a universal base.

This result has been proved only for ambiguity assignments, but it seems quite likely that it can be proved for other aspects of descriptive adequacy as well. Thus, if true, III shows that the implications of the preceding paragraph can be generalized to all aspects of descriptive adequacy. No empirical evidence can be found in this realm to tell us whether the Universal Base Hypothesis is true or false. (For discussion of these results and their implications, see Peters, 1970, 1972.)

It is obvious that the excessive power of transformational grammars lies in the transformational component. In proving Theorem I, Peters and Ritchie showed how a set of transformational rules, obeying the recoverability condition and operating cyclically, is able to imitate an arbitrary Turing machine.

Now let us make one further observation. The testing of an evaluation metric depends on tests of descriptive adequacy. It follows from III that we can never use arguments about explanatory adequacy (stated in terms of an evaluation metric) to confirm or disconfirm particular versions of transformational theory in its unrestricted form. For suppose someone proposes a theory with a particular evaluation metric that leads to descriptively adequate grammars. We can always propose an alternative theory using a universal base and invent an evaluation metric that will favor particularizations of the theory giving us whatever structural descriptions we need to achieve descriptive adequacy.

From these considerations, we can conclude that syntactic theory is at an impasse, resulting from the extreme power of transformations. It follows also that the more powerful systems of generative semantics and extended interpretive semantics, which we considered briefly in Chapter 9, are in an even worse impasse, if that is possible. Moreover, until the theories can be restricted in some way that makes them less powerful than the standard theory, the thesis of the strong equivalence of the two systems (Section 9.61) must be considered valid.

Consider, for example, one of the major issues between generative and extended interpretive semantics. Generative semantics holds that the deepest structures of the base are essentially the same as semantic representations. If we make the assumption that, given time and patience and paraphrase possibilities, it is possible to express any semantic content in any language, the thesis of generative semantics must entail the existence of a universal set of base rules. But this thesis is devoid of empirical content at present. Further, if the intertranslatability thesis is denied (if it is insisted that semantic representations must be distinct from language to language), the generative semanticist must deny the existence of a universal set of base rules. But either consequence is beyond empirical research.

Further, we can never show that a particular set of base rules (such as those in Chomsky, 1970) for a given language is correct. For if it were possible to show that such rules for individual languages are correct, then we could refute the Universal Base Hypothesis by finding the right sets of base rules for two languages and noting that they are different. But then the Universal Base Hypothesis would be falsifiable, which it is not.

One may ask how linguists are able to carry on serious discussions about syntax under these conditions. The answer is that there is a gross mismatch between what is explicitly given by the theory of transformational grammar (in any of its variants) and the implicit working hypotheses that linguists in fact use. For example, no linguist would ever seriously propose a transformation for a natural language like the ones used by Peters and Ritchie for their proofs.

It is apparent that the Universal Base Hypothesis should be an empirical hypothesis that could be disconfirmed. What is wrong with the present theory is its extreme power. There are two possibilities: we must limit the power of transformations in linguistically reasonable ways, or we must enlarge the range of evidence beyond that given by ordinary considerations of descriptive adequacy. In the remainder of this chapter we will look at some possibilities of both sorts.

11.5 Universal Transformations

In Section 11.2 we noted similarities in certain syntactic features that can be found among unrelated languages. In this section we will consider some hypotheses about the transformational part of a grammar. It seems clear that we can account for such similarities only if we make strong assumptions about substantive limitations both on the base rules and on the rules that relate basic structures and surface structures. Moreover, if we place heavy enough restrictions on the content of transformations, it may be that we will be able to circumvent the difficulties of excessive power noted by Peters and Ritchie.

One possible set of hypotheses embodies the idea that there is a fixed list of transformations of a certain sort — call them **major transformations** — available to every language. For example, it has been argued that both German and Amharic have a Verb-final rule of the form (Bach 1970, 1971b):

$$Y \; [\; V \; X \;] \; Z \qquad\qquad\qquad X \; [\; Y \; V \; W \;] \; Z$$
$$\quad\; S \qquad\qquad\qquad\qquad\qquad\; S$$

$$1 \quad 2 \; 3 \quad 4 \Rightarrow \qquad \text{or} \qquad 1 \quad 2 \; 3 \; 4 \quad 5 \Rightarrow$$
$$1 \quad \emptyset \;\; 3{+}2 \; 4 \qquad\qquad\qquad 1 \quad 2 \; \emptyset \; 4{+}3 \; 5$$

In German, this rule applies only in subordinate clauses; in Amharic, in all clauses. Ross's argument in his 1967 paper on Gapping (Ross, 1970a) requires the availability of this rule but also the assumption that no rule in any language does the opposite of such rules (takes a verb from final position and puts it into a position at the head of its clause, or of its *VP*). Thus it is necessary to posit not only the permissibility of certain rules but the unavailability of other rules. These two sorts of requirements are embodied in the notion of a fixed list[1] of major transformations. I stress again that such hypotheses must be considered only tentative first steps in the explanations we are seeking for universal limitations on the content of grammars. For some initial ideas about such universal rules see Bach (1965, 1970, 1971a, 1971b, 1974) and Ross (1970a). Hankamer (1971) also considers hypotheses about universal orderings of rules.

We will take up here two interrelated sets of phenomena (both discussed in Section 11.2): relative clauses and word order. Our method of argument will be to set up some general hypotheses and then show that certain facts about individual languages follow from these assumptions.

11.51 Restrictive Relative Clauses

Relative clauses are especially well suited to the sort of study that we are proposing here. First of all, it is relatively easy to identify relative clauses cross-linguistically. They are constructions in which some form of dependent sentence is used to specify more closely the interpretation

---

1. Of course, actually providing a list is not the only way to meet these two requirements. We might also provide certain positive and negative substantive conditions that must be met by any grammar, or attempt to recursively specify an infinite set of possible rules, and so on. The idea of a fixed set is the most restrictive hypothesis, and may need to be modified.

of a "head" nominal expression. Second, as we saw in Section 11.2, the kinds of relative clauses encountered in the languages of the world seem to be quite limited and closely related to general characteristics of language in terms of Greenberg's typology of basic word-order. Third, with apparently very few exceptions (see Hale, to be published) every language exhibits such structures. We will deal here only with so-called restrictive relative clauses of the type of (1), not with appositive (nonrestrictive) clauses such as (2):

1. the man that I saw . . .
2. John, who lives in the East Village, . . .

Numerous analyses have been proposed for relative clauses (I shall drop the qualification "restrictive" hereafter), but they fall into a few general types. We will take up two such classes of analyses, show that certain hypotheses about universal grammar require us to choose one over the other, and then look at evidence for the correctness of this choice in English and a few other languages.

Our two analyses of English are those in which the underlying structures of relative clauses are as follows:[2]

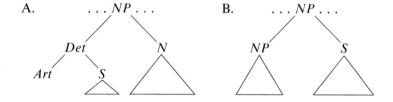

---

2. Since I am interested here more in the form of the argument than in the particular conclusions we draw, I will not consider at length a number of questions and alternative analyses, but they should at least be mentioned. One alternative is that in which relatives are derived from conjoined sentences, as in Thompson (1971). The other is an analysis in which there is a third type of nominal category, *Nom*, distinct from *N* and *NP*, so that *NP*'s with relative clauses have the structure

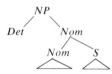

Some of the arguments below are invalid as they stand if either of these alternatives is followed. See Stockwell, Schachter, and Partee (1973) for discussion of the alternatives and references, and for a defense of the *Nom-S* analysis. Partee (1972) also argues for the last analysis on semantic grounds.

Analysis A posits a structure in which the relative clause is part of the *Determiner* constituent (this analysis goes back ultimately to Lees, 1960, and Smith, 1964). Let us refer to this analysis as the *Det–S* analysis. The other has been followed in much recent work, for example Ross (1967a and subsequent works). In analysis B, the clause follows a head *NP*. Let us call this the *NP–S* analysis.

The hypotheses that we will consider are the following:

    I. The base rules for all languages are identical.
   II. Among the categories of the base rules are S, NP, and V, but not N. Moreover, not every language has the surface category N.
  III. There is a restricted set of rules for forming relative clauses.

We have just seen (Section 11.4) that Hypothesis I is not an empirical hypothesis. I will assume here that the general theory has been amended either by adding formal constraints of the sort considered in the last chapter or by adding substantive constraints on transformations of the sort we are taking up here, so that the Peters-Ritchie results do not follow. Hypothesis II has some independent support, in that there are apparently languages without either a deep or a surface category N (Nootka, Tagalog), but no languages without a fundamental category like NP, and by evidence of the sort given in Bach (1968) against the existence of a deep N category in English.

Hypothesis III is too unspecific to be of much help in carrying out any deductions. Some way is required of getting predictions across languages about the nature of relative clause structures. Let us assume first that (restrictive) relative clauses are all derived from a single type of base structure. Given Hypothesis I, the Universal Base Hypothesis, it follows that this underlying structure is present in every language, and from II it follows that this universal source may involve the categories NP and S but not N, since only the former two are in the set of universal categories. Thus, the $NP–S$ analysis is a possible one for any particular language, but not the $Det–S$ analysis. As a partial support for this conclusion, we may note that the category of *Determiner* seems to be a much more language-specific category than NP or S. I will now try to show (1) that the $NP–S$ analysis is to be preferred for English over the $Det–S$ analysis, and (2) that the $NP–S$ analysis is preferable to a third analysis that would also be consistent with our assumptions above, one in which the clause precedes its head ($S–NP$).

Under the $Det–S$ analysis, a phrase like *the house that is on the left* has a basic structure roughly like this:

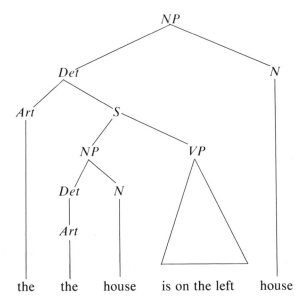

To reach the surface form of the phrase, we need to make two changes:

   1. Move the clause around its head noun.
   2. Introduce *that* and delete the *NP* from the clause.

Assuming that both changes take place in a single rule, we might posit something like this:

$$X \, [\atop NP] \quad Y \, [\atop S] \quad Z_1 \, [\atop NP] \quad Det \; N]Z_2]N]W$$

1	2	3	4	5	6	7	8	$\Longrightarrow$
1	2	∅	∅	∅	∅	7+that+3+6	8	

where 5 = 7

This rule will take care of simple cases of relative clauses, but not more complicated ones in which there is a relative clause attached to a head that itself has a relative clause, that is, so-called stacked relatives:

   the house that is on the left that has three windows

The underlying structure for this phrase would presumably be something like the following one:

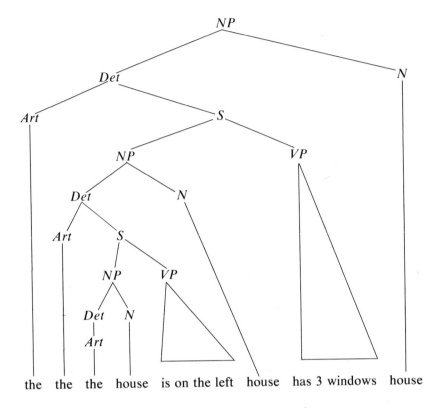

Applying the rule above, we get on the second cycle:

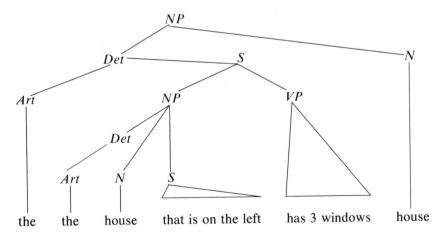

As the reader can easily work out, the rule given above will no longer apply; it has to be revised. But even if we do revise the rule in a minimal way (to allow some term to follow the *N* in its *NP*), the result of applying the rule to the structure above will be:

the house that that is on the left has 3 windows

In order to get a grammatical stacked relative it is necessary to complicate the rule even further to reposition the clause in the inner sentence after the new relative clause, or else to add a new rule to effect the repositioning. In either event it is necessary to complicate the grammar in order to take care of a more general class of expressions.

On the other hand, the *NP–S* analysis requires a rule something like this:

$$X \ [\quad NP \ [\qquad Y \ NP \ Z]]W$$
$$ NP \qquad S$$
$$1 \qquad 2 \qquad \ \ 3 \ 4 \ 5 \ \ 6 \Rightarrow$$
$$1 \qquad 2 \ \ that{+}3 \ \ \emptyset \ \ 5 \ \ 6$$

(I am ignoring certain problems about determiner identity and so on, some of which may be relevant in reaching a decision about the proper Relative-clause rule). Now, without any change at all, this rule will produce the correct form for stacked relatives. Thus the *NP–S* analysis not only allows a simpler rule (which is not very compelling evidence in itself), but the rule takes care of the most general class of expressions in its simplest form; in fact, to *exclude* stacked relatives we would have to complicate the rule.[3]

The force of the argument just given depends on the assumption that the phenomenon of stacked relatives must be accounted for in any adequate syntax of English. One question that arises is whether there is any difference between the interpretations of stacked relatives and of relatives in which there is a conjunction of clauses, that is, between phrases like (1) and (2):

1. the house that is on the left that has three windows
2. the house that is on the left and (that) has three windows

Although the difference is subtle, such phrases do differ in their interpretations. It has been pointed out by Asa Kasher (lecture at the University of Texas at Austin, April 1972) that a restrictive relative clause

---

3. The foregoing argument would also apply to a decision between the *Det–S* analysis and the *Nom–S* analysis of the footnote on p. 267. Stacked relatives are also accounted for automatically by the simplest formulation of a *Nom–S* rule.

presupposes the existence of entities of which the description given in the relative clause is not true. Thus, *the man that I saw* presupposes at least one man that I didn't see. Now, (1) presupposes at least one house on the left that does not have three windows (and a house that is not on the left), while (2) presupposes only at least one house that either is not on the left or does not have three windows. Thus, there is a difference in the acceptability of (3) and (4):

3. The house that is on the left that has three windows is the only house on the left.
4. The house that is on the left and that has three windows is the only house on the left.

The principal assertion of both sentences contradicts one of the presuppositions of (3) but not of (4).

A second argument for the *NP–S* analysis as against the *Det–S* analysis has to do with the rule(s) for getting adjectival and other modifiers into the correct order with respect to their head nouns. I shall assume here (without argument) that sets of phrases like these are to be derived from a common source:

the house that is on the left
the house on the left

the house that is big
the big house

the train that is approaching rapidly
the rapidly approaching train

Under either analysis it will be necessary to reposition some modifiers. G. Lakoff has pointed out (1970a) that modifiers can be preposed just in case the last element is *Verb* or *Adjective* and is directly covered by the highest *VP* (or *S*) in the relevant *NP*. Thus, compare these phrases with those above:

*the on the left house

 the man that is seeing Sally
*the seeing Sally man

 an elephant (that was) bigger than a house
*a bigger than a house elephant

Under the *NP–S* analysis, this preposing rule can be stated straightforwardly. Under the *Det–S* analysis we must either first postpose the clause, reduce, and then reposition the right set of modifiers before the noun, or state a much more complicated condition for postposing the right set of postnominal modifiers. Moreover, the preposing rule that can be used in the *NP–S* analysis ties in with further cross-linguistic facts. In general, languages that have the verb in final position prepose their relative clauses. We can thus suppose that the preposing rule is itself a (structure-dependent) universal transformation. This argument, it should be noted, favors any analysis in which relative clauses follow their heads in underlying structure, and thus would also count against an *S–NP* analysis that would be consistent with our general assumptions and the argument from stacked relatives.

It seems, then, that our predictions from Hypotheses I–III are borne out by facts about English. Let us turn our attention to some implications of our hypotheses for the analysis of relative clauses in other languages. If the assumptions about universal grammar are correct, then whatever structure we posit for English must be correct for all other languages. There are languages in which relative clauses always precede their heads, for example, Japanese and Mandarin Chinese. We could refute our hypotheses by showing that in such languages the underlying structure for relative clauses should be *S–NP* (say), and some weaker set of assumptions would have to be adopted. But there are some indications that even in Japanese and Mandarin the correct underlying structure is *NP–S*. Muraki (1970) has argued from facts of reflexivization and other considerations that the Japanese relative clause should follow its head in underlying structure. And Tai (1973) has given an argument based on pronominalization for the same conclusion about Mandarin. In Mandarin, relative clauses contain pronominal copies of the head. But relative clauses are the only structures in Mandarin in which a pronoun may precede its antecedent. This fact follows automatically from assuming that pronominalization always takes place forward, that it precedes relative clause movement, and that the underlying structure of noun phrases with relatives is *NP–S*.

One further argument from cross-linguistic data supports the universality of the *NP–S* analysis. (This argument must be considered fairly speculative, since not enough data are readily available on different languages.) Let us suppose that relativization includes a number of interrelated rules, some independently needed. Among these rules is probably Pronominalization. For example, the regular way of forming relatives in many languages is just like that in two types of English clauses. One was cited in Section 11.2:

That's a movie that you cry when you see it.

The other is a formal type of structure with *such that:*

> Construct a triangle such that its sides are equal.

There are some languages in which the shared nominal, *Antecedent,* remains in the embedded sentence, while the nominal head is represented by a pronoun. But as far as I know this possibility is confined to languages and constructions in which the relative clause precedes its head. Thus, the possible and impossible patterns appear to be these:

1. [. . . *Antecedent* . . .] *Pronoun*
2. [. . . *Pronoun* . . .] *Antecedent*
3. *Antecedent* [. . . *Pronoun* . . .]
4. **Pronoun* [. . . *Antecedent* . . .]

If in general Pronominalization cannot occur backwards except into a subordinate clause (and in some languages not under any circumstances), then these facts follow from the universality of the *NP–S* analysis, so long as we make the reasonable assumption that no grammar would contain a rule shifting the order of relative and head and then shifting it back again to the original order. Pattern (4) could never arise, because *Pronoun* always precedes and commands its *Antecedent*. On the other hand, an *S–NP* analysis would allow for the possibility that some language might have a forward pronominalization and then a shifting of relative and head:

Pronominalization	[. . . *NP* . . .] *NP*
	[. . . *NP* . . .] *Pro*
Relative shift	*Pro* [. . . *NP* . . .]

11.52 Word Order

There appear to be three main types of languages according to the position of the verb in the sentence (see Section 11.2): those like English, which usually have the subject *NP* before the verb; those like Japanese, which have the verb at the end of the clause; and those like Kwakiutl, which have the verb at the head of each clause. These are only surface characteristics and are only rough descriptions. In English, for example, some special constructions depart from the subject-first order. If we lump together objects and other complements, we may, following Greenberg (1963), speak of three basic types:

1. *V S O*   2. *S V O*   3. *S O V*

Many other features seem to correlate with these order-types. It seems that the number of actually possible order-types is severely limited. For example, there appear to be no languages that require the verb to stand in the third position of the clause, as in the following sentences of a fictional dialect of a kind of pidgin English:

>Boy girl saw.
>Boy book gave to girl.
>Yesterday boy gave book to girl.
>*Boy saw girl.
>*Boy book to girl gave.

It is generally assumed that the order of constituents in underlying structures is the same as that of surface structures, unless one can give cogent reasons for assuming a difference. Where variant orders exist, as in English or German, the linguist is forced to choose one among them as basic and to derive the others, or to set up some basic order from which all the others are to be derived.

It is obvious that general syntactic theory is faced with the problem of accounting for these restrictions on the order of constituents among the languages of the world. Within the theory we are following here, it is necessary to take into account various possibilities for deriving these surface orders from various possible underlying orders. The assumption of the theory that the underlying structures have some order defined on their constituents has been called into question. I shall not attempt to defend this aspect of the theory here (some linguists who have questioned this assumption are Shaumjan, Staal, Lamb, Sanders, Hudson, and, most recently, Postal). Instead, I shall present several alternative accounts within some variant of the standard theory, in which it is assumed that underlying structures are phrase-markers of the same general sort as surface structures.

The first hypothesis to consider is one in which the basic order of constituents is held to be identical with the dominant surface order, that is, the order of simple declarative sentences with no special focus or topicalization features. Thus, given the facts cited above, there would be just three possible underlying orders corresponding to the three surface orders $V S O$, $S V O$, and $S O V$.[4] As we noted above (Section 11.3), the

---

4. It has been claimed that there are other types of languages besides the ones noted above, for example, free word-order, $O V S$, and $V O S$ languages. I am inclined to believe that the phenomenon of "free word-order" is always the result of special, possibly context-dependent rules for focus, emphasis, and the like. As to the last type (see Keenan, 1972), the languages usually cited are Malayo-Polynesian, especially Philippine languages. Here I believe that the order of constituents is determined by a thematization rule moving the theme to the right, and that it is a mistake to think of this item as the subject. To settle this question it is necessary to have a good language-independent characterization of surface subjects, so far lacking. In any event, these questions must be considered very much open.

existence of *V S O* languages like Kwakiutl or Zapotec (Rosenbaum, 1973) taken together with the assumption of the congruence of deep and surface orders is inconsistent with the assumption that grammatical relations are universally defined on deep structures in the spirit of Chomsky (1965). Hence, either the theory of grammatical relations or the assumption of the identity of deep orders and dominant surface orders (or both) must be wrong.

Independently of such considerations, however, arguments have been given for various languages that the dominant order hypothesis about underlying structures is false. Thus, in Bach (1970) it is argued that the underlying order of Amharic, a surface *S O V* language, is either *V S O* or *S V O* (see Hudson, 1972, for an argument against this hypothesis from the point of view that there is no order defined on deep structures). Several linguists have argued that the basic order of Modern German is that of dependent clauses (*S O V*) rather than that of independent clauses (*S V O*) (Bach, 1962; Bierwisch, 1963) or that the underlying order is neither of these, but rather *V S O* (Bach 1971a,b). McCawley (1970) has argued that English is also an underlying *V S O* language (further arguments in Muraki, 1970; Bach, 1971a; but see a reply to McCawley in Berman, to be published).

Within the framework of his structure-preserving hypothesis, Emonds (1969) must also conclude that the underlying order of German is that of dependent clauses rather than that of root clauses. In fact, Emonds's hypothesis leads to a general prediction for all languages: the order of elements in the deep structure is identical to that of nonroot sentences (except for special positionings for relative pronouns and the like) wherever there is a difference in order between independent sentences and dependent (nonroot) sentences.[5]

Thus, there is a certain amount of admittedly inconclusive discussion tending to show that the hypothesis of identity of deep and dominant orders is wrong. A literal version of the Universal Base Hypothesis would require that the underlying order of all languages be identical. In the last section we noted some slim evidence that the basic structures for relative clauses are identical in all languages, a hypothesis that would follow from the view that all underlying structures are identical. To the extent that arguments for the universality of the relative clause structure stand up, we may take them as partial support for the Universal Base Hypothesis.

---

5. Emonds's predictions would be falsified by the *V S O* or *S V O* analysis of German and, given sufficient restrictions on the possible deep structures, by the *V S O* analysis of Amharic. In a number of recent lectures Ross has argued from general considerations of "primacy relations" that English has an underlying *S O V* order.

Within the Universal Base Hypothesis, one could account for the typological facts by assuming an underlying *V S O* order and two universal rules: Subject-formation and Verb-final (see beginning of Section 11.5). Unfortunately, a great deal more work on individual languages needs to be done before this idea can be considered well-supported. The difficulty is compounded by the fact that we do not yet understand sufficiently the way in which typological facts of the sort noted by Greenberg (1963) are to be tied into a general theory of syntax. Once again we must end our discussion on an inconclusive note.[6]

11.6 Functional Explanations

Recently, a good deal of work has been done that either goes beyond the speculations of the last sections or takes an entirely different tack in attempting to account for cross-linguistic facts. The common denominator in the two avenues has been the consideration of psychological functions for linguistic structures. Thus, the attempt is made to knit together a theory of linguistic structures and theories about performance, or more general theories of cognition, perception, or the like.

On the one hand, we may consider the relevant principles to be constitutive of linguistic theory. On this approach we ask with respect to some feature of universal syntax, a rule or constraint, why it should be this way rather than some other way, and try to find an answer in terms of psychology. On the other hand, we may consider more or less independent constraints or principles and try to show how they interact with more specifically linguistic systems to account for language behavior. In both approaches, a move is made toward a more explanatory theory (see the end of Chapter 10).

As an example of the first sort of consideration, let us take up again the rule of Extraposition (see Section 7.4). We want to show that there is a reason why the rule has the form that it does.

It seems that of the following pairs of sentences, the second is easier to understand and utter than the first:

That John is a fink is true.
It's true that John is a fink.

For us to prove that theorem would be difficult.
It would be difficult for us to prove that theorem.

---

6. For some discussion of the problems of underlying word-order, see Ross (1970a), Bach (1971a,b), and H. Rosenbaum (1973).

The difference is especially clear if we introduce a further level of embedding:

> That that the sun is hot is true is uninteresting.
> That it's true that the sun is hot is uninteresting.
> It's uninteresting that it's true that the sun is hot.

The first sentence is virtually unintelligible, the second is somewhat better, and the third is perfectly acceptable and understandable. Suppose we could explain this difference in terms of some general properties of human memory, perception, or whatever. Suppose further that we require our theory of grammars to choose those analyses in which optional transformational rules perform some function of increasing ease of processing, intelligibility, or the like. Then our choice between the two analyses of sentences like those just given is clear: the Extraposition analysis must be chosen over the Intraposition analysis, since only the former can be shown to perform the function of decreasing self-embedding. To the extent that we can associate such functions with transformations in a way that determines their form, and find independent evidence for the correctness of the analyses so chosen, we can extrapolate to the case at hand and make a strong argument for the Extraposition analysis. The arguments that were given for the form of Extraposition in Section 7.4 confirm the correctness of the prediction.

In general, it appears to be the case that structures with embedded and self-embedded *S*'s are more difficult to process than structures in which the *S*'s have been reduced or pruned, or removed to one or the other end of the sentence. Transformations that have such results include Extraposition, Raising, Equi, and relative clause reductions with subsequent preposing of adjectives. Further, some movement transformations seem to have the function of allowing us to put complex and long elements after shorter ones, presumably thus decreasing the load on temporary memory. Compare these pairs, for example, illustrating the operation of various movement rules:

> The man that the police were looking for stole it.
> It was stolen by the man that the police were looking for.

> I gave the book that Sally wanted to John.
> I gave John the book that Sally wanted.

> I was talking to the shrink that Henry knows about Extraposition.
> I was talking about Extraposition to the shrink that Henry knows.

As we saw above, it is possible to think about psychological explanations not as constitutive of grammatical rules or constraints but as independent systems (either specifically linguistic or more general).

Consider, for example, the following sentences:

1. The man arrived yesterday that we were supposed to interview.
2. The man saw the woman yesterday that we were supposed to interview.

In (2), the extraposed relative clause must be interpreted to modify the second rather than the first *NP*. We could account for this fact grammatically by placing a restriction on the rule of Extraposition from *NP* (so that it could not be derived from *The man that we were supposed to interview saw the woman*). Or we might suppose that it is to be accounted for by a perceptual constraint, quite independent of the rules of English grammar, that rules out ambiguous surface structures in some way, or by a strategy that says: "Associate a modifier with the nearest possible head." Different predictions arise from these two views. If we construct a sentence of the form *NP V NP X that S,* in which the association of the relative clause with the second *NP* is blocked either by semantic constraints or by failures of agreement and the like, and if the result is a possible English sentence, then we have confirmed the perceptual account. Judgments vary, but it seems that this conclusion is correct:

3. The man made a statement whom we were supposed to interview.
4. ?The men saw the woman who were in the room.

For some reason that I am unable to give, (3) seems much better than (4). This choice is confirmed when we see that a subsequent rearrangement of constituents for sentences like (2) restores the connection that would be blocked by a constraint on the extraposition rule:

Who(m) had the man seen that we were supposed to interview?

Serious proposals along these lines cannot be made without considerable independent investigation of the psychological factors at work. If we simply take some supposed grammatical constraint and term it a perceptual strategy, we have obviously only made a terminological proposal. The strength of arguments for perceptual accounts is largely a function of the strength of the arguments for an independently needed strategy or constraint. A good example of such an analysis is Langendoen and Bever (1973), in which it is shown quite convincingly that a certain class of expressions (*a not unhappy man*) are best considered ungrammatical, although perfectly acceptable. In carrying out the argument, the authors show that the grammatical account can be considerably simplified, syntactic theory kept relatively constrained, and the facts of interpretation better explained by assuming an interaction of grammar and interpretive strategies that would be needed in any event.

Work of the sort touched on in this section has been done by Kuno (to be published), Grosu (1972, 1973), Bever and Langendoen (1971), and Bever (1970). Bever especially has argued for the necessity to account for linguistic behavior in terms of a complex interaction of various cognitive and perceptual systems.

EPILOGUE

It should be evident from the last few chapters that there is at present no wholly satisfactory theory of syntax for natural language. At present, almost every assumption of syntactic theory as outlined in the first part of this book has been called into question. This fact may cause dismay to some readers. But against this dismay one may put the potential excitement of a developing field. The whole point of a book like this is not to pass along well-established truths (if there are such things), but to put the reader into the position of throwing the book away and participating in the search for the understanding of natural language. We learn more from our mistakes than from our successes. The best answers are always those that lead to further questions. And one of the most rewarding fruits of trying to answer questions about language, this most characteristic and mysterious of human gifts, is that we are led to other questions about the fundamental nature of man, this most fascinating, terrible, and noble of the animals.

Bibliography

I have included a few items that are not referred to specifically in the text. Works have been listed in what seem to me the most convenient sources. Where pertinent I have added a date of first appearance or circulation.

Aarsleff, Hans. 1970. "The History of Linguistics and Professor Chomsky." *Language* 46:570–585.

Anderson, Stephen R., and Paul Kiparsky, eds. 1973. *A Festschrift for Morris Halle*. New York.

Ashton, E. O. 1947. *Swahili Grammar*. Second edition. London.

Bach, Emmon. 1962. "The Order of Elements in a Transformational Grammar of German." *Language* 38:263–269.

———. 1964. *An Introduction to Transformational Grammars*. New York.

———. 1965a. "Structural Linguistics and the Philosophy of Science." *Diogenes* 51:111–128.

———. 1965b. "On some Recurrent Types of Transformations." *Georgetown University Monograph Series on Languages and Linguistics* 18:3–18.

———. 1967. "*Have* and *Be* in English Syntax." *Language* 43:462–485.

———. 1968. "Nouns and Noun Phrases." In Bach and Harms, 1968.

———. 1970. "Is Amharic an SOV Language?" *Journal of Ethiopian Studies* 8:9–20.

———. 1971a. "Questions." *Linguistic Inquiry* 2:153–166.

———. 1971b. "Syntax since *Aspects*." *Georgetown University Monograph Series on Languages and Linguistics* 24:1–17.

[———.] Cabnomme (pseud.) 1971c. "On Concrete Syntax." In Arnold M. Zwicky, Peter Salus, Robert I. Binnick, and Anthony L. Vanek, eds., *Studies Out in Left Field: Defamatory Essays Presented to James D. McCawley on the Occasion of His 33rd or 34th Birthday*. Edmonton and Champaign.

———. 1974. "Explanatory Inadequacy." In David Cohen, ed., *Explaining Linguistic Phenomena*. Washington, D.C.

Bach, Emmon, and Robert T. Harms, eds. 1968. *Universals in Linguistic Theory*. New York.

Baker, C. L. 1970. "Double Negatives." *Linguistic Inquiry* 1:169–186.

Baker, C. L., and Michael K. Brame. 1972. "'Global Rules': A Rejoinder." *Language* 48:51–75.

Bar-Hillel, Yehoshua. 1953. "A Quasi-arithmetical Notation for Syntactic Description." *Language* 29:47–58. (Reprinted in Bar-Hillel, 1964.)

———. 1964. *Language and Information*. Reading, Mass., and Jerusalem.

Bar-Hillel, Yehoshua, and E. Shamir. 1960. "Finite-State Languages: Formal Representation and Adequacy Problems." *The Bulletin of the Research Council of Israel* 8F:155–166. (Reprinted in Bar-Hillel, 1964.)

Bates, Roberta Reed. 1969. *A Study in the Acquisition of Language*. Ph.D. Dissertation, University of Texas at Austin.

Berlin, Brent, and Paul Kay. 1969. *Basic Color Terms*. Berkeley and Los Angeles.

Berman, Arlene. Forthcoming. "On the VSO Hypothesis." (To appear in *Linguistic Inquiry*.)

Bever, T. G. 1970. "The Cognitive Basis for Linguistic Structures." In R. Hayes, ed., *Cognition and Language Development*. New York.

Bever, T. G., and D. T. Langendoen. 1971. "A Dynamic Model of the Evolution of Language." *Linguistic Inquiry* 2:433–463.

Bierwisch, Manfred. 1963. *Grammatik des deutschen Verbs* (identical with *Studia Grammatica* Vol. 2). Berlin.

———. 1966. "Regeln für die Intonation deutscher Sätze." *Studia Grammatica* 7:99–201.

Bierwisch, Manfred, and Karl Erich Heidolph, eds. 1970. *Progress in Linguistics*. The Hague and Paris.

Bloch, Bernard, and George L. Trager. 1942. *Outline of Linguistic Analysis*. Baltimore.

Bloomfield, Leonard. 1933. *Language*. New York.

Bolinger, Dwight L. 1971. "Semantic Overloading: A Study of the Verb *Remind*." *Language* 47:522–547.

Bresnan, Joan. 1970. "On Complementizers: Toward a Syntactic Theory of Complement Types." *Foundations of Language* 6:297–321.

Carden, Guy. 1970. "A Note on Conflicting Idiolects." *Linguistic Inquiry* 1:281–290.

Carnap, Rudolf. 1939. *Foundations of Logic and Mathematics* (identical with *International Encyclopedia of Unified Science*, Vol. I, No. 3). Chicago.

Carrell, Patricia L. 1970. *A Transformational Grammar of Igbo.* (Revised version of 1966 University of Texas at Austin Ph.D. Dissertation; identical with *West African Language Monographs* No. 8.) Cambridge, England, and Ibadan.

Casagrande, Jean. 1970. "A Case for Global Derivational Constraints." *Papers in Linguistics* 2:449–459.

Chomsky, Noam. [1955.] *The Logical Structure of Linguistic Theory.* (An unpublished dittoscript, available from Massachusetts Institute of Technology library on microfilm.)

———. 1956. "Three Models for the Description of Language." *I.R.E Transactions on Information Theory*, Vol. IT-2, *Proceedings of the Symposium on Information Theory*, 113–124.

———. 1957. *Syntactic Structures.* The Hague.

———. 1959a. Review of B. F. Skinner, *Verbal Behavior. Language* 35:26–58.

———. 1959b. "On Certain Formal Properties of Grammars." *Information and Control* 2:137–167.

———. 1963. "Formal Properties of Grammars." In Luce, Bush, and Galanter, 1963.

———. 1964 (1962). "Current Issues in Linguistic Theory." In Fodor and Katz, 1964.

———. 1965. *Aspects of the Theory of Syntax.* Cambridge, Mass.

———. 1966. *Cartesian Linguistics.* New York.

———. 1970. "Remarks on Nominalization." In Jacobs and Rosenbaum, 1970.

———. 1971. "Deep Structure, Surface Structure, and Semantic Representation." In Steinberg and Jakobovits, 1971.

———. 1972a. "Some Empirical Issues in the Theory of Transformational Grammar." In Peters, 1972.

———. 1972b. *Language and Mind.* New York.

———. 1973. "Conditions on Transformations." In Anderson and Kiparsky, 1973.

Chomsky, Noam, and Morris Halle. 1965. "Some Controversial Questions in Phonological Theory." *Journal of Linguistics* 1:97–138.

———. 1968. *The Sound Pattern of English.* New York.

Chomsky, N., and G. F. Miller. 1958. "Finite State Languages." *Information and Control* 1:91–112.

Cohen, David. 1971. *On the Linguistic Representation of Presupposi- tions.* Ph.D. Dissertation, University of Texas at Austin.

Davidson, Donald, and Gilbert Harman, eds. 1972. *Semantics of Na- tural Language.* Dordrecht.

Davis, Martin. 1958. *Computability and Unsolvability.* New York.

Dougherty, Ray. 1969. "An Interpretive Theory of Pronominalization." *Foundations of Language* 5:488–519.

_____. 1970. Review of Bach and Harms, 1968. *Foundations of Lan- guage* 6:505–561.

Downing, Bruce Theodore. 1970. *Syntactic Structure and Phonological Phrasing in English.* Ph.D. Dissertation, University of Texas at Austin.

Elliott, Dale, Stanley Legum, and Sandra Annear Thompson. 1969. "Syntactic Variation as Linguistic Data." *Papers from the Fifth Regional Meeting, Chicago Linguistic Society,* pp. 52–59.

Emonds, Joseph. 1970. *Root and Structure-preserving Transformations.* Ph.D. Dissertation, Massachusetts Institute of Technology.

_____. 1972. "A Reformulation of Certain Syntactic Transformations." In Peters, 1972.

Fillmore, Charles J. 1963. "The Position of Embedding Transforma- tions in a Grammar." *Word* 19:208–231.

_____. 1965. *Indirect Object Constructions in English and the Ordering of Transformations.* The Hague.

_____. 1968. "The Case for Case." In Bach and Harms, 1968.

_____. 1969 (1966). "Toward a Modern Theory of Case." In Reibel and Schane, 1969.

Fillmore, Charles J. and D. T. Langendoen, eds. 1971. *Studies in Lin- guistic Semantics.* New York.

Fodor, J. A., and T. Bever. 1965. "The Psychological Reality of Lin- guistic Segments." *Journal of Verbal Learning and Behavior* 4:414– 420.

Fodor, J., and Jerrold J. Katz, eds. 1964. *The Structure of Language.* Englewood Cliffs.

Ginsburg, S., and Barbara Hall Partee. 1969. "A Mathematical Model of Transformational Grammar." *Information and Control* 15:297– 334.

Gleason, H. A., Jr. 1961 (1955). *An Introduction to Descriptive Linguis- tics.* Revised edition. New York.

Gleitman, Lila R. 1969 (1965). "Coordinating Conjunctions in English." In Reibel and Schane, 1969.

Greenberg, Joseph H. 1963. "Some Universals of Grammar with Par- ticular Reference to the Order of Meaningful Elements." In Joseph H. Greenberg, ed., *Universals of Language.* Cambridge, Mass.

Grinder, John. 1972. "On the Cycle in Syntax." In Kimball, 1972b.

Grinder, John, and Paul M. Postal. 1971. "Missing Antecedents." *Linguistic Inquiry* 2:269–312.

Grosu, Alexander. 1972. "The Strategic Content of Island Constraints." *Ohio State University Working Papers in Linguistics,* No. 13.

———. "On the Status of the So-called Right Roof Constraint." *Language* 49:294–311.

Hale, Kenneth. Forthcoming. "Gaps in Culture and Language."

Halle, Morris. 1962. "Phonology in Generative Grammar." *Word* 18:54–72. (Reprinted in Fodor and Katz, 1964.)

Hankamer, Jorge. 1971. *Constraints on Deletion in Syntax.* Ph.D. Dissertation, Yale University.

Harms, Robert T. 1968. *Introduction to Phonological Theory.* Englewood Cliffs.

Harris, Zellig S. 1951. *Structural Linguistics.* Chicago.

———. 1952. "Discourse Analysis." *Language* 28:1–30. (Reprinted in Fodor and Katz, 1964.)

———. 1957. "Co-occurrence and Transformation in Linguistic Structure." *Language* 33:283–340. (Reprinted in Fodor and Katz, 1964.)

Harwood, F. W. 1955. "Axiomatic Syntax: The Construction and Evaluation of a Syntactic Calculus." *Language* 31:409–414.

Hasegawa, Kinsuke. 1968. "The Passive Construction in English." *Language* 44:230–243.

Hempel, Carl G. 1966. *Philosophy of Natural Science.* Englewood Cliffs.

Hill, Archibald A. 1958. *Introduction to Linguistic Structures.* New York.

———, ed. 1962. *Third Texas Conference on Problems of Linguistic Analysis in English.* Austin.

Hockett, Charles F. 1954. "Two Models of Linguistic Description." *Word* 10:210–233. (Reprinted in Joos, 1957.)

———. 1955. *A Manual of Phonology.* Bloomington, Ind.

———. 1958. *A Course in Modern Linguistics.* New York.

———. 1968. *The State of the Art.* The Hague.

Householder, F. W., Jr. 1965. "On some Recent Claims in Phonological Theory." *Journal of Linguistics* 1:13–34.

Hudson, Grover. 1972. "Why Amharic Is Not a VSO Language." *U.C.L.A. Studies in African Linguistics* 3:1:127–166.

Jackendoff, Ray. 1969. *Some Rules of Semantic Interpretation for English.* Ph.D. Dissertation, Massachusetts Institute of Technology.

———. 1972. *Semantic Interpretation in Generative Grammar.* Cambridge, Mass., and London. (Substantial revision and expansion of Jackendoff, 1969.)

Jacobs, Roderick A., and Peter S. Rosenbaum, eds. 1970. *Readings in English Transformational Grammar.* Waltham, Mass.

Jespersen, Otto. 1964 (1922). *Language*. New York.

———. 1924. *The Philosophy of Grammar*. New York.

Johnson, N. F. 1965. "The Psychological Reality of Phrase-Structure Rules." *Journal of Verbal Learning and Behavior* 4:469–475.

Joos, Martin, ed. 1957. *Readings in Linguistics*. Chicago.

Katz, Jerrold J. 1966. *The Philosophy of Language*. New York and London.

———. 1972. *Semantic Theory*. New York.

Katz, Jerrold J., and J. Fodor. 1963. "The Structure of a Semantic Theory." *Language* 39:170–210. (Reprinted in Fodor and Katz, 1964.)

Katz, Jerrold J., and Paul M. Postal. 1964. *An Integrated Theory of Linguistic Descriptions*. Cambridge, Mass.

Keenan, Edward L. 1972. "Relative Clause Formation in Malagasy." In Paul M. Peranteau, Judith N. Levi, and Gloria C. Phares, eds., *The Chicago Which Hunt*. Chicago.

Kimball, John. 1970. " 'Remind' Remains." *Linguistic Inquiry* 1:511–523.

———, ed. 1972a. "Cyclic and Linear Grammars." In Kimball, 1972b.

———. 1972b. *Syntax and Semantics*. Vol. 1. New York and London.

King, Robert D. 1969. *Historical Linguistics and Generative Grammar*. Englewood Cliffs.

Kiparsky, Paul. 1968. "Linguistic Universals and Language Change." In Bach and Harms, 1968.

Kiparsky, Paul, and Carol Kiparsky. 1970. "Fact." In Bierwisch and Heidolph, 1970.

Klima, Edward S. 1964. "Negation in English." In Fodor and Katz, 1964.

Koller, Alice. 1967. *A Hornbook of Hazards for Linguists*. New London, Conn. (A research report to the U.S. Air Force, listed as AFOSR 67–0770.)

Koutsoudas, Andreas. 1966. *Writing Transformational Grammars: An Introduction*. New York.

———. 1972. "The Strict Order Fallacy." *Language* 48:88–96.

Kuno, Susumu. Forthcoming. "Natural Explanations for Some Syntactic Universals." (To appear in *Linguistic Inquiry*.)

Kuroda, S.-Y. 1964. "Classes of Languages and Linear-bounded Automata." *Information and Control* 7:207–223.

Lakoff, George. 1970a (1965). *Irregularity in Syntax*. New York.

———. 1970b. "Global Rules." *Language* 46:627–639.

———. 1970c. "An Example of a Descriptively Inadequate Interpretive Theory." *Linguistic Inquiry* 1: 539–542.

———. 1970d. "Repartee, or a Reply to 'Negation, Conjunction, and Quantifiers.'" *Foundations of Language* 6:389–422.

_____. 1971. "On Generative Semantics." In Steinberg and Jakobovits, 1971.

_____. Ms. *Deep and Surface Grammar.* (Available mimeographed from the Indiana University Linguistics Club.)

Lakoff, Robin. 1968. *Abstract Syntax and Latin Complementation.* Cambridge, Mass.

_____. 1969. Review of Brekle, ed., *Grammaire générale et raisonnée. Language* 45:343–364.

Lamb, Sydney M. 1966. *Outline of Stratificational Grammar.* Washington, D.C.

Langacker, Ronald W. 1968. *Language and Its Structure.* New York.

_____. 1969. "On Pronominalization and the Chain of Command." In Reibel and Schane, 1969.

_____. 1972. *Fundamentals of Linguistic Analysis.* New York.

Langendoen, D. Terence. 1969. *The Study of Syntax.* New York.

_____. 1970. *Essentials of English Grammar.* New York.

Langendoen, D. Terence, and Thomas G. Bever. 1973. "Can a Not Unhappy Person Be Called a Not Sad One?" In Anderson and Kiparsky, 1973.

Lees, Robert B. 1960. *The Grammar of English Nominalizations.* Bloomington, Ind.

Lenneberg, Eric H. 1967. *Biological Foundations of Language.* New York.

Luce, R. Duncan, Robert R. Bush, and Eugene Galanter. 1963. *Handbook of Mathematical Psychology,* II. New York and London.

Lyons, John. 1966. "Towards a 'Notional' Theory of the 'Parts of Speech.'" *Journal of Linguistics* 2:209–236.

_____. 1968. *Introduction to Theoretical Linguistics.* Cambridge, England.

McCawley, James D. 1968a. "The Role of Semantics in a Grammar." In Bach and Harms, 1968.

_____. 1968b. "Concerning the Base Component of a Transformational Grammar." *Foundations of Language* 4:243–269.

_____. 1970. "English as a VSO Language." *Language* 46:286–299.

_____. 1971. "Prelexical Syntax." *Georgetown University Monograph Series on Languages and Linguistics* 24:19–33.

Miller, George A., and Noam Chomsky. 1963. "Finitary Models of Language Users." In Luce, Bush, and Galanter, 1963.

Moore, Edward F., ed. 1964. *Sequential Machines: Selected Papers.* Reading, Mass.

Muraki, Masatake. 1970. *Presupposition, Pseudo-clefting and Thematization.* Ph.D. Dissertation, University of Texas at Austin.

Olmsted, D. L. 1967. "On some Axioms about Sentence Length." *Language* 43:303–305.

Partee, Barbara Hall. 1971. "On the Requirement that Transformations Preserve Meaning." In Fillmore and Langendoen, 1971.

———. 1972. "Some Transformational Extensions of Montague Grammars." In R. Rodman, ed., *Papers in Montague Grammar*. University of California at Los Angeles.

———. Forthcoming. *Fundamentals of Mathematics for Linguistics*.

Perlmutter, David M. 1970. "Surface Structure Constraints in Syntax." *Linguistic Inquiry* 1:187–255.

———. 1971 (1968). *Deep and Surface Structure Constraints in Syntax*. New York.

Peters, Stanley. 1970. "Why There Are Many 'Universal' Bases." *Papers in Linguistics* Vol. 2, No. 1, pp. 27–43.

———. 1972a. "The Projection Problem: How Is a Grammar to Be Selected." In Peters, 1972b.

———, ed. 1972b. *Goals of Linguistic Theory*. Englewood Cliffs.

Peters, Stanley, and Robert W. Ritchie. 1969. "A Note on the Universal Base Hypothesis." *Journal of Linguistics* 5:150–152.

———. 1971. "On Restricting the Base Component of Transformational Grammars." *Information and Control* 18:483–501.

———. 1973. "Nonfiltering and Local-filtering Transformational Grammars." In K. J. J. Hintikka, J. M. E. Moravcsik, and P. Suppes, eds., *Approaches to Natural Language*. Dordrecht.

———. Forthcoming a. "On the Generative Power of Transformational Grammars." (To appear in *Information Sciences*.)

———. Forthcoming b. *Formal Properties of Transformational Grammars*.

Popper, Karl. 1959. *The Logic of Scientific Discovery*. New York.

Postal, Paul M. 1964. "Limitations of Phrase Structure Grammars." In Fodor and Katz, 1964.

———. 1970a. "On the Surface Verb 'Remind.'" *Linguistic Inquiry* 1:37–120.

———. 1970b. "On Coreferential Complement Subject Deletion." *Linguistic Inquiry* 1:439–500.

———. 1971. *Crossover Phenomena*. New York.

Prideaux, Gary D. 1970. "On the Selection Problem." *Papers in Linguistics* 2:238–266.

Quine, Willard Van Orman. 1961. *From a Logical Point of View*. Second edition, revised. New York and Evanston.

Rabin, M. O., and D. Scott. 1959. "Finite Automata and Their Decision Problems." In Moore, 1964.

Reibel, David A., and Sanford A. Schane. 1969. *Modern Studies in English*. Englewood Cliffs.

Reich, Peter A. 1969. "The Finiteness of Natural Language." *Language* 45:831–843.

Robson, R. A. 1972. *On the Generation of Passive Constructions in English*. Ph.D. Dissertation, University of Texas at Austin.

Rosenbaum, Harvey. 1973. *Language Universals and Zapotec Syntax*. Ph.D. Dissertation, University of Texas.

Rosenbaum, Peter S. 1967. *The Grammar of English Predicate Complement Constructions*. Cambridge, Mass.

Ross, John R. 1967a. *Constraints on Variables in Syntax*. Ph.D. Dissertation, Massachusetts Institute of Technology.

————. 1967b. "On the Cyclic Nature of English Pronominalization." In Reibel and Schane, 1969.

————. 1969. "Guess Who?" *Papers from the Fifth Regional Meeting, Chicago Linguistic Society*, pp. 252–286.

————. 1970a (1967). "Gapping and the Order of Constituents." In Bierwisch and Heidolph, 1970.

————. 1970b. "On Declarative Sentences." In Jacobs and Rosenbaum, 1970.

————. 1972. "Double-ing." *Linguistic Inquiry* 3:61–86.

Sanders, Gerald. 1970. "Constraints on Constituent Ordering." *Papers in Linguistics* 2:460–502.

Sapir, Edward. 1921. *Language*. New York.

————. 1925. "Sound Patterns in Language." *Language* 1:37–51. (Reprinted in Joos, 1957.)

Schane, Sanford A. 1966. "A Schema for Sentence Coordination." *Information System Language Studies* No. 10. The Mitre Corporation, Bedford, Mass.

Schwartz, Arthur. 1971. "General Aspects of Relative Clause Formation." *Working Papers on Language Universals* 6:139–171. (Stanford University Language Universals Project.)

Searle, John R. 1969. *Speech Acts*. Cambridge, England.

Sebeok, Thomas., ed. 1968. *Animal Communication*. Bloomington, Ind.

Shannon, Claude L., and Warren Weaver. 1949. *The Mathematical Theory of Communication*. Urbana, Ill.

Smith, Carlota S. 1964. "Determiners and Relative Clauses in a Generative Grammar of English." *Language* 40:37–52. (Reprinted in Reibel and Schane, 1969.)

Smullyan, Raymond M. 1961. *Theory of Formal Systems*. Revised edition (identical with *Annals of Mathematics Studies,* Vol. 47). Princeton, N.J.

Staal, J. F. 1967. *Word Order in Sanskrit and Universal Grammar*. Dordrecht.

Steinberg, Danny D., and Leon A. Jakobovits, eds. 1971. *Semantics: An Interdisciplinary Reader in Philosophy, Linguistics, and Psychology*. Cambridge, England.

Stockwell, Robert P., Paul Schachter, and Barbara Hall Partee. 1973. *The Major Syntactic Structures of English*. New York.

Swift, Lloyd B. 1963. *A Reference Grammar of Modern Turkish*. Bloomington, Ind., and The Hague.

Tai, James H.-Y. 1973. "Chinese as a SOV Language." *Papers of the Ninth Regional Meeting, Chicago Linguistic Society*.

Thompson, Sandra Annear. 1971. "The Deep Structure of Relative Clauses." In Fillmore and Langendoen, 1971.

Twaddell, W. Freeman. 1935. "On Defining the Phoneme." *Language Monographs* No. 16. (Reprinted in part in Joos, 1957.)

Wall, Robert. 1972. *Introduction to Mathematical Linguistics*. Englewood Cliffs.

Index